"Russ has yet again written an extre
common problems that we all encounter when doing acceptance and commitment therapy (ACT), this book is reassuring, open, funny, irreverent, and at the same time, supremely wise. It is full of practical strategies, guidance, and helpful resources, that are also grounded in theory. With illuminating new material on self-compassion, exposure, and functional analysis, as well as well-known ACT classics, Russ's down-to-earth examples of how to use this wisdom in therapy will prove helpful to all levels of experience with ACT."

—**David Gillanders**, academic director of the doctoral program in clinical psychology at the University of Edinburgh, United Kingdom; peer-reviewed ACT trainer; and former chair of the ACBS training committee

"In *ACT Questions and Answers*, Russ Harris once again uses humor and clear language—this time to address the complex subtleties of 150 common ACT sticking points. The book is full of practical solutions for handling problems that arise when things don't go as planned. Harris does a brilliant job showing how the six core processes interact, and he emphasizes behavior analytic concepts with simplicity. Further, several misconceptions about ACT are clarified. The appendix has incredible resources and links to even more, including worksheets, videos, and handouts. Highly recommended!"

—**Amy R. Murrell, PhD**, associate professor of psychology at the University of North Texas, and coauthor of *The Joy of Parenting*

"Russ Harris has produced another gem. In these pages, newbies and seasoned ACT veterans alike will find many, many useful clarifications, concepts, strategies, and resources for getting their clients, and themselves, unstuck in session. And all in a playful, compassionate, jargon-busting style. A must-read."

—**Christopher McCurry, PhD**, clinical psychologist, and author of *Parenting Your Anxious Child with Mindfulness and Acceptance*

"Russ Harris has done a spectacular job of addressing the most common questions and challenges that therapists face in using ACT. His writing is clear, charming, and honest, making for a very enjoyable read. The inclusion of chapters detailing the Choice Point model and loads of clinical examples and handouts make this an essential read for clinicians, both novice and seasoned. I am sure you will find something of value in *ACT Questions and Answers*."

—**Sheri Turrell, PhD, C. Psych**, adjunct lecturer in the department of psychiatry at the University of Toronto, clinician, ACT therapist, and coauthor of *ACT for Adolescents*

"ACT *Questions and Answers* is an excellently written book both in terms of its prose and tips. In Harris's typical witty and charming style, this book will help any ACT practitioner get out of the tricky spots that inevitably crop up. The question and answer format make it an easy and accessible read. It is a perfect adjunct to introductory ACT materials for practitioners who want get that extra edge to their work."

—**Louise McHugh, PhD**, associate professor in the school of psychology at University College Dublin, peer-reviewed ACT trainer, and coauthor of *The Self and Perspective Taking*

"Russ Harris has done it again! Inviting, fun, and practical, ACT *Questions and Answers* is a real-life reference in doing ACT and overcoming hang-ups for clinicians. In an approach where the answer to difficult questions is often "it depends," Russ Harris gives you new, ACT-consistent ways to think about tricky situations we all find ourselves in with concrete techniques and sound advice. This will book will motivate you to use ACT in your practice."

—**Timothy Gordon, MSW, RSW**, social worker, peer-reviewed ACT trainer, and coauthor of *The ACT Approach*

"Wouldn't it be great to have a book on everything you always wanted to know about ACT but were too afraid to ask? With answers that are practical and understandable? Written by one of the leading ACT trainers in the world? Good news! Your search is over with Russ Harris's *ACT Questions and Answers*. He answers questions he's compiled from the literally hundreds of trainings he's run around the world. Questions like: 'How do we work with clients who keep saying *I don't know*?' or 'Can people fuse with both thoughts and feelings?' and 'How can we talk about self-as-context without making it weird or mystical?' Dive inside to find out the answers to these questions, laid out in a clear and helpful way, illustrated with lots of real-life clinical examples. This book is a super accessible, engaging, must-have companion, whether you are just starting out on your ACT journey, or you're well down the track."

—**Joe Oliver, PhD**, coauthor of *ACTivate Your Life*

"The book you are holding captures the questions and nuances missing in the field. Harris offers a gift to allied health professionals and consultants. This is the definitive guide to answer your questions for how to improve lives when no two people are the same."

—**Todd B. Kashdan, PhD**, professor of psychology and senior scientist at the Center for the Advancement of Well-Being at George Mason University, and coauthor of *The Upside of Your Dark Side*

"Finally! It's about time someone answered the ubiquitous questions that often perplex therapists after their introductory training. Harris's book answers the hard questions with no-nonsense, real-world practical ideas and applications that ACT therapists can effectively and immediately use with their clients. Even experienced ACT practitioners can benefit from Russ's fresh perspective on some of the thorny issues that come up during the application of ACT."

—**Daniel J. Moran, PhD**, coauthor of *ACT in Practice*

"ACT *Questions and Answers* offers an invaluable opportunity to learn about core ACT processes and their direct application, in a straightforward, unique, and refreshing format. In this easy-to-read and highly informative book, Russ Harris shares his wealth of expertise to skilfully address a range of obstacles and questions which commonly arise in practice. This incredibly useful resource is packed full of relevant advice, guidance, and practical tips, and is sure to support and enrich your work with clients. Every ACT practitioner should grab a copy. Highly recommended."

—**Michael Sinclair**, coauthor of *Mindfulness for Busy People* and *The Little ACT Workbook*

"I've been studying ACT for fourteen years, and yet Russ Harris continues to educate me. For any person using the ACT model: this book will teach you many new ways of improving your applied work."

—**Nic Hooper, PhD**, coauthor of *The Research Journey of Acceptance and Commitment Therapy (ACT)*

"In *ACT Questions and Answers*, Russ Harris continues his long history of providing clear, direct, thorough, and readily applicable insights into both basic and nuanced aspects of ACT. This highly readable work not only addresses processes and approaches that have been part of ACT since its inception, it also provides up-to-date innovations such as Choice Point, and usefully distinguishes dysfunctional 'fusion' with language from adaptive 'absorption.' Not only does Harris 'know what he is talking about,' his gift for clear, concise description and explanation allows readers to acquire that knowledge with the sense of having spent time with a warm, open, and fun-loving individual who genuinely wants to be helpful. If you have questions about ACT, this book will almost certainly answer them, and do so in a way that will actually make you glad you asked!"

—**Hank Robb, PhD, ABPP**, Oregon (USA)-licensed psychologist in private practice, peer-reviewed ACT trainer, and fellow of the Association for Contextual Behavioral Science

"A long-needed book that breaks new ground in responding to the most troublesome moments of any ACT therapist.... Harris does an incredible job identifying those moments of 'stuckness' in our clinical work; he recognizes specific challenges when putting the hexaflex in practice, acknowledges motivation-related problems, clarifies how to do exposure-based interventions, explains how to conduct functional analysis in session, even in complex situations, and with clarity, silliness, and competence of a master clinician, he shows us, hands-on, how to get unstuck in our clinical work.... Whether you're a beginner, an intermediate, or an advanced ACT clinician, this book is a must-read between sessions, a great source for teaching ACT, and a vital resource.... Here are my last words: read it, try it, track it, and read it again!"

—**Patricia E. Zurita Ona, PsyD**, director of the East Bay Behavior Therapy Center, author of *Parenting a Troubled Teen*, and coauthor of *Mind and Emotions*

"Internationally renowned ACT expert Russ Harris has accomplished the seemingly impossible with this book. While *ACT Questions and Answers* is a brilliant and user-friendly guide to some of the trickiest parts of being an ACT therapist, it is also something more. It is delightful. It is fun. It is empowering. How rare is it that a book can tackle such challenging questions and help you enjoy the ride?"

—**Dennis Tirch PhD**, director at The Center for Compassion Focused Therapy, and associate clinical professor at the Icahn School of Medicine at Mount Sinai

"Russ Harris has written a useful adjunct to any core ACT text. Clinicians who find themselves stumbling as they implement ACT for the first time will find well-considered answers to just about any question they have. More seasoned ACT therapists can also learn a lot: reading it will be like having a long conversation about what ACT looks like on the inside with a trusted colleague. And best of all, Russ includes a helpful chapter on how to use functional assessment in your practice, an essential part of doing ACT well."

—**Matthew S. Boone, LCSW**, ACBS peer-reviewed ACT trainer, editor of *Mindfulness and Acceptance in Social Work*, creative director for clinical content at Lyra Health, and adjunct instructor at the University of Arkansas at Little Rock School of Social Work

"**Q:** Where can you find an indispensable set of guidelines offered by a seasoned ACT trainer and therapist, with just the right sprinkling of self-effacing humor, to help practitioners of ACT, from the most veteran to beginners, overcome bumps in the road? **A:** Look no further than this latest contribution by Russ Harris that you now hold in your hands."

—**Robert Zettle, PhD**, professor and director of clinical training in the department of psychology at Wichita State University, and author of *ACT for Depression*

"Accessible, actionable, practical, engaging, and user-friendly. This book will help ACT practitioners to overcome the blocks they are experiencing in simple, yet effective ways. A must-read for those who want to take their ACT skills and competencies to the next level."

—**Aisling Leonard-Curtin**, chartered psychologist, codirector of ACT Now Purposeful Living, coeditor of *Mindfulness and Acceptance for Gender and Sexual Minorities*, and coauthor of *The Power of Small*

"This book provides a treasure trove of answers to the questions that arise in doing ACT: especially when conversations, exercises, and techniques do not go as planned, and when the messy business of living requires creativity from the therapist and client! In this very engaging book, Russ Harris describes the common challenges in doing ACT well, and provides guidance about the ACT model and its foundations that will broaden any therapist's practice. Highly recommended as a friendly companion to the standard ACT textbooks."

—**Eric Morris, PhD**, director of the La Trobe University Psychology Clinic, Melbourne Australia; and coauthor of *Activate Your Life* and *ACT for Psychosis Recovery*

"Russ Harris uses the Choice Point to anchor the reader's understanding of ACT, and then takes a deep dive into the subtleties of everyday applications. With humor and excellent examples, he offers guidance to new and experienced students of ACT. 'Vicious Values' was my personal favorite of the sixteen chapters. It's a quick read, and the 'Clinician's Guide to Getting Unstuck' in the appendices is a treasure. Thank you again, Russ, for moving the field forward!"

—**Patricia J. Robinson, PhD**, Mountainview Consulting Group; master clinician and international ACT trainer; coauthor of *The Mindfulness and Acceptance Workbook for Depression* and *In This Moment*

"This book is an indispensable resource for any clinician learning and practicing ACT. Russ Harris skillfully provides practical guidance and answers to questions commonly asked by ACT therapists. The reader is guided through an accessible approach to learning effective responses to challenging clinical situations. The real-world applicability provided in the pages of this book is bound to be greatly appreciated those who are learning, teaching, and/or practicing ACT."

—**Laura Silberstein-Tirch, PsyD**, clinical psychologist and director at The Center for Compassion Focused Therapy

ACT QUESTIONS & ANSWERS

A Practitioner's Guide *to* 150 Common Sticking Points *in* Acceptance & Commitment Therapy

RUSS HARRIS

CONTEXT PRESS
An Imprint of New Harbinger Publications, Inc.

Publisher's Note

This publication is designed to provide accurate and authoritative information in regard to the subject matter covered. It is sold with the understanding that the publisher is not engaged in rendering psychological, financial, legal, or other professional services. If expert assistance or counseling is needed, the services of a competent professional should be sought.

Distributed in Canada by Raincoast Books

Context Press
An imprint of New Harbinger Publications, Inc.
5674 Shattuck Avenue
Oakland, CA 94609
www.newharbinger.com

Cover design by Amy Shoup

Acquired by Tesilya Hanauer

Edited by Rona Bernstein

Library of Congress Cataloging-in-Publication Data on file

20 19 18

10 9 8 7 6 5 4 3 2 1 First Printing

Contents

Introduction

How to Use This Book (Please don't skip this—it's important!)

Have you ever read an ACT (acceptance and commitment therapy) textbook and wondered, *Hmm—but what if a client doesn't react that way? What if he does* X, Y, Z *instead?* Have you ever tried out an ACT tool, technique, process, or strategy and found it had radically different results from what you'd expected? Have you ever found ACT seems to work differently with your clients than what you saw, heard, or read about during your introductory ACT training?

If your answer to all three questions is yes, then welcome to the club! That means you're normal! Almost all ACT therapists have these experiences sooner or later. And that's why I wrote this book: to help you out when things go awry and standard textbooks don't really tell you how to fix them.

I've assembled this textbook from literally thousands of questions I've been asked over the years by therapists training in ACT. At this point, I've run over 500 ACT workshops around the world, in addition to training thousands of therapists through my online courses. And I've picked the questions that keep cropping up again and again. (And again.)

In some cases, I've modified and broadened the questions so that they are relevant to the widest possible range of ACT practitioners and their clients. And I've answered them in ways that are not just theoretical but highly practical, so you can take that information and immediately apply it in useful ways to help both yourself and your clients. I'm confident that this book will help you take your ACT skills and knowledge to the next level, no matter what kind of practitioner you are (therapist, coach, nurse, counselor, doctor), what type of clients you have, and what type of issues you deal with.

Now having said all of that, ACT is not a one-size-fits-all approach. There is no stock standard response that will always suffice for a specific problem. There will always be exceptions to the answers I give in these question and answer (Q&A) discussions, because I can't realistically account for all the possible variables of every possible situation. To do ACT well, we need to be flexible, to adapt what we do to meet the demands of the situation. So please make sure to adapt and modify all the answers I give throughout this book to suit the unique circumstances of your unique client. This is especially so when working with children and adolescents. The answers in this book all refer to adult clients, and some of them may need to be dramatically modified when working with children and adolescents.

My hope is that you'll use this as an adjunct to any other core ACT textbook. I've written it to cover the main issues that tend to get missed, be skimmed over, or simply leave people a bit confused. You'll note that several chapters are much longer than the rest—most notably chapter 6, Vicious Values, and chapter 9, Dastardly Defusion. This reflects the disproportionate number of questions that I get asked on those topics. (And if you're wondering about the unusual chapter titles, they are an homage to the British TV show *Horrible Histories*, which has many playful names for different periods of history: "Rotten Romans," "Vicious Vikings," "Measly Middle Ages," and so on.)

I recommend you begin by reading the opening chapter on the choice point because I refer back to this in almost every other chapter. Then I recommend you read the next four chapters, in order, because they cover many of the essentials for effective therapy, so later chapters often refer back to them. The rest of the chapters, from chapter 6 onward, aren't in any specific order (at least that I'm consciously aware of), so feel free to work through them in your own way, however it suits you. (How's that for flexibility?) You can pick a chapter of interest and read it from end to end. Or you can just open it at random and read from wherever your eyes happen to land.

At the end of the book, there are several appendices in which you'll find a variety of useful scripts and worksheets. Of special note is appendix 9: A Clinician's Guide to Getting Unstuck from Just About Anything. This is a quick reference to use—after you've gone through the whole book at least once—to help you out when you're feeling really stuck with a client. You can download all these appendices, as well as many other resources mentioned throughout the book, from the free resources page on http://www.ImLearningACT.com. To access them, click on the "Free Stuff" tab on the home page and then click the link for The Complete Set of Worksheets and Handouts for ACT *Questions and Answers*.

I hope you enjoy reading this book as much as I enjoyed watching *La La Land* during a break from writing it—but even if you don't, I trust there will still be plenty in here to help you take your ACT skills to the next level. Good luck!

—Russ Harris

Melbourne, Australia, May 2017

CHAPTER 1

Playing with the Choice Point

It's easy to get overwhelmed by the vast and ever-expanding range of tools, techniques, and strategies available to us in ACT, so I want to kick off this book by introducing you to a very simple but comprehensive tool that will allow you and your clients to rapidly get to grips with the ACT model. It's called the choice point, and you'll find that I refer to it in many of the questions and answers throughout this book, especially to two aspects of it: "towards moves" and "away moves."

This chapter is different from all the other ones in this book. Instead of Q&A discussions, I'm going to cover the topic as in a standard textbook. At the time of writing, the choice point is a relatively unknown tool, outside of Australia, where it originated. Over the next few years, as I write new editions of my textbooks and self-help books, I'll be including this tool in all of them, so it will steadily gain more attention. But for now, there's a good chance that you, dear reader, are unfamiliar with it. So what follows is a quick introduction.

What Is the Choice Point?

The choice point is a simple tool for building psychological flexibility in just about anyone, at any time, in any place. We can use it for many purposes, including to explain the ACT model, take a history, set an agenda for a session, summarize a session, and actively develop all of the core ACT processes. In this chapter, I'm just introducing you to a few of its most basic applications. There are many more ways to use it as a tool in therapy in addition to those described here, and you can find more materials on the free resources page on http://www.ImLearningACT.com

When Ann Bailey, Joe Ciarrochi, and I created the original choice point for our book on ACT and weight loss, *The Weight Escape* (Ciarrochi, Bailey, & Harris, 2013), we were "standing on the shoulders of giants," inspired and influenced by a range of powerful and creative tools that came before us. Our two main influences were

- the ABC model of behavior analysis (Antecedents => Behavior => Consequences) and
- the "bull's-eye," created by Tobias Lundgren (Dahl & Lundgren, 2006), which first introduced the terms *towards moves* and *away moves* to ACT.

We were also influenced by the great simplicity, practicality, and user-friendliness of

- the "Four Square Tool" (Strosahl, Robinson, & Gustavsson, 2012) and
- the "Matrix" (Polk & Schoendorff, 2014).

In recent years, I have modified the original choice point, and what I present to you now is a new version, which I sometimes call the *choice point 2.0*, or *CP2* (but more commonly just refer to as the *choice point* because it's shorter).

The diagram below shows what a CP2 looks like in its most basic form. I think it's better to draw this by hand in a session rather than print it out, but on the web page mentioned at the end of this chapter, you'll find several printable versions with various degrees of text on them.

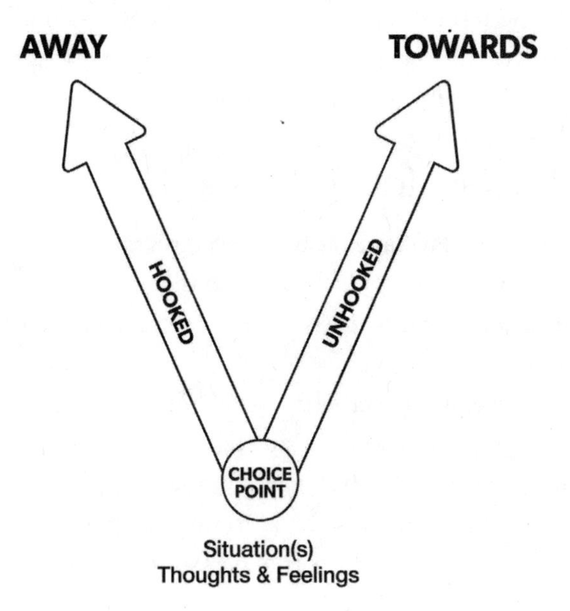

Here is what a hand-drawn CP2 looks like:

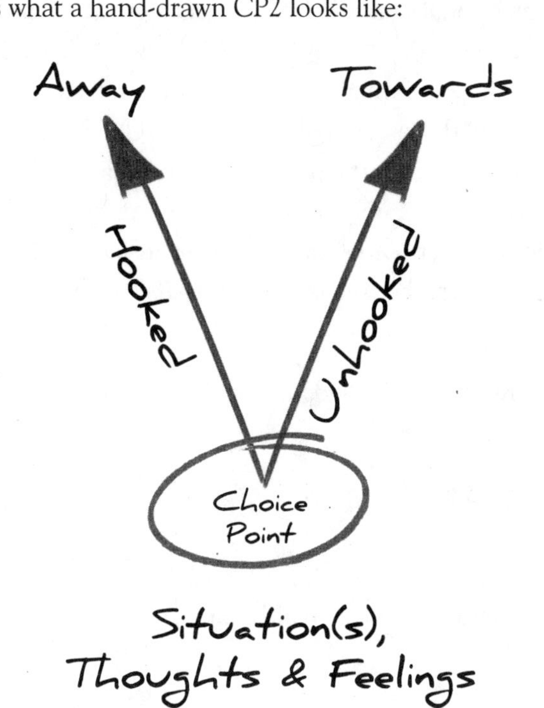

Note that the term *thoughts & feelings* in the diagram is short for all private experiences: thoughts, feelings, emotions, memories, images, urges, sensations, beliefs, cravings, schemas, and so on.

What Do We Mean by "Hooked"?

Hooked is a useful layman's term for *cognitive fusion*. All emotions and feelings involve cognition. So I like to talk to therapists about "fusion with thoughts *and feelings*," and to clients about "getting hooked by thoughts *and feelings*."

Fusion is the overarching problem we address in ACT. The term *fusion* implies that thoughts and feelings are having a negative influence on behavior—such that behavior becomes so inflexible or rigid that it's self-defeating, problematic, and detrimental to well-being. In other words, the behavior takes you away from the sort of person you want to be, away from the sort of life you want to build.

And one of the most common ways we get hooked is by fusion with the agenda of emotional control: *I must avoid (get rid of) my unpleasant thoughts and feelings*. This is known in ACT as *experiential avoidance*. Experiential avoidance is normal and only reaches problematic levels when there is fusion with the emotional control agenda. When this occurs, experiential avoidance tends to dominate our behavior. But note that experiential avoidance is rarely if ever the only problem we address in ACT. Rather, it's a subset of the many problems fusion creates.

In addition to getting hooked by the emotional control agenda, we can also get hooked by

- reason-giving, rules, judgments, the past, the future, our self-concept;
- looking good and being right;
- perfectionism;
- seeking pleasure, power, wealth, fame, status, and other coveted goals;

- a sense of entitlement or righteousness;
- any emotion, such as anxiety, fear, sadness, anger, shame, guilt, greed, envy, jealousy, lust;
- urges, cravings, desires;
- and much more!

Towards and Away Moves

In both the choice point and the bull's-eye (appendix 3), *away moves* mean ineffective, values-incongruent action—in other words, moving away from the person you want to be, or moving away from the life you want to build. These away moves are often but not always due to experiential avoidance. They are also often due to fusion with reasons, rules, "being right," "looking good," seeking pleasure, or any combination of positive or negative thoughts, feelings, emotions, and memories. *Towards moves*, in contrast, involve effective, values-congruent actions that are in line with the person you want to be.

If you're familiar with the ACT matrix, it's important to note that this is a massive difference from the way the term *away moves* is commonly used with that tool. In all current textbook descriptions of the matrix, the term *away moves* does *not* mean moving away from values or moving away from the life you want to build. Instead, the term means moving away from difficult thoughts and feelings, or moving away from inner obstacles. This difference is vital to recognize; moving away from painful or difficult thoughts and feelings is not the same thing as moving away from values. This doesn't make the choice point right or the matrix wrong; it's simply a difference between the tools.

Before we go any further, it's essential to recognize that towards moves and away moves are always from the client's perspective, not the therapist's. For example, if the client sees his behavior of going out and getting completely drunk with his buddies as life enhancing, effective, and in line with the person he wants to be, then it would be a towards move (even if the therapist sees it as destructive or self-defeating).

At the start of therapy, some clients will class certain behaviors as towards moves even though in the therapist's eyes they are obviously self-defeating. This is common in addictions and eating disorders. The therapist should not question the client's view if this happens. At this point in therapy, we just want to introduce the client to looking functionally at his behavior; it's okay if he doesn't yet see the self-defeating consequences of a behavior; it's a new skill he's learning.

As therapy progresses and values clarification happens in depth, such behaviors can be revisited and compassionately and respectfully explored to see if they truly are values-congruent and effective for the client in terms of being the person he wants to be and building the life he wants in the long term. At this later point, clients will often change their minds and class these towards moves as away moves.

Also note that a behavior may be towards or away depending on the situation. Here's an example from my own life. When I eat cake mindfully, truly savoring it, as part of a special occasion like a birthday celebration, I class it as a towards move. But when I eat cake mindlessly, wolfing down a second and third slice when I'm hooked by greed and sugar cravings, I class that as an away move. (Please don't tell anyone I do this, by the way. I want everyone to think I am a true mindfulness guru.)

The Choice Point 2.0 and the Six Core ACT Processes

The choice point 2.0 easily maps onto the ACT "hexaflex": the six core processes of acceptance, defusion, contacting the present moment, self-as-context, values, and committed action. The next diagram illustrates this:

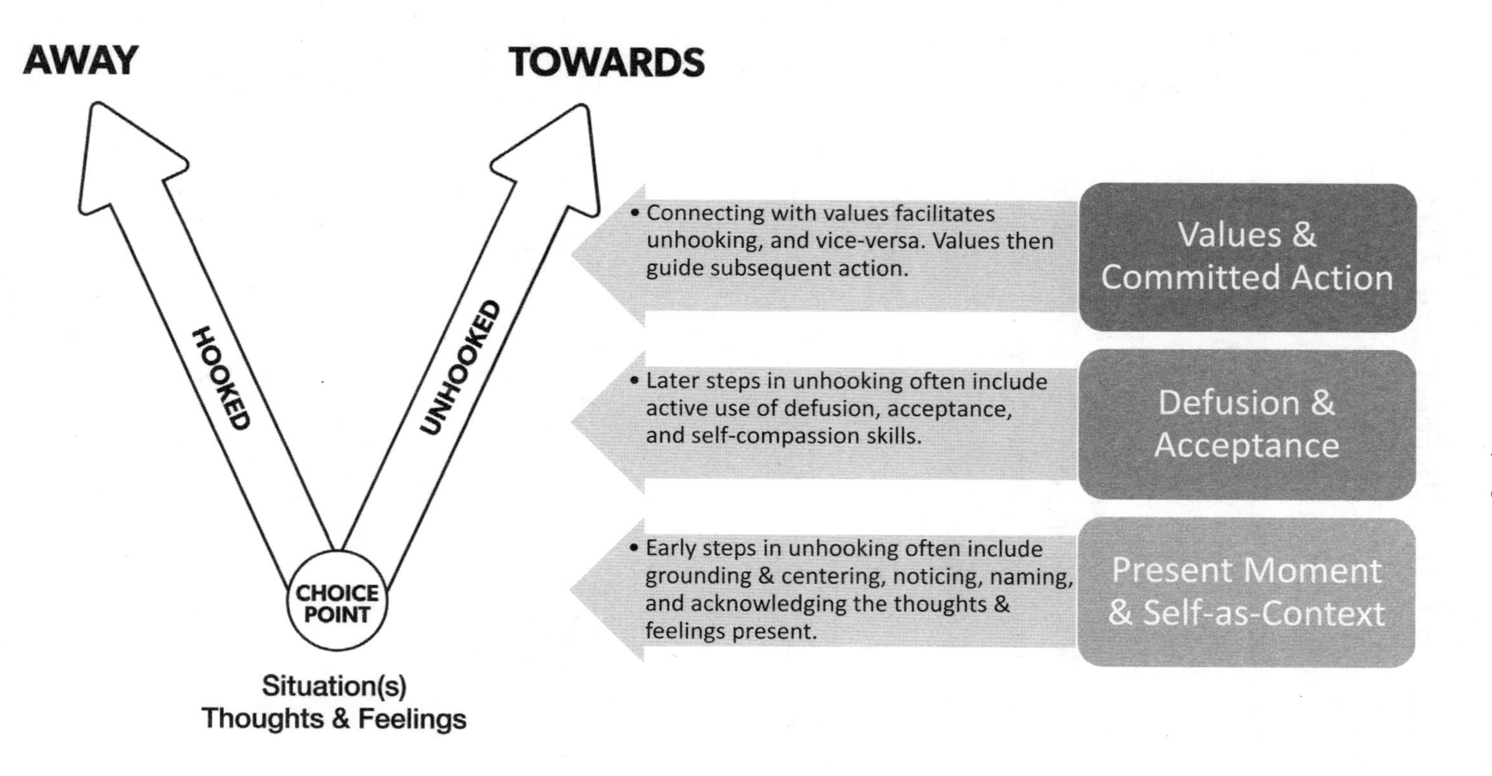
AWAY
TOWARDS
HOOKED
UNHOOKED
CHOICE POINT
Situation(s)
Thoughts & Feelings
• Connecting with values facilitates unhooking, and vice-versa. Values then guide subsequent action.
Values & Committed Action
• Later steps in unhooking often include active use of defusion, acceptance, and self-compassion skills.
Defusion & Acceptance
• Early steps in unhooking often include grounding & centering, noticing, naming, and acknowledging the thoughts & feelings present.
Present Moment & Self-as-Context

Introducing the Choice Point 2.0 to Clients

When introducing the CP2 to clients, I like to explain it as I draw it, as follows:

Therapist: Can I draw you something? It's a kind of map, to help us keep track of what we do here. All day long, humans do things—cook dinner, drink coffee, play with the kids, watch movies... We're always doing something, even if it's just sleeping in bed. Now some things we do move us toward the life we want to live—acting effectively, behaving like the sort of person we want to be—and we can call these *towards moves*.

Therapist draws and writes:

Therapist: And some things we do move us away from the life we want to live—acting ineffectively, behaving unlike the sort of person we want to be—and we can call these *away moves*.

Therapist draws and writes:

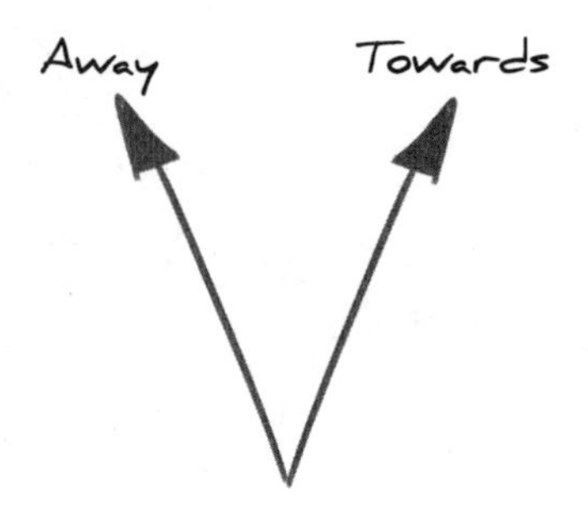

Therapist: (*continuing*) Now when life is easy, giving us what we want, it's usually fairly easy for us to choose towards moves: to act effectively, treat ourselves and others the way we want to deep in our heart, do the things that make life better in the long term, rather than worse. But unfortunately, life just isn't that easy most of the time, and it doesn't give us what we want for very long. So as we go about our day, all sorts of challenging situations and difficult thoughts and feelings arise.

Therapist draws and writes: "Situation(s), Thoughts & Feelings"

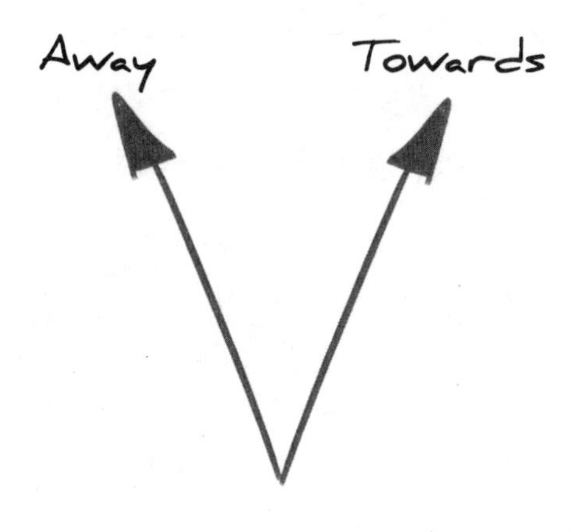

Therapist: And unfortunately, we tend to easily get "hooked" by those difficult thoughts and feelings; they hook us, and they reel us in, and jerk us around, and pull us off track—and once we're hooked, we start doing all those away moves. Almost every psychological disorder, from stress and anxiety to depression and addiction, boils down to this basic process: we get hooked by difficult thoughts and feelings and we do away moves.

Therapist writes: "Hooked"

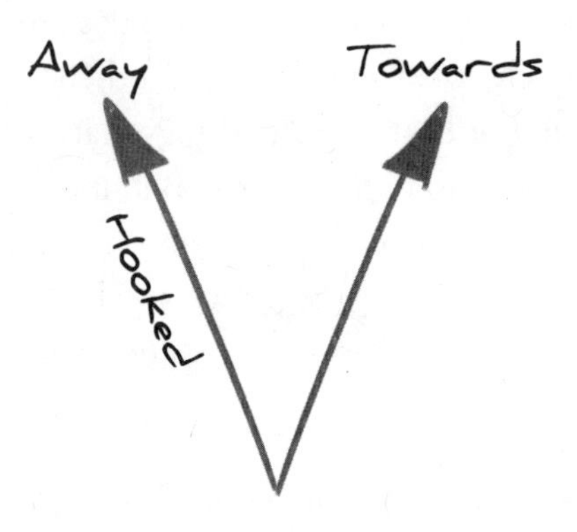

Therapist: However, there are times when most of us are able to unhook ourselves from those difficult thoughts and feelings, and do towards moves instead—doing things that move us toward the life we want to live—acting effectively, behaving like the sort of person we want to be. And the better we get at doing this, the better life gets.

Therapist writes: "Unhooked"

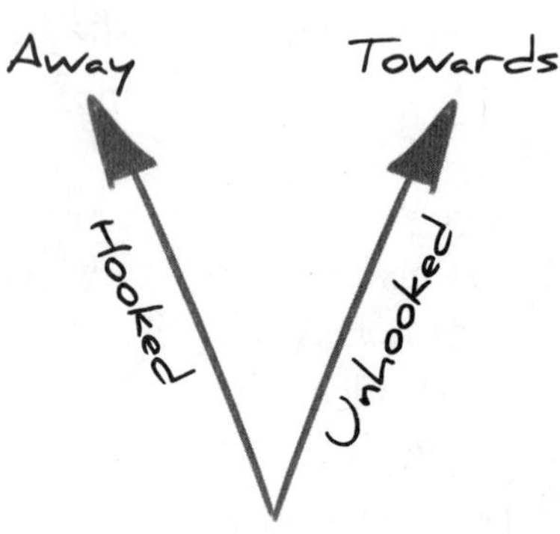

(Therapist draws a little circle around the part where the arrows converge and writes in the words "choice point" or the initials "CP.")

Therapist: So when we're in these challenging situations, experiencing difficult thoughts and feelings, there's a choice for us to make: How are we going to respond? Do we unhook and do towards moves? Or do we get hooked and do away moves?

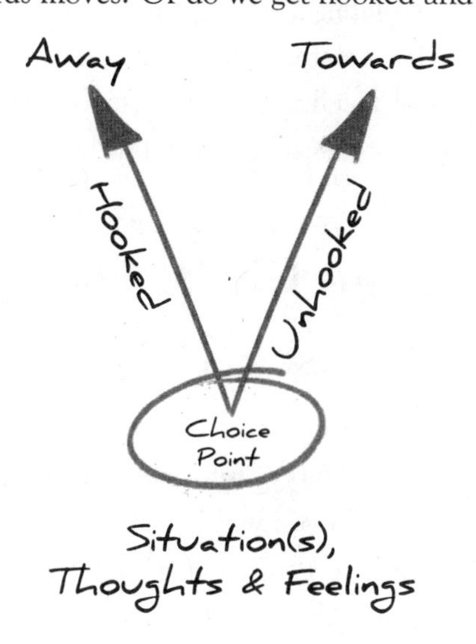

Therapist: For most of us, our default setting is that we get hooked, we do away moves. But as we develop our unhooking skills, and we get clear about what matters to us, we find we have a lot more choice about how we respond. It gets easier for us to choose this way (*points to towards arrow*) over that way (*points to away arrow*). So that's what this approach is all about. Basically, it's about helping you to get a lot better at doing this stuff (*pointing to "towards" section*)—if and when that's what you want to do.

So one of our aims is to help you identify your values—in other words, to get clear on what matters to you and who you care about and what sort of person you want to be—and use those values to guide and inspire and motivate you to do more of these towards moves.

And another aim is to develop *unhooking skills*, so you can get much better at unhooking from all those difficult thoughts and feelings (*pointing to "unhooked" section*).

These towards moves also include taking action to solve your problems, and overcome challenges, and change those difficult situations for the better, if and when they can be changed (*pointing to "situations"*).

So the greater our ability to unhook from difficult thoughts and feelings, and choose towards moves, the greater our quality of life, our health, our happiness and well-being.

Applications of the Choice Point

CP2 Model Overview and Informed Consent

The preceding setup of the choice point provides a quick overview of the model and can become a part of informed consent for ACT by demonstrating the therapy approach you will be taking. You can also show your client the YouTube video I've created that demonstrates the CP2 in the form of an animation. Just search on https://www.YouTube.com for Russ Harris Choice Point.

Taking a History and Case Formulation

We can use the choice point 2.0 for taking a history, case formulation, or both, as the next diagram illustrates. Using the CP2, we can map out a broad overview of life as it is today—writing in a wide range of situations, thoughts, feelings, away moves, and towards moves across a number of life domains—or we can use it to narrow the focus to one specific situation.

The example in the diagram below shows a narrow-focus CP2, zooming in on a specific situation: a teenage boy who is avoiding math homework.

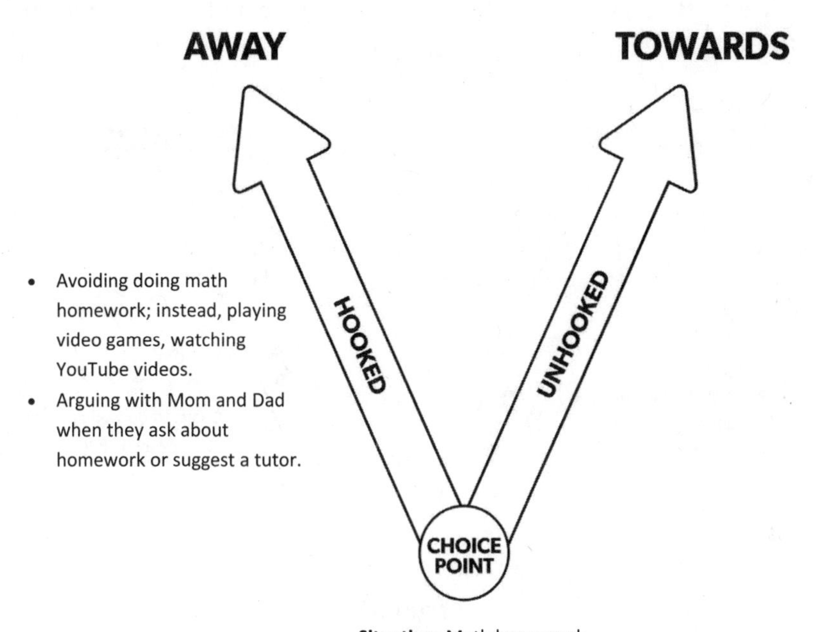

Having highlighted the fusion, avoidance, and unworkable action, we can go on to fill in the right side of the diagram. This is a dynamic process that involves an ongoing dance between goals, actions, and values. Often, it's easier to identify goals and actions initially, and tease out values later.

For example, suppose we ask the client what he wants to be doing instead of his away moves: what he'd like to have happen with his math lessons, and what he'd like to have happen in his relationship with his mom and dad. He answers that he doesn't want to argue with Mom and Dad and he doesn't want to keep doing badly at math. Notice these goals are worded in the negative. Those are *dead person's goals*—goals that a corpse could do better than the client, as we'll explore in chapter 3—so we reframe them as *live person's goals* (get along well with Mom and Dad, do well at math) and we write them in as helpers, about halfway down on the right side, as shown on the next diagram.

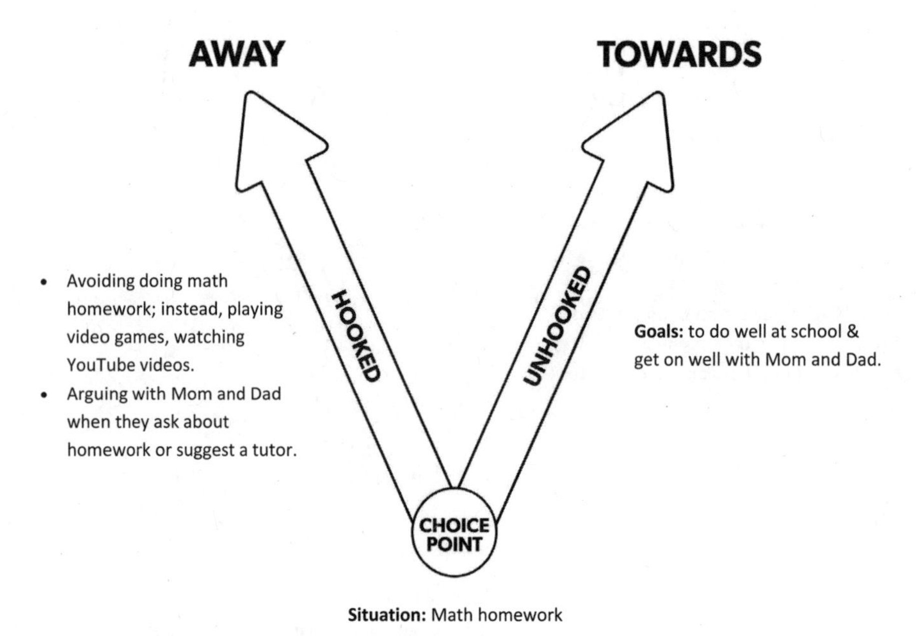

We flesh out the right side by "dancing" between values, goals, and actions. Dance moves can include clarifying values, setting goals, creating action plains, exploring the values implicit in any goal or action, using values to set goals and guide actions, building actions up into larger goals, and breaking goals down into actions. We can do this in any order we like; there's no fixed sequence.

Keep in mind as you do this: towards and away moves are always from the client's perspective. So if the parents or therapist see doing math homework or getting a math tutor as a towards move, but the teenager does not, then it does not go down as a towards move!

In this specific case, we move from goals to actions and values: the client identifies towards moves that will take him toward the goals specified, as the next diagram shows.

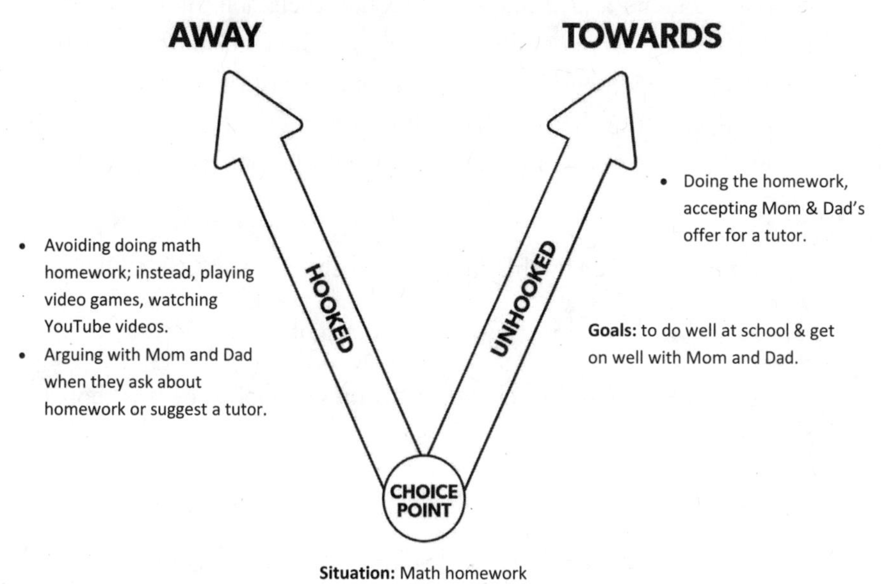

Remember that you can make a choice point diagram as specific, narrow, and focused as you'd like. For example, for this client you might do a very broad diagram on his relationships in general, a more focused one on his relationship with one or both of his parents, or a very specific one focused on the situation of his parents asking him about homework.

Developing Unhooking Skills

Unhooking often refers specifically to defusion, but unhooking skills can include any or all of the main four ACT mindfulness skills:

- Defusion
- Acceptance
- Contacting the present moment

- Self-as-context

These are all unhooking skills in the sense that they can help us to notice our thoughts and feelings and reduce their dominance over our behavior; they help us respond more flexibly to thoughts and feelings that typically trigger rigid, self-defeating behavioral repertoires.

If you're using the choice point with your clients, you can run through this simple five-step questioning process, which can help them to unhook from any thought or feeling:

1. Are you hooked by this thought or feeling? (If no, go to 3.)
2. If yes, what effect is it having on you right now?
3. How do you usually behave when you get hooked by this thought or feeling?
4. What towards moves would you do if you weren't hooked?
5. What unhooking skills can you use right now, if necessary?

Running through the first four questions often helps the client to rapidly unhook. However, if the client remains hooked, question 5 prompts him to use additional unhooking skills, such as grounding techniques, acceptance and self-compassion exercises, or other defusion techniques. It can be helpful to print these questions out and give them to the client to take home and use between sessions.

Identifying Helpers

We don't have to use the term *helpers*, but many clients like it. *Helpers* is a convenient term for all the stuff we place on the right side of the diagram to facilitate towards moves:

- Values and goals: What matters to you? Who do you care about? What sort of person do you want to be?
- Values and actions: How do you want to treat yourself, others, the world around you? What do you want to do more of, less of, or differently? What do you want to stop or start doing?

- Unhooking skills: defusion, acceptance, contacting the present moment, self-as-context, self-compassion.
- Additional life skills: problem solving, goal setting, action planning, and others as needed (e.g., assertiveness, communication, empathy).

We can write "Helpers" in on the right side of the diagram as therapy progresses. The next diagram illustrates this.

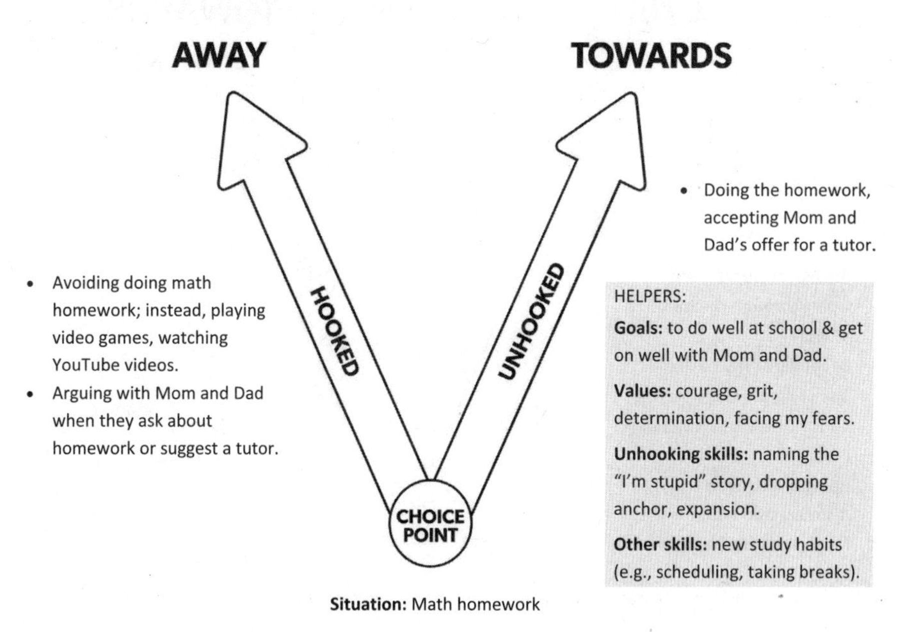

DSM-5 and ICD-10 ACT Formulation

Almost any disorder included in the *Diagnostic and Statistical Manual of Mental Disorders* (5th ed.; *DSM-5*; American Psychiatric Association [APA], 2013) or the *International Classification of Diseases* (10th ed.; *ICD-10*; World Health Organization, 1992) can quickly and simply be summarized and reformulated in terms of ACT, via the bottom and left side of the choice point 2.0.

For example, in the next diagram, we meet a client with depression. Note how the diagram reformulates depression in terms of ACT processes: fusion with or experiential avoidance of thoughts and feelings (HOOKED), values-incongruent, ineffective behavior (AWAY MOVES), and challenging life situations that require problem solving and committed action (SITUATIONS). You can easily map this out as you take a history of the client's presenting complaint(s).

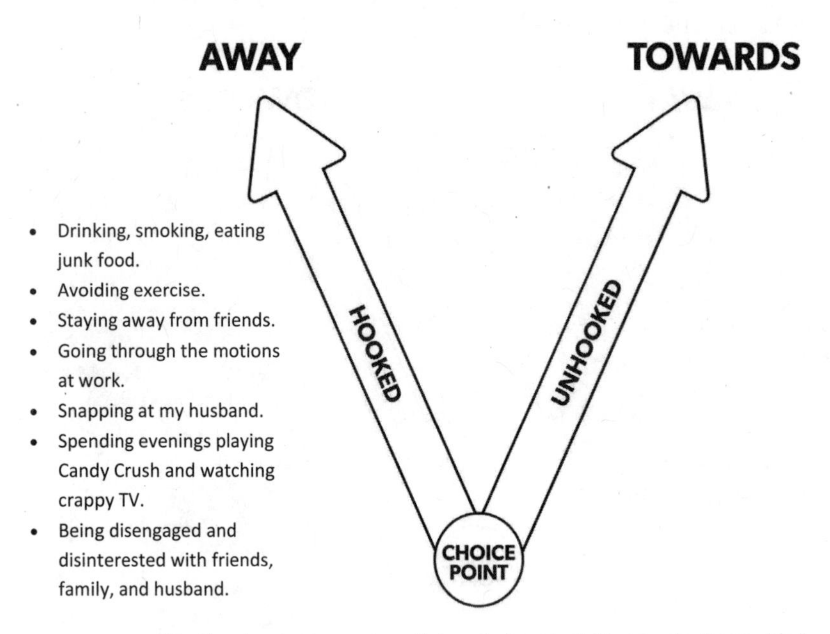

Situation: tension in marriage, "job sucks," overweight and unfit, "boring life."

Thoughts & Feelings: anxiety, sadness, guilt, shame. I'm dull/stupid/boring. I'm fat, I can't change, life sucks, I hate myself and my job, my husband will leave me.

As therapy progresses, we can fill in the right side from session to session—identifying current towards moves and desired towards moves, and writing down "helpers" as they are introduced.

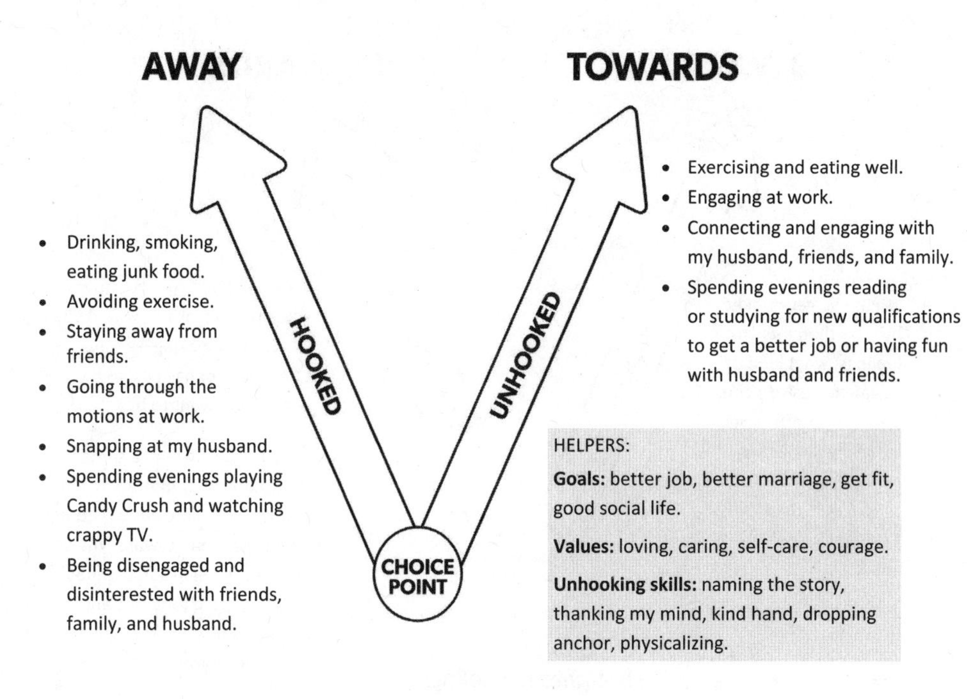

Situation: tension in marriage, "job sucks," overweight and unfit, "boring life."

Thoughts & Feelings: anxiety, sadness, guilt, shame. I'm dull/stupid/boring. I'm fat, I can't change, life sucks, I hate myself and my job, my husband will leave me.

So, as shown in the next diagram, there are four broad areas to explore when using the choice point 2.0 for taking a history and case formulation, for any *DSM-5* disorder or client issue.

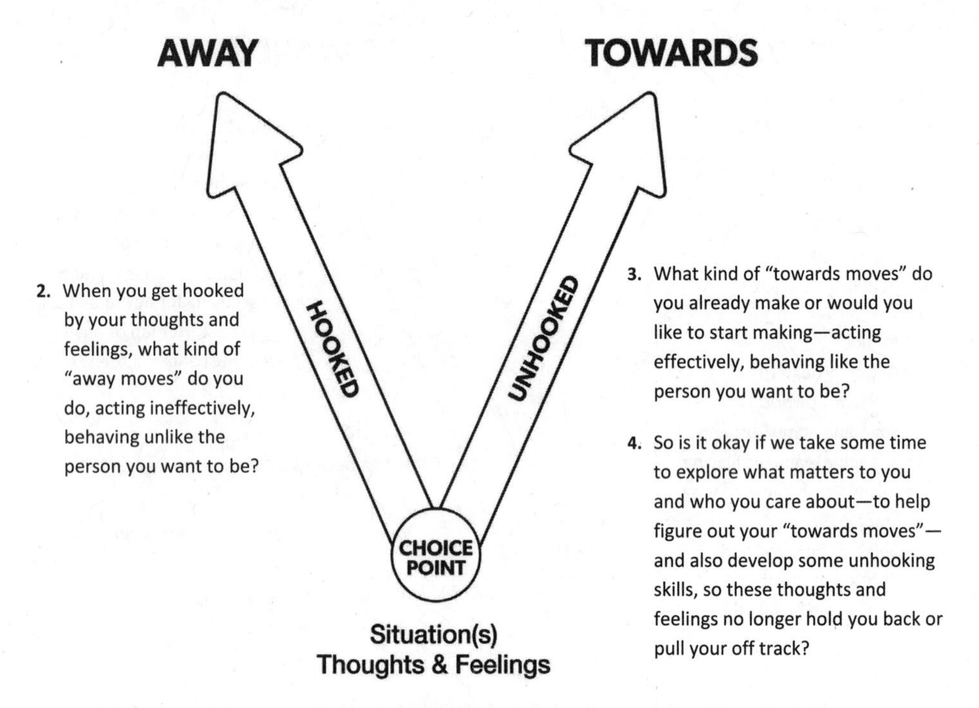

Treatment Considerations

Aversive Vs. Appetitive Control

The main problem we treat in ACT is narrow, rigid, inflexible behavior. Inflexible behavior is often under *aversive control*, meaning it is motivated by trying to avoid or escape something you don't want: an *aversive stimulus*. An example is taking drugs primarily to escape feelings of anxiety or traumatic memories.

However, inflexible behavior is also often under *appetitive control*; that is, it is motivated by trying to get something you do want: an *appetitive stimulus*. An example of this is taking drugs primarily to have fun, party on with friends, or fit in with a social scene.

One of our main aims in ACT is to help people develop broader, more flexible repertoires of behavior in the presence of both appetitive stimuli and aversive stimuli that normally tend to cue rigid, self-defeating behaviors. In other words, the core issue is not about whether behavior is under aversive or appetitive control, but whether behavior is flexible or inflexible.

The Language of Choice

I have sometimes had clients say, "But I have no choice." And I'm sure you can imagine just how badly it would go if I started to insist, "Oh yes you do!" We never want to get into struggles with our clients about what's right or wrong or true or false. So if clients say they have no choice, I validate this response. I say, "Yes, that's the way it's been for you for a long time. Without unhooking skills we effectively have no choice; we get hooked and we do away moves. It's automatic. So a big aim of our work here is to help you to have some choice, and that will involve learning new skills. Without these new unhooking skills, you'll keep on doing the same things, over and over."

It's a good way of reaffirming the need to learn or practice new skills. If the client doesn't learn them, she is likely to just keep going through the left side of the choice point: repeating the same old away moves.

We can also use this strategy when clients with impulsive, compulsive, aggressive, suicidal, addictive, or self-harming behaviors make the same argument: "I can't control it, I have no choice, it just happens before I realize it." We validate: "Yes, right now, that's exactly the way it is. Right now, you can't control it, you have no choice, it just happens before you realize it. Would you like to change that? If so, it's going to require learning some new skills."

The Wrap-Up

Hopefully you can see how the CP2 lends itself easily to several ACT applications:

- *Informed consent*
- *ACT case formulation*
- *Setting an agenda ("Which part of this shall we focus on today?")*
- *Summarizing a session ("Here's what we covered today.")*
- *Clarifying values, setting goals, planning actions*
- *Identifying difficult thoughts and feelings for defusion and acceptance*
- *Identifying difficult situations that require problem solving and committed action*

We can also use the CP2 in many other ways, but that's beyond the scope of this basic overview. As I mentioned earlier, you'll find more information and a variety of printable versions on the free resources page of http://www.ImLearningACT.com. So now, let's get started with our Q&A!

CHAPTER 2

Miserable Mindfulness

Among all the different mindfulness-based models of therapy, there is not one agreed-upon definition of mindfulness. In most ACT textbooks and research papers, mindfulness is used as an umbrella term for four interconnected skills: defusion, acceptance, self-as-context, and contacting the present moment. However, in a small number of ACT textbooks and research papers, the term mindfulness is used synonymously with contacting the present moment. I strongly prefer the former usage over the latter. Like the majority of ACT authors, trainers, and researchers, I see all four core processes mentioned above as types of mindfulness skills.

So, keeping in mind there isn't an official, universally agreed-upon definition of the term (neither inside ACT nor in the broader field of psychology), I tend to define mindfulness as "a set of psychological skills for effective living, based on a special way of paying attention: with flexibility, openness, curiosity, and warmth." But you don't have to use that definition if you don't want to; I won't be offended!

Discussions in This Chapter:

- How do I sell mindfulness to my clients?
- What if the client reacts negatively to the word mindfulness?
- Is mindful breathing a relaxation technique?
- What if focusing on the breath increases a client's distress?

- What if clients drift off, zone out, or find it hard to engage in mindfulness exercises?
- What if clients don't want mindfulness to "take away from time to talk"?
- Is a state of absorption, such as reading a book or watching a movie, the same as a state of mindfulness?
- What if clients say they "don't know how to apply mindfulness in everyday life"?

Q: How do I sell mindfulness to my clients?

Russ: I think it's best to avoid trying to sell mindfulness. Personally, I hardly ever use the word these days because it's become such a vague and muddied term; many people now think it means things such as meditation, Buddhism, relaxation, feeling good, having a still mind with no thoughts, a form of distraction, a way to get rid of painful thoughts and feelings, positive thinking, and so on. Given all this confusion, and given that in ACT the term *mindfulness* usually refers to at least four different skills (defusion, acceptance, contacting the present moment, and self-as-context), I think it's better to use different words.

Ideally, we want everything we recommend to clients to be clearly and directly relevant and applicable to whatever they're struggling with, and I believe we're often better off doing this without ever mentioning the word *mindfulness*. For example, if clients are hooked by difficult thoughts or worrying or rumination, we could talk about helping them to "unhook" or learn some "unhooking skills." Or if making room for difficult feelings will help clients live their values and pursue their goals, we can talk about helping them "expand around" or "open up and make room for" those feelings and then refer to "expansion skills" or "opening up skills." Another option is "flow skills," as in learning how to let feelings flow through them. And if they're having difficulty focusing on important tasks, engaging in life, or being present with their kids, then we can help them "focus," "refocus," "engage," "train their attention," or "be present." Basically, as a term, *mindfulness* is often just too abstract, too heady, too generic, and too far removed from clients' issues.

One thing to watch for is the enormous difference between "practicing mindfulness" and "practicing mindfulness meditation." They aren't the same thing. There are zillions of ways to practice mindfulness in everyday life, without ever meditating. The simple fact is, most clients won't get into meditation in a big way, if at all. And for many, even the thought of meditation will be a turn-off. If you're running a mindfulness meditation program and that's what people are coming along for, great. But in a therapy context, if you start trying to sell meditation, you'll likely find it a very hard sell.

The bottom line is that we need to link each of the four specific mindfulness skills covered in ACT—defusion, acceptance, contacting the present moment, and self-as-context—to clients' specific issues and their goals for therapy. We need to make sure that they not only see why this is relevant but also get to experience the benefits during the actual session.

After every experiential mindfulness exercise you do in session, it's a good idea to ask your client, "How can this be useful to you outside the room? How can this help you with the issues you are coming here for?" If clients can't answer those questions, then why on earth would they bother to practice? It just doesn't seem relevant to them. Of course, if clients *can* answer those questions, then there's no "selling" or "buy-in" needed; we can simply go on to ask, "So would you be willing to practice this between sessions?" And from there, we can go on to brainstorm when, where, and in what manner they'll do so.

Q: What if the client reacts negatively to the word *mindfulness*?

Russ: As I indicated above, these days I'm increasingly advising therapists not to use the word *mindfulness*, as it can so easily trigger a negative reaction. (For a dramatic example, a psychologist I know recently had a new client say to him angrily, "I know what mindfulness is! You can take that mindful raisin and shove it up your arse!") So I recommend you use alternative terms, such as those mentioned in the previous Q&A, at least early on in therapy. But if you do use the "m" word with a client, and it does elicit a negative reaction, then you want to respectfully explore that response. Does the client see it as a religious practice? Has he heard bad things about it? What are his past experiences with mindfulness? What mindfulness practices has he already tried? What was he hoping would happen, and what actually did happen?

One of the most common reasons for a negative reaction to the "m" word—such as rolled eyeballs and a loud groan, or a protest ("I hate that mindfulness stuff. It's all bullshit!")—is that the client equates mindfulness with a formal meditation practice. Typically, she has been to therapy or a mindfulness training of some sort and has sat through long, formal, mindfulness meditation exercises, without clearly understanding the purpose or how to apply it in everyday life. She has likely found such experiences boring, frustrating, confusing, or unhelpful. Typically, she won't have any inkling of the kind of flexible, nonmeditative, intensely practical mindfulness practices we do in ACT.

So we want to respectfully tease out that information from the client. We might say, "Thanks for being so upfront with me. I'm certainly not going to push you into anything you aren't open to. I'm guessing you've had a bad experience with mindfulness in the past. That's not uncommon. The word mindfulness is a bit like the word music; there are many different styles and variants. If you hate hip-hop but you love reggae, you wouldn't dismiss all music; you'd just be selective about which type of music you listen to. It's much the same with mindfulness; there are so many different types of stuff that come under that heading. When my clients have reactions like yours, it's almost always because they've been through something that's radically different from what I do. So can you tell me a bit about what you did, and what happened—so I can make sure that what you and I do is significantly different?"

Having elicited that information, we can say something like, "Well given all that, I can understand your negative reaction to the word mindfulness. What we do here is so different; can we just forget I ever used the word? What I meant was learning new skills to handle difficult thoughts and feelings more effectively, and get more satisfaction out of life."

Q: Is mindful breathing a relaxation technique?

Russ: Breathing exercises in ACT have different functions in different contexts. We may use mindful breathing:

- as a way to train attention: to learn the skills of narrowing focus (zooming in on the breath), sustaining focus (keeping it on the breath), and refocusing attention after it's wandered away from the breath. This kind of breath-focused attention training is especially useful where distractibility is a big problem, such as in ADHD and anxiety disorders.
- for grounding and centering: to "drop an anchor in the midst of an emotional storm."
- to facilitate acceptance, which we might refer to as "breathing into a feeling."
- as an element of self-compassion—as a form of kind self-soothing.
- for homeostasis. When clients hyperventilate, carbon dioxide levels in the blood drop to below normal, which can create unpleasant symptoms of flushing, dizziness, tingling fingers, and light-headedness. So we may help clients regulate their breathing in order to return their carbon dioxide levels to normal.

When mindful breathing is used for any of these purposes, it may well give rise to feelings of relaxation. If so, this is a pleasant bonus or by-product; it is not the main aim or intention, and it certainly won't always happen. In the ACT model, relaxation skills and mindfulness skills are fundamentally different.

To make this crystal clear, the aim of relaxation skills is to *control* or *change* feelings—to reduce or eliminate feelings such as anxiety and stress—in order to feel more relaxed or calm. With mindfulness skills the aim is to *allow* our feelings to be as they are in the moment, enabling clients to notice them with openness and curiosity, make room for them, drop the struggle with them; to let them come and stay and go in their own time, without trying to control or change them.

So ask yourself, *What is the purpose of this exercise? How will it help the client? What outcome is the client expecting to achieve?* If the answers to these questions are about reducing anxiety, feeling calmer, or relaxing, it's a "relaxation technique." If the answer is that it's about being in the present moment, engaging in life, increasing awareness, and allowing the client's feelings to be as they are, it's a mindfulness technique.

Q: What if focusing on the breath increases a client's distress?

Russ: Some clients may become dizzy, light-headed, or more anxious while doing a breath-focused exercise. The bottom line is, there's no law that proclaims mindfulness must involve a focus on the breath. If clients don't like to focus on breathing or they find that it increases their distress, making them dizzy, anxious, or light-headed, then they don't have to do it! There are many, many other things in the present moment that they can focus on instead: anything they can see, hear, touch, taste, or smell; any activity; any part of the body; any type of physical movement; any thought, feeling, or sensation.

To develop the broadest range of mindfulness skills, clients need to notice that they're distracted, notice what distracted them, notice what it's like to be distracted, and notice what it's like to refocus. But there's no fixed set of instructions that everyone has to follow in ACT; you can modify and adapt any exercise as you wish.

Q: What if clients drift off, zone out, or find it hard to engage in mindfulness exercises?

Russ: If we're going to do a mindfulness exercise with a client, and we know or suspect she might struggle to stay engaged, remain focused, and keep her attention on the task, then we want to modify it. Break it down. Make it shorter, simpler, easier. And most importantly, keep it interactive. In other words, don't let your client sit there in silence with her eyes closed while you slavishly "follow the script." Instead, respond to the unique client in front of you. Check in, ask what's going on for her, what's happening for her. Don't wait until the end of the exercise to see if the client's following your guidance. Talk to her throughout it, check if she's following you, and address any issues she's having. If necessary, your mindfulness exercise may go for just thirty seconds initially. Then you can build up. Treat these skills like any new skill: break them up into small, easy-to-digest chunks. The more difficulty the client has concentrating or focusing, the shorter and simpler your exercise should be.

Also, be alert for problems with visualization. If clients find it difficult to visualize, then do exercises that don't require it. Most mindfulness exercises don't require visualization, but for those that do (such as putting your thoughts onto leaves floating down a stream or clouds drifting through the sky), offer a nonvisual alternative (such as closing your eyes and simply noticing the thoughts that appear).

Some Tips to Reduce "Drifting Off"

The longer the experiential exercise, and the more meditative it is in style, the greater the risk of the client "drifting off," especially if the client's eyes are closed. So here are a few tips to help you with this:

- If clients are drowsy, sleep-deprived, or prone to dissociate, encourage them to keep their eyes open.
- Keep your own eyes (and ears) open so you can tell if your client has fallen asleep.
- Keep it interactive; regularly ask your client questions: What are you noticing? What's happening now? Are you with me? What's showing up? What's your mind saying? How are you finding this? This is especially important if an exercise involves accepting painful feelings; we want an ongoing report about what is happening inside the client. How regularly should you check in with your client? Trust your intuition. Personally, I rarely go for more than two minutes without checking in—but in early sessions, when clients are new to these skills, I usually don't let even a minute pass by.

Q: What if clients don't want mindfulness to "take away from time to talk"?

Russ: I'm guessing that if you are getting such a response from a client, then she's not coming to you for ACT; she's probably just coming to vent and have supportive counseling. If so, you'll need to go through informed consent again (see appendix 2), and if she's not open to ACT then either (a) refer her on, or (b) stop trying to do ACT with her and offer supportive counseling instead. (Think of it this way: if she wants to buy a fridge and you're selling TVs, you've got an issue!)

On the other hand, maybe she doesn't see the relevance of developing mindfulness skills. She may not see how it will help her with her issues, so she sees it as a waste of time. If so, you need to make it crystal clear how it's relevant and useful. A good way to find out is to ask, "Do you see how practicing this skill or doing this exercise would be helpful for you? Do you see how it will help you to achieve the goals we've established for therapy?" If the answer is no, then that's your issue right there!

Sometimes clients will say, after completing a mindfulness exercise, that they had difficulty concentrating because they were thinking about what they wanted to discuss later in the session. If so, one option is to have them write down before the session what they want to talk about, so they know they won't forget it. We can also look at it as a great opportunity to make the mindfulness practice more relevant and impactful: "Notice how your mind keeps pulling you to the future—to what's coming later—and bring your attention back to what's happening here and now." It's a great opportunity for the client to learn about getting hooked by (and unhooking from) thoughts about the future.

Q: Is a state of absorption, such as reading a book or watching a movie, the same as a state of mindfulness?

Russ: Good question! TV, radio, video games, and books readily create a state of absorption that is quite different from mindfulness; one becomes absorbed in the words and the imagery and transported out of the present moment and into the content of the media. If we were to practice mindfulness during these activities, it would disrupt them, ruin their enjoyment. For example, while watching a movie at a cinema, you don't want to be mindful of where you are, the other people in the cinema, the projector flickering behind you, your thoughts and feelings, the sounds of people eating; nor do you want to be mindful of the movie elements: the performance of the actors, the editing, the lighting, the camera moves, the sound effects; you just want to get absorbed in the story.

Knowing this, we can actually use mindfulness to disrupt a values-incongruent behavior in which we are absorbed. If we're mindlessly watching TV instead of doing something else that we'd consider more meaningful and life affirming, becoming mindful of that pulls us out of our absorption in the experience, so it's easier for us to choose to do something different.

Q: What if clients say they "don't know how to apply mindfulness in everyday life"?

Russ: That's golden feedback for the therapist. It means the therapist has failed to clearly link these skills to the client's therapy goals. So before we do a mindfulness exercise, it's a good idea to

1. clearly establish the client's therapy goals and make sure they're ACT-congruent (see chapter 3: Ghastly Goals), and

2. explain what skill the exercise is going to help the client develop and how this is going to help the client achieve her therapy goals.

Without this preamble, the client will likely think you've given her a relaxation technique or a way to feel good and avoid pain.

It's also a good idea to ask, after any experiential exercise, "So how might this help you with [therapy goals XYZ]?" If the client can't answer, the therapist then needs to make it clear. If the client *can* answer, the therapist can then go on to ask, "How can you apply this?" "When, where, and with whom?" "Would you be willing to practice this?" and so on.

The Wrap-Up

Mindfulness is often a confusing term for both clients and therapists, not least because it refers to a whole set of skills that serve different purposes. And unfortunately, as the term continues to grow in popularity, it becomes ever more confusing; people increasingly use it to mean different things, such as meditation or relaxation. In view of this, I recommend you use the term as rarely as possible, and instead come up with names for the specific skills you're teaching. And always be clear with your clients about the purpose of the exercise and how it's likely to help with their therapy goals.

CHAPTER 3

Ghastly Goals

ACT involves a lot of goal setting, and this starts from the very first session, where we establish goals for therapy. One of the trickiest aspects of ACT for many therapists is shifting the focus from emotional goals to behavioral goals. Emotional goals are all about what a person wants to feel. Behavioral goals are all about what a person wants to do. Massive difference, right?

Clients almost always come to therapy with emotional goals: "I want to get rid of my anxiety" or "I want to stop feeling depressed" or "I want to be happy." Basically: "I want to feel X, and I want to stop feeling Y." This is completely natural, of course; we all like to feel good, and none of us likes to feel bad. But if therapists agree to such emotional goals, they'll run into all sorts of problems.

Of course, we do want to obtain this information. It's important that we know what thoughts and feelings and emotions and memories the client is struggling with. And as therapy progresses, we are going to encourage the client to change his agenda from one of trying to avoid or get rid of these unwanted thoughts and feelings to one of defusion from and acceptance of these thoughts and feelings.

However, in addition to knowing the client's emotional goals, we also want to know about her behavioral goals—in other words, what she wants to do differently in important areas of her life.

Behavioral goals for therapy can include:

- *Ways the client wants to act differently (to treat herself, others, the world differently)*

- *Extrinsic goals the client wants to pursue (e.g., get a job, find a partner, change careers, have a baby) and the actions he wants to take to increase the chance of achieving those goals*
- *Effective behavioral repertoires from the past that the client wants to reinstate, continue with, or do more of*
- *Skills-training to develop any type of skill (which can include defusion skills, acceptance skills, and self-compassion skills)*
- *Action plans to solve problems or access help and support*
- *Anything and everything in the behavioral goals section of the ACT Case Formulation worksheet in appendix 1*

I've found that many therapists seem reluctant or unwilling to elicit this information, but we really do need it if we are to work effectively with ACT. Before reading this chapter, I encourage you to read through the ACT Case Formulation worksheet (appendix 1), paying special attention to the second box on page 1: "What does the client want from therapy/coaching?"

Discussions in This Chapter:

- How can we elicit behavioral goals early on in therapy?
- Why is it so important to establish behavioral goals?
- But don't values come before goals?
- Why is it so important to avoid phrasing goals in terms of dead person's goals?
- What if the client's only goal is "I just want to be happy"?
- What if clients don't want to change because they feel there aren't any problems?
- What if anxious clients just "want to get rid of anxiety," and nothing else?

- What if the client's answer to all questions about therapy goals is "I don't know"?
- What if our clients become defensive or aggressive during goal setting?
- What if clients' goals are focused on things that are out of their control?
- What if clients can't set goals because they are limited by fatigue or pain?
- What if a client's only goal is to help someone else, such as a loved one suffering from addiction or a life-threatening illness?
- What if a client's goals are dangerous to others or self-destructive?
- What if asking about goals triggers shame?
- What if clients keep changing their goals from session to session?
- What if the client's goal is something like "to manage my mind better"?
- Do we have to do formal goal setting in ACT?

Q: How can we elicit behavioral goals early on in therapy?

Russ: There are so many ways, it's hard to choose. But here are a few of my favorites. I find these questions are more powerful if you set them up with a "magic wand" and a "duck's back," like so:

Therapist: Suppose I had a magic wand here, one that does really powerful magic, and I wave it right now—and magic happens! And what happens next is that all these thoughts, feelings, emotions, and memories that you've been struggling with are no longer an issue for you. They no longer jerk you around,

> hold you back, bring you down, get in your way. They lose their impact and influence over you; they're like water off a duck's back.

Immediately following this setup, I like to ask questions such as:

- What would you stop doing or start doing?
- What would you do more of or less of?
- How would you treat yourself, others, life, the world, differently?
- What goals would you pursue?
- What activities would you start or resume or do more of?
- What people, places, events, activities, or challenges would you approach or start or resume or contact—rather than avoid, give up, or withdraw from?
- What relationships would you work on improving? What would you say and do differently in those relationships?

Note: we can modify the magic wand and duck's back setup when clients ask for help with a specific diagnosis, as follows: "If I had a magic wand here, one that does really powerful magic, and I wave it, so that your [depression, alcoholism, social phobia, borderline personality disorder, schizophrenia, addiction] were no longer a problem, what would you stop doing or start doing, or do more of or less of?"

Another variant is for the therapist to say something like "I can see this is a big problem for you. I just need to know more about how this is a problem for you; in other words, what is it getting in the way of? If I could wave a magic wand so that this were no longer a problem for you, what would you stop doing or start doing, do more of or less of?"

A useful avenue to explore is discovering extrinsic goals the client wants to pursue, such as getting a job, finding a partner, changing careers, or having a baby. Useful questions include "What would you like to have that you don't already?" "What would you like to achieve?" "What do you feel is lacking?"

Once you've identified the extrinsic goal, you can then elicit behavioral goals: explore what actions the client needs to take, and the behavioral changes she'll need to make, in order to increase her chances of success.

One of my favorite lines of questioning is this: "If our work here could make a positive difference in just one important relationship you have, who would you pick? How would your relationship improve? What will you do differently in this relationship if our work here is successful?"

You could ask similar useful questions by replacing the word *relationship* with *area of life* or *activity*: "If our work here today could make a positive difference in just one important area of life, which would you pick: work, education, relationships, health, leisure, or something else? How would this area of life improve? What will you be doing differently in this area of life if our work here is successful?"

For more ideas, look at the second section of the ACT Case Formulation worksheet (appendix 1). And also make sure you've read chapter 1: Playing with the Choice Point. As you work through these tools with your client, you'll usually find it's quite simple to establish behavioral goals. Finally, keep in mind that even something as simple and fundamental as running through the informed consent script (appendix 2) with your client establishes overarching behavioral goals for therapy.

Q: Why is it so important to establish behavioral goals?

Russ: ACT is a behavior therapy. We're looking for an outcome of behavioral change: we want to see people guided by and acting on their values to actively create better lives. So the sooner we establish behavioral goals for therapy, the better. When we take the time to do this, the following occurs:

- It often provides motivation and inspiration. For many clients, it's the first time they've started to create any kind of plan for the future.

- It gives therapy a direction and makes it easy to assess if therapy is working or not.

- It provides motivation for the hard work of learning mindfulness skills, especially acceptance skills: "If learning this skill could help you to do X, Y, and Z (behavioral goals), would you be willing to try it, apply it, and practice it?"

- It paves the way for values work right from the start of therapy. Even if values aren't made explicit at this point, they will be implicit in the chosen behavioral goals.

- It makes it possible to use the core ACT construct of *workability*: "If you do action A when feeling B or when thought C or memory D or sensation E shows up, will that take you into towards moves or away moves? Make you more like the person you want to be, or less? Move you closer to building the life you want, achieving your goals, doing the things that matter—or further away?"

When we take the time to gather this information early on in therapy, it enables both therapist and client to be sure they have the same agenda. Without such information, often the therapist will have a different therapy agenda from that of the client, which creates confusion, tension, and stuckness in both.

For example, when clients express therapy goals such as "reduce depression," "reduce anxiety," "increase self-worth," "build self-esteem," "feel calm," "feel in love again," "recover from [DSM disorder X]," "get over what happened," "stop feeling Y," "get my confidence back"...they are basically saying, "Teach me how to control my feelings. I want to get rid of these unpleasant thoughts and feelings and memories. I want to feel good and happy and have pleasant, positive thoughts and feelings instead." This is what ACT calls the *emotional control agenda*. It is the very agenda that ACT aims to undermine. So if you agree to these as your goals of therapy, you will soon encounter confusion, resistance, or stuckness.

Note that behavioral goals should always be stated in terms of what the client *will* do (not what the client *won't* do). If a client states a goal in the negative—"I'll stop doing this," "I won't do that"—we call those *dead person's goals* because a dead person can do them better than the client can. (After all, a corpse will stop or cease all bad habits instantly and permanently.) It's okay to start off with a dead person's goal, but as soon as possible, we want to turn it into a live person's goal—something the client can do better than a corpse. This is best done with simple questions such as "So what will you do instead?" or "So if you're not doing that, what will you be doing?"

Also, be wary of goals such as "spending less time" on something. We need to ask, "So what would you like to be doing instead, with all that time you free up?"

Q: But don't values come before goals?

Russ: Well, it depends. In the earliest ACT protocols, the four core ACT mindfulness processes were introduced first, then came values clarification, and then came goal setting based on values. The reasoning was that fusion and experiential avoidance would get in the way of values work—so defusion and acceptance skills needed to come first. However, over time, many ACT protocols began to start with values work upfront. The reasoning was that this would motivate the client to do the hard work of therapy, and would facilitate acceptance.

Keeping this in mind, let's look at the arguments for and against clarifying goals first, before values. As you already know, I'm a big believer in establishing behavioral goals for therapy on the first session, for all the reasons outlined in the previous Q&A.

The argument against addressing goals first is that in traditional ACT protocols, goals are derived from and based on a client's values. In other words, we first clarify values, then we discuss specific goals that we derive from these values. Indeed, some issues with goal setting arise because of a fundamental problem: the therapist or client (or both) is not really clear about what the client's values are.

Now as you may have guessed, I personally don't agree with this argument. I believe we want to get the broad goals for therapy established in the first session, again, for all the reasons given in the previous Q&A. The simple fact is that values clarification for some clients is very hard, and unlikely to be possible without some defusion, acceptance, and grounding skills. Thus, it may be quite a few sessions before we are able to get to values with such clients. But we can establish behavioral goals with everyone in the first session, even if it is just agreeing to the basic goals of ACT as discussed during the informed consent process (see appendix 2).

Once we have informed consent and an agreement on goals for therapy, then we can start exploring values whenever we like—right away or in later sessions. For example, if we suspect that some of the initial goals for therapy may be values-incongruent, we would probably want to explore values immediately. But if there is too much fusion and avoidance, this may not be possible, and so we will have to postpone such work until later in therapy, once the client has developed defusion and acceptance skills. Once these mindfulness skills are in place, we can revisit values and clarify if the goal is values-congruent or not. At this point, clients may well change their minds about behaviors they initially saw as towards moves, and reclassify them as away moves.

Keep in mind that behavioral goals are a great starting point to explore values. For example, suppose a socially withdrawn client gives a behavioral goal of going out more or spending more time with friends. We can ask questions such as:

> "How would you like to treat your friends when you see them?"
>
> "What kind of friend do you want to be?"
>
> "Can you remember a time when you and a friend were doing something you enjoyed or found meaningful? Where, when, what, with whom? What was that like? Can you close your eyes, remember it vividly, describe it to me? Look at yourself in this memory: what qualities are you showing? How are you treating your friend?"

Let's suppose, as a result of this, the client identifies values such as kindness, caring, and being playful. We now can go on to explore small actions the client can take and small goals the client can pursue in the service of these values—even though she's not yet willing or able to achieve her initial goals (of going out or spending more time with friends).

Q: Why is it so important to avoid phrasing goals in terms of dead person's goals?

Russ: Good question. Once again, ACT is a behavior therapy. And behavior is defined as "something an organism does." To "not do something" is not a behavior; behavior is what you are doing (as opposed to the things you are not doing).

We wouldn't class "to not smoke" as a behavior because it describes something you are *not* doing, as opposed to something you *are* doing. To take a deep breath and accept an urge to smoke without acting on it—well, that *is* a behavior, because it's something you *are* doing.

Basically, to phrase a goal in terms of "what I won't do" is next to useless in terms of giving us some specific behavior to develop and reinforce in therapy. The goal of "quitting smoking" is fine as a starting point, but we immediately want to turn it into a live person's goal by posing these types of questions: "What will you need to start doing differently (to achieve that desired outcome)?" "What will you do instead of smoking when a craving for a cigarette shows up?" "What will you do with the extra hour a day that you'll have after you quit smoking?"

Similarly, you might agree as a starting point to a dead person's goal—what the client *is not* going to do—such as not yelling at the kids, not eating junk food, or not staying up late binge-watching *Game of Thrones*. But as fast as possible you want to move to live person's goals—what the client *is* going to do: "So what do you want to do instead?" "What do you want to do differently?" "What skills do you need to learn, develop further, or apply more effectively?"

Right now, my behavior is "typing on the computer." That is what I am doing. It's a behavior.

Right now, there are an infinite number of things I am not doing: not playing guitar, not eating dinner, not hunting rabbits, not poking Donald Trump in the eye, not watching *Game of Thrones*, not polishing my shoes, not driving a taxi, not patting the dog, not making love, and so on. None of these descriptions of what I'm "not doing" tells you anything about my behavior in this moment; my behavior can only ever be described in terms of what I am doing.

So we don't want dead person's goals—"what I would like to not do"—to guide our therapy; it's impossible to do behavioral therapy with something that's not a behavior.

What we aim to do is differential reinforcement of a new, more desirable behavior over the older, less desirable one, for example, urge surfing and mindful stretching over smoking, or dropping anchor (chapter 7) and talking in a calm voice over yelling.

Q: What if the client's only goal is "I just want to be happy"?

Russ: My immediate response is to validate it: "Of course you do. Me too. I think almost everyone wants to be happy. So I'm guessing that you *don't* feel happy right now? So what kind of difficult thoughts and feelings are showing up for you?… What sort of things do you do when those difficult thoughts and feelings show up?… And how does that affect your life when you do that?" This information can then be drawn or written on a choice point (chapter 1) if desired, and used to structure the session. From there I'd say something like, "So a big part of our work here will be learning new skills to handle those difficult thoughts and feelings more effectively, so they have less impact on you."

And then I'd segue into setting behavioral goals for therapy, as described in the previous Q&A.

However, sometimes even after I've tried all those questions, clients will insist that they already do everything they need to be doing, despite their emotional difficulties. They say the issue is their feelings, not how their feelings impact their behavior.

When this happens, I usually probe a little bit more: "So can you tell me how these feelings are a problem for you? Do they make anything harder for you? What do they make it harder for you to do, or to focus on, or engage in? Do they make it harder for you to treat yourself or others well?"

I might also ask, "If these feelings were no longer an issue for you, who would notice the difference? What difference would they notice in you? Would your kids, wife, husband, friends, or coworkers notice any difference in your facial expressions, your words, your gestures, your actions, the way you interact with them, or what you talk about?"

And if the person is in an intimate relationship: "What would your partner say is most difficult for her when you are caught up in these feelings? What does she complain that you are doing or not doing?"

If this still draws blanks, then the behavioral goals, at least for now, are simply "learning new skills to handle these difficult thoughts and feelings more effectively so they have less influence and impact on you."

Q: What if clients don't want to change because they feel there aren't any problems?

Russ: Well, the first thing we want to know is what such clients want from therapy. If everything is going well in their life, they have no problems, everything is fine...why have they come to see you? A useful question to ask is, "What will need to be different in your life in order for you to say therapy was successful?"

If nothing will change, if she'll be doing the same things, feeling the same way, and her life will be exactly the same, then what's the point of coming to therapy?

If the answer is that nothing will change except she'll be feeling good or feeling happy, then as outlined in the earlier Q&A on "I just want to be happy," identify what difficult thoughts and feelings she's struggling with, and agree that your work is to learn new ways to handle them more effectively so they have less impact and influence. If the client doesn't want to learn new ways to handle them, then what does she want?

This is why informed consent (appendix 2) is so essential. If she's not interested in ACT, or if she "just wants someone to talk to," then it's best to find out in the first session. Then you have a choice to make: refer her to a different therapist, or work from a different model.

Q: What if anxious clients just "want to get rid of anxiety," and nothing else?

Russ: Some clients cling very tightly to the emotional control agenda. This is especially common with anxiety disorders: anxiety is the enemy, and the client's goal is to get rid of it. With any client who's strongly fixated on the goal of avoiding or getting rid of emotional or psychological pain, we'll need to do creative hopelessness to undermine the control agenda (see chapter 8: Crummy Creative Hopelessness).

After creative hopelessness, I like to do the Pushing Away Paper exercise (appendix 6). After finishing the exercise, I say, "I don't know how to eliminate anxiety. Everyone has it. But as long as you keep responding to it like this (*pushing away*), it will make your anxiety bigger, more unpleasant, more painful. If you want to reduce the impact of anxiety, you'll need to learn how to do this (*dropping the paper on the lap*). There's no way to have a life free of anxiety—so it's about finding new ways of responding to anxiety. You've tried so many things to get rid of anxiety. You've tried... (*quickly recapping all the main avoidance strategies identified during the creative hopelessness intervention*). And in the short term, they give you some relief, but in the long term, your anxiety continues to be a problem. So are you open to trying something different? Everything you've been doing is basically this (*pushing away*), and in the long term, it's not working. So are you open to trying something radically different—learning how to do this (*dropping the paper on the lap*)?"

Some clients will of course be disappointed. If we get that kind of reaction, we want to (a) validate and normalize it, and (b) be compassionate. And we can tell them that symptoms of anxiety *will* improve with this approach. We can also tell them ACT is an empirically supported treatment for anxiety disorders. And then we clarify that this improvement *won't* happen by going into battle against anxiety, trying to avoid or get rid of it. The improvement will come through responding differently to it: by dropping the struggle with it, as in the Pushing Away Paper exercise.

If the client is obviously disappointed, we might say something like "I'm sorry you're disappointed. That's a completely normal reaction. But please don't misunderstand what I'm saying here. I'm not saying your anxiety will stay the same as it is now. I'm not saying it will continue to push you around and restrict your life and hold you back. What I'm saying is, given that what you've been doing until now isn't giving you the sort of life you want, are you open to a new way of responding to anxiety? Are you willing to try something radically different? A way of handling it differently, so it has less impact and influence, so it doesn't jerk you around and run your life?"

Q: What if the client's answer to all questions about therapy goals is "I don't know"?

Russ: If this happens, therapy may initially focus just on this behavioral goal: "So it seems our main aim at this point is to work together as a team to help you develop some new skills to handle your difficult thoughts and feelings more effectively—so they have much less impact and influence over you." Or, said more colloquially, "So it seems our main aim at this point is to work together as a team to help you learn how to unhook from these difficult thoughts and feelings, so they no longer jerk you around, hold you back, or bring you down."

Yes, this is a behavioral goal. To learn any new skill is a behavioral goal; learning a skill is something you do. To "feel happy" or "to feel calm" is an emotional goal: it describes what you want *to feel.* But to "learn new skills to unhook from difficult feelings" is a behavioral goal: it describes what you want *to do.*

Q: What if our clients become defensive or aggressive during goal setting?

Russ: Establishing behavioral goals often triggers at least some degree of discomfort in clients. Usually this isn't a problem. But if the client is becoming aggressive or hostile or fused or shut down, we need to back off and change tack. And we need to trust our intuition and experience about when to do this. In such cases, it may be that initially we get agreement on the vaguest of behavioral goals:

We are working together as a team...

- *To help you do things that build a better life*
- *To help you take action to solve your problems more effectively*
- *To help you handle difficult thoughts and feelings more effectively*

This is fine as a starting point; it's basically just restating what the client agreed to during informed consent (appendix 2). And notice how even these vague goals are radically different from the vague goals therapists often agree to, such as "reduce depression," "reduce anxiety," "increase self-worth," "recover from PTSD," "get over X," "stop feeling Y," "get my confidence back," or "feel happy."

Q: What if clients' goals are focused on things that are out of their control?

Russ: In ACT, we aim to empower people. This means it's important to establish locus of control early on: What do you have most control over? What do you have least control over? Many clients come in fused with unrealistic ideas of control—expecting or wanting to have control of things they simply can't control (especially other people); it's important that we address that early in therapy.

Initially we sit with the clients' stuckness and validate their pain, but not for too long (definitely not a whole session!), otherwise we'll simply reinforce their stuckness, fusion, and psychological inflexibility. We want to sit with the stuckness and suffering, listen and respond compassionately, empathize, validate their experience while encouraging them to freely express themselves—and then guide them kindly and gently into ACT processes.

We want to explain, "The more we focus on things we want to change that are *not* in our control, the more powerless and upset we feel. This can manifest as helplessness, hopelessness, anger, anxiety, guilt, sadness, rage, despair, and so forth. So it's important that we learn to focus on what is in our control, and to channel our energy and time into that stuff. This is at the core of self-empowerment."

We might say to a client, "When life is challenging or difficult, we have far more control over our actions—what we do with our arms and legs, and how and what we say—than we do over our thoughts and feelings. For example, if I hold a cocked and loaded gun at your head and say, 'Have no feelings of fear or anxiety; have no negative thoughts about bad things that might happen,' could you do that? Of course not. But if I hold a cocked and loaded gun at your head and demand, 'Dance like a penguin and sing Happy Birthday,' could you do that? Of course you could."

Often we encounter clients fused with the story "My life will be great when I achieve goal X, and miserable until it happens." Goal X might be anything from getting a good job to finding a partner to getting a payout from a compensation claim to recovering from an injury or illness. The thing is, it's actually not in the client's control as to if and when X will be achieved. So first we need to run through everything I mentioned above, and then we might kindly and gently say:

"The fact is, we don't know exactly when X (the desired outcome) will happen. Fact is, we don't even know if it will happen, although obviously that's what you are hoping for. So there are two aspects to our work here: (a) create an effective action plan to increase the chances that X will happen; and (b) given that we don't know how long X will take—days, weeks, months, years, or never—let's look at how you can make the most of your life each day until X happens (if it does)."

Also, quite commonly, we have clients whose goals are to change other people. In this case, we might kindly and gently say something like "Although we all try to do it, it's actually impossible to *control* other people. We can *influence* the behavior of other people, but we can't *control* them. And the thing is, if we want to influence them in a constructive and healthy way, then we will need to have a lot of control over our arms, and legs, and mouth; a lot of control over the manner in which we speak to them and interact with them."

After that, we could run through everything mentioned above about what we can and can't control, and from there move on to learning, developing, and applying relevant relationship skills, as covered in my book *ACT with Love* (Harris, 2009b).

And we want to make sure we're clear about the limits of relationship skills, saying something like "These skills increase the chances of getting what you want in a relationship, but they aren't magic; they won't always get your needs meet; they will fail at times. So perhaps a part of our work here that could be really useful to you would be learning to handle such disappointments and frustrations more effectively, so they have less impact on you."

Q: What if clients can't set goals because they are limited by fatigue or pain?

Russ: Good question. This is especially relevant to clients with chronic pain, chronic illness, and chronic fatigue syndrome. They have problems setting behavioral goals because there's so much variability in their functioning; they may be okay one day, but on other days, extreme tiredness, pain or exhaustion may make it seem impossible to even get out of bed.

The aim with such clients is to help them develop the psychological flexibility to adapt and modify their goals and actions to suit the situations and circumstances they are in. For example, we could help a client create a hierarchy of goals that she can adapt to her physical status: things she can do when she is so tired that she can't get out of bed, and other things she can do if she can get out of bed. Obviously, a huge amount of self-compassion is called for. And we'd want to help her find little ways to live her values even when she can't do the things she really wants to do. For example, suppose your client wants to play music and travel. If she's too unwell to actually play music, can she listen to music that she enjoys, and mindfully appreciate it? If she's too unwell to travel, can she watch travel documentaries or read travel books?

Such clients will often state goals like "I want to have more energy to do the things I want to." We'd want to convert that into two behavioral goals:

A. to change what you are doing in order to have the best chance of increasing your energy levels—focusing on sleep, diet, exercise, and so on; and

B. to get better at doing things that are important even when your energy levels are not good and you don't feel like doing them.

I highly recommend reading the book *Tuesdays with Morrie* by Mitch Albom (1997). It's a true story and a great example of how we can live our values even when completely physically incapacitated (in Morrie's case, by a motor neuron disease that paralyzed his entire body).

Q: What if a client's only goal is to help someone else, such as a loved one suffering from addiction or a life-threatening illness?

Russ: We can modify the type of questioning covered earlier in this chapter so that it's suitable for any context. So let's suppose the client is the parent of a child with cancer. And initially all she wants from therapy is to help her child. After much validation and compassionate acknowledgment of her intense suffering, we might agree to something like this: "Part of our work here is to help you be the most effective and caring parent you can possibly be, to do the best possible to help your child. In order to do that, part of our work here is to help you handle the difficult thoughts and feelings showing up for you, to reduce their impact and influence over you, so you can be effective for your child."

After that we could talk about the fact that if we wish to be effective caregivers for others, we need to look after ourselves. I often introduce this concept by asking, "Have you ever been on a plane? Do you remember the instructions they gave you about what to do if the oxygen masks drop? Who did they say needs to put the oxygen mask on first: the parent or the child?" The client will usually answer "the parent." We could then add, "Yes. And you probably know the reason for that is that humans lose consciousness in about 30 seconds without oxygen—and an unconscious parent is no use to a child. But if the child is unconscious, the parent can still help her."

We might then say, "So if you could handle all these difficult thoughts and feelings more effectively, so they weren't holding you back, or bringing you down, or getting in the way of you being the sort of mother you want to be, then...

- What would you do differently, to enable you to more effectively support your child?
- What would you stop doing or start doing, do more of or less of, that could help your child directly? Or help your partner cope, so that you can both better support your child?
- What goals would you pursue—shorter-term, smaller goals, that is—little things that might help your child, or help you to be there for her?
- What activities could you start or resume that could help you to be in better shape or look after yourself, so you can more effectively be there for your child?
- What would you like to be able to say and do in response to your child when he's suffering?"

Of course, all these questions can be adapted to accommodate a partner, a parent, a friend, or a relative.

Q: What if a client's goals are dangerous to others or self-destructive?

Russ: We want to be very clear with clients that we can't work with them on agendas that compromise our professional ethics. We could say something like "If you want me to help you do things that seem to me to be destructive to yourself or others, I can't help you with that. However, if you want support in cutting down on those behaviors, replacing them with more effective ones, then I'm with you."

Bottom line for me: I need to know we're a team, with the same agenda. If the client is wanting help from me to commit suicide, lie, deceive, manipulate others, hurt others, hurt herself, abuse children, sell illegal drugs, break the law, or be violent, I'm going to talk openly about my ethical stance. I can't help her to do those things. I will, however, help her to do less of those things, to break those patterns. And I will support her as she goes through the pain of changing those patterns.

All of this of course hinges on first getting informed consent for ACT (appendix 2), which establishes that at the very least you are (a) a team, (b) learning skills to handle difficult thoughts and feelings, and (c) working to build a richer, fuller life.

Q: What if asking about goals triggers shame?

Russ: This isn't common, but it does happen at times. A client may feel shame about the fact that he doesn't yet have his life sorted out, or isn't clear about what he wants, or has failed at his goals in the past. One thing to keep in mind here is that the word *goal* can in itself be a problem. That word freaks a lot of people out. So it's often a smart move to avoid the "g" word. For example, we may say, "Can we establish a focus for the session, or one aspect of life you want to work on improving, or one important thing that we can zero in, or one main problem or issue that we can keep center stage for this session?" And we can experiment with phrases like "What matters?" "What's important?" "What would you like to get out of this?" "If this could make a difference for you, what would that be?" "What would you like to improve or do differently as a result of this?" All of these questions establish goals without ever using the word *goal.*

Shame-prone clients can of course experience shame at any point in a session—almost anything can trigger it. Even something as simple as asking the client if she'd like a glass of water can trigger her "I am undeserving" story. The therapist will become rigid if he tries to run the session based on the rule "This client must not experience shame during my session." The main thing is for the therapist to be compassionate, respectful, caring, and validating. When shame appears in session, the therapist compassionately responds to it, unpacks it, and addresses it via noticing and naming it, dropping anchor (chapter 7), defusion, acceptance, and self-compassion. It's rich fuel for us to work with, not something to be avoided.

It's also good to preempt shameful feelings with clients and groups: "These kinds of questions about what you want to do differently, or work on improving, often bring up uncomfortable feelings for most people. But we need to spend some time on them if we want our lives to improve, to have more direction, to have more meaning and purpose. So even though it's uncomfortable for most people, can we spend a bit of time on it please?"

Q: What if clients keep changing their goals from session to session?

Russ: The aim is to be flexible. As long as we're actively working the core ACT processes in our session, it doesn't usually matter if the goals change from week to week. The outcome we want is higher levels of psychological flexibility, so as long as we are always working on that, we can freely shift our focus to differing goals. Indeed, this is exactly what we need to do when clients turn up suicidal or in crisis mode. Therapy doesn't stop to deal with the crisis or the suicidality; instead, coping with these challenges becomes the new goal to focus on for that session. (Also see the Q&A on setting an agenda for the session in chapter 11: Sticky Structure.)

Q: What if the client's goal is something like "to manage my mind better"?

Russ: We'd really need to clarify what the client means by "manage my mind." He likely wants to control his thoughts, control his feelings, or get rid of unwanted thoughts and feelings. We'd need to establish behavioral goals, using some of the methods I've suggested. Personally, I'd just be honest with him: "I don't really understand what you mean by 'manage your mind'—can you tell me what that means?" And then go on to ask, "What would you do differently if you managed your mind better? How would other people be able to tell you were doing that?"

Sometimes I've had clients go on to say they want to "increase optimism and reduce negative thinking." I aim to reframe this as "learning new skills to handle difficult thoughts more effectively, so they have less impact" and "learning to act more effectively even when feeling pessimistic." As part of this process, it's useful to ask questions such as "If you were feeling optimistic, what would you do differently? How about if our work could be about learning how to do that stuff, regardless of whether you feel optimistic or pessimistic, happy or sad, energized or flat?"

Q: Do we have to do formal goal setting in ACT?

Russ: I often get asked this question by therapists who are uncomfortable with goal setting. Usually it turns out they've trained in other models that are more open ended and that don't include formal goal setting. Often the therapist worries he is forcing his clients into things they don't want to do.

Of course, we don't want to force clients to do anything—ever! And if a client is making good progress without formal goal setting during the sessions, no problem. But the more stuck a client becomes, the more important formal goal setting becomes. For example, it's hard to imagine a client who is depressed making progress quickly without investing time in setting realistic goals, planning ahead for obstacles and creating contingency plans to deal with them, identifying barriers, and so on. If clients aren't making progress from session to session, lack of effective goal setting is one of the most likely culprits.

The main purpose of formal goal setting is to activate behavioral change; without goals to strive for, many clients make no changes at all. Goal setting also helps clients establish a sense of how the future might look; this is particularly important for clients who see the future as bleak and gloomy, or don't see any future at all. And of course, another important function of goal setting is to help us gauge whether therapy is successful. So no one says you *have* to do it, but you'd be missing out on a huge chunk of ACT if you skipped it.

However, please note that it doesn't always have to be that very formal, very specific type of goal setting. It can be informal, and quite vague. For example, it might be looking for opportunities to practice doing X, looking for opportunities to live values A and B, noticing your towards and away moves, or playing around with this unhooking technique. If clients are coming back and reporting making progress with these types of more informal goal setting, that's fine.

The Wrap-Up

In my experience, one of the most common reasons for therapists feeling lost, stuck, confused, or directionless in session is that they have not taken the time to clarify the client's behavioral goals for therapy. The same issue is often at the core of resistance from clients: basically, they are expecting something different from what the therapist is offering. So it's well worth your while to develop this skill.

And remember, in the worst-case scenario, if the client can't come up with any behavioral goals, then we can at least start with the basics that apply to every client: working together as a team to build a better life, and learning new skills to unhook from difficult thoughts and feelings.

CHAPTER 4

Beastly Barriers

There are many barriers to working with ACT that show up early—often in the first session. Sometimes clients aren't open to ACT. Sometimes they react negatively to the word mindfulness (see chapter 2). Sometimes they actively oppose ACT because of things they've heard about it or past experiences with other therapists who did ACT poorly. Sometimes they want to do ACT, but their own fusion and avoidance gets in the way. Sometimes they start doing ACT, but it doesn't go well because of a breakdown in therapeutic rapport. Sometimes the client is willing to do ACT, but the therapist is too pushy—moving too fast, being too directive. At other times the therapist is too passive, falling into a "supportive listening" mode for fear of being too pushy. As you read through these Q&A discussions, keep in mind the therapeutic relationship is of central importance in the ACT model. ACT sees therapist and client as equals. We are both "in the same boat," both dealing with the human condition, both experiencing psychological suffering as a natural and inevitable by-product of a normal human mind. The ACT therapist aims to model psychological flexibility for the client: to be compassionate, respectful, caring, and authentic.

We aim to see our clients as rainbows rather than roadblocks. When we encounter a rainbow, we admire it, we appreciate it, we recognize it as a unique work of nature. When we encounter a roadblock, we see it as a nuisance, as something getting in our way, as a problem we need to solve.

Unfortunately, the more stuck or resistant or unwilling our clients are, the more likely we are to look at them as roadblocks. Our aim then is to unhook from all those judgmental thoughts that so easily enter our heads when therapy stalls. Instead of seeing the client as a roadblock—a barrier to successful therapy—can we see him as a rainbow? Can we pay attention to him with openness and curiosity? Can we appreciate him as a unique and magnificent work of nature to be appreciated—rather than a barrier to get past?

A strong therapeutic relationship makes all the difference. So if you use any of the strategies outlined in this chapter (or any chapter, for that matter), make sure you always come from that compassionate, respectful place of mindful appreciation for your client.

Discussions in This Chapter:

- What if clients don't want to continue after informed consent?
- Being directive with clients feels like I'm being too pushy. Any advice?
- Can moving too quickly destroy rapport?
- How can I avoid falling into supportive listening—especially when I feel bored?
- How can I switch my CBT clients to ACT?
- What if clients just want to vent?
- What if the client is skeptical of ACT?
- What if clients resist doing exercises?
- What if clients insist on exploring the past in great depth?
- How does ACT address systemic factors such as relationship issues?
- How does ACT address readiness to change?

Q: What if clients don't want to continue after informed consent?

Russ: If clients don't want ACT, the therapist has a choice to make: refer them on, or work from a different model. However, if we adopt the compassionate, respectful, appreciative therapeutic stance outlined above—seeing our clients as rainbows, not roadblocks—and we validate the client's suffering, and explain the model simply as in the informed consent script (appendix 2) or with the choice point (chapter 1), then it's highly unlikely she won't want to continue. (Obviously, if the therapist were authoritarian, controlling, demanding, and condescending, it would be a far more likely scenario.) To be honest, I've only ever had this happen twice, and both cases were when I first made the switch to ACT from traditional CBT (cognitive behavioral therapy). I told all my existing clients that I was switching over to ACT, explained what this new approach involved, and all except two were willing to try it. I referred them both to a traditional CBT therapist because I no longer wanted to work that way.

On the first session, we take a history, establish what's hard for the client, and get a sense of what matters to her and what the issues are. And at some point in that session, we gently, kindly, and respectfully run through informed consent. (Remember, you don't have to follow the script word-for-word; modify the language so it suits you and your clients.) If we do this, the client is likely to respond well. But if she doesn't, we want to find out what her barriers are. Does she have some misconceptions about ACT? Has she had negative experiences with another ACT therapist? If you used the word *mindfulness*, for example, did that trigger negative connotations (as covered in chapter 2)? Is she fusing with shame or fear or the "I can't do it" story?

We'd need to clarify and address this client's specific barriers to ACT. There's no standard response; we need to individualize our response for each unique client. And if after doing all that, she still isn't open to ACT, then we'd either refer her on or use a different model. For example, I personally don't do this, but I know some therapists who initially opt to do supportive counseling for a few sessions to build rapport, and then introduce ACT later.

Q: Being directive with clients feels like I'm being too pushy. Any advice?

Russ: Thanks, great question. Many new ACT therapists struggle a bit with establishing goals, encouraging clients to actively commit to action, and otherwise being directive in session.

As a first step, consider this: what are your own barriers to being directive? Identify the thoughts and feelings that you are fusing with or avoiding and respond with defusion and acceptance. Are you willing to make room for anxiety and discomfort in order to learn a new way of working? ACT will raise your anxiety and discomfort in the short term; in the service of your own values as a therapist are you willing to make room for it? And to unhook from all the reasons your mind is giving you not to do it?

Second, ask permission often: "Is it okay if…?" "Do you mind if…?" "Can I just…?" "Would it be okay if…?" Set up the "press pause" (as part of informed consent, appendix 2), explain it goes both ways, and say to the client, "Please 'press pause' if I'm ever being too pushy."

Third, observe the client's responses to what you do in session. If the client is responding well, you're on the right track. If not, change course.

Fourth, give clear rationales for everything you do. "The reason I'm asking you to do this is…" "Is it okay if I bring us back to this, because…" "I notice we've gone off-topic, and is it okay if we go back to the topic, because…" Everything of course needs to be clearly linked back to the client's behavioral goals for therapy. If you haven't established those, you're in trouble. (See chapter 3 for help with setting goals.) But if you have, then explaining the rationale for shifting back to the topic will help you gently guide the session back on track to help the client achieve those goals.

Fifth, use self-disclosure, authenticity, and openness, if and when appropriate: "My mind's telling me I'm being too pushy here. Can I just check in with you… Is it just my mind having a go at me, or am I being a bit too pushy?"

Finally, pushy is not the same as directive. The client's goals direct the therapy. Without these goals, typically both therapist and client lose direction and get stuck. The therapist facilitates the client's process of establishing goals and taking action to achieve them. But this should never be done in a pushy, controlling, arrogant, demanding, or condescending manner. It should be done in a compassionate, respectful way, keeping the client's best interests at heart.

Q: Can moving too quickly destroy rapport?

Russ: This is a good point to raise, and one that's relevant for any model of therapy. If we rush in too quickly, we may invalidate the client. She may, for example, feel that we're not really listening to her needs, but just trying to give her a quick behavioral fix. On the other hand, if we hold back too long, we may do the client a disservice. Timing is not about following a formula; it's about being mindful of where both you and the client are, trusting your judgment, and being willing to modify and adapt depending on what happens. At times, we need to slooooow down or back off. At other times, we need to speed up and jump in. And the truth is, we will all get it wrong sometimes—and right at other times.

Q: How can I avoid falling into supportive listening—especially when I feel bored?

Russ: Ah, yes. When we're bored in session, it's easy for us to fall into a supportive counseling role: we nod our heads and listen compassionately, and let go of trying to do any active goal setting, skills building, or experiential work. I have to confess that since embracing ACT, I am never bored in a session for long. In the old days, I used to fall into supportive listening mode too—but no longer. As soon as I'm aware that I'm bored, that's an instant wake-up call; it tells me that I'm no longer doing effective therapy, so I take it as a cue to launch into ACT mode.

Boredom indicates fusion on the part of the therapist: she's hooked by the story "There's nothing of interest here." So a good first step is to ground and center ourselves: to get present, reengage with the client, notice him with curiosity and openness, appreciate him "like a rainbow." And a good second step is to get clarity about what we are working on in session.

I often say something like "I'm willing to be wrong about this, but I have a sense that we're not working with a clear agenda here. Can we just take a moment to clarify what we are working on, and what the desired outcome is?" Then I get active, often pulling out a choice point (chapter 1) or bull's-eye (appendix 3) to get clear about what we're working on and what outcome we're moving toward.

This approach will pull us out of supportive counseling mode and into active therapy mode. If the client is willing, we could also do some mindful stretching together at this point to help us both wake up.

Q: How can I switch my CBT clients to ACT?

Russ: I'd been reading about ACT for a few months before I went to my first workshop (which, as luck would have it, was with Steve Hayes himself. Awesome experience!). After the workshop, I went back and told all my clients, with whom I was doing traditional CBT, "I've just discovered this new model of therapy, and I absolutely love it. Wish I'd discovered it years ago. And at the workshop, I thought about you. I thought this would be a really good approach to help you with these difficulties. It's very different from the way we've been working. In fact, some of it is the complete opposite of what we've been doing. But I have to say, I applied it to myself during the workshop, and it was just so powerful. So I'm going to be making it my new model that I use with everyone. Would you be interested in trying it?"

All but two of my clients enthusiastically agreed. As for those two who didn't agree, I did a couple more sessions of CBT with them, but my heart wasn't in it anymore. So I referred them on. For all the other clients who agreed to change over, I said, "I'm a novice at this. I may be a bit shaky at times. There are a lot of new techniques and I may need at times to read an exercise from this book, because I haven't yet learned it all by heart." In doing this I was not only being authentic and vulnerable, useful qualities for an ACT therapist, but I was creating a space where I could make mistakes, be shaky, and read from a script if needed.

I'm not saying that this is how you have to do it—just that this is what worked for me. And because I switched everyone over, literally overnight,

I ended up getting a huge amount of experience very quickly. Having said all of that, if you're not ready to make such a dramatic shift, I fully understand. For me, ACT was love at first sight, and I wanted to plunge in headfirst. But it may not be that way for you.

Q: What if clients just want to vent?

Russ: A little bit of venting isn't a problem. It's important that we allow clients enough time to talk about their issues, problems, and concerns, and that we compassionately acknowledge and validate their suffering. But if that's all the session involves—the client venting and the therapist listening supportively—it's a bit of a waste of time in terms of ACT. It certainly won't help the client develop psychological flexibility.

When clients are venting, we can work with it constructively. For example, we might ask them to pause for a moment, notice what they are thinking and feeling, and from there segue into self-compassion.

In my own experience, I've found problematic or excessive venting is most common with relationship difficulties; the more upset the client is with the other person, the more protracted the venting is about all the hurtful things the other person is doing.

Suppose, for example, a client presents as deeply distraught by the bad behavior of her boyfriend. I'd certainly want to hear what has happened and to validate how painful and difficult the situation is. But I wouldn't want to spend a whole session on that! Fairly quickly I'd want to ask, respectfully and compassionately, what the client would like to get from therapy, and translate her answers into behavioral goals (see chapter 3: Ghastly Goals). If her answer is "I don't know," I'd offer her some options. We could work on handling her pain better and looking after herself better, or on taking action to improve the relationship, or even on ending the relationship.

Once we're clear on the behavioral goals for therapy, we can focus the session constructively. And we can respectfully have the client note whenever her mind pulls her off track to start venting about her boyfriend, and then gently and kindly redirect her back to the behavioral goal we are working on.

Q: What if the client is skeptical of ACT?

Russ: First, I recommend normalizing and validating that response: to be skeptical and dubious and hesitant is completely understandable, completely natural. Then you could talk a bit about "how your mind is trying to protect you" and emphasize that this is a good thing.

Second, specify that the client never has to do anything she doesn't want to, that you'll always tell her in advance what the exercise is and how you think it will help, and that you can always modify it to suit her needs, or ditch it if she doesn't want to do it.

Third, consider using the word *experiment* with the client as a preamble to experiential exercises. For example, you might say, "Can we try an experiment? I'd like to take you through an exercise. I call it an experiment because I'm asking you to try something new, and although I hope it will be helpful, I can't know that for sure. I never actually know what the outcome will be, in advance. But can we give it a go? See what happens? See if it's helpful or not?" If the client reacts negatively to the term *experiment*, you might add that the outcome will be unknown for any type of intervention from any type of professional from any model of therapy for any type of condition.

We might also say something like "Just coming in here today for your first session is an experiment, in the sense that I mean it. It's new—you haven't done it before—and we don't yet know if it will be helpful." After that, we might go on to explore: "Did you have some doubts, skepticism, or hesitation about coming here today? Did your mind try to talk you out of it? Did anxiety show up?" The client will likely answer yes.

Then we can normalize that again: "Whenever we try new things, step out of our comfort zone, these sorts of thoughts and feelings are normal. Anxiety shows up. Our mind tells us, *watch out, be careful, don't do it, it might go wrong, you might get hurt.* So I expect these kinds of thoughts and feelings to show up again and again and again as we work together."

Note that we now have an excellent recent example of committed action to draw upon: the client experienced fear, doubt, anxiety—and yet still took action to come to the first session, in the service of important values such as self-care.

Also notice, there are quite a few elements of defusion in there. First, noticing and naming the thoughts. Second, couching them it in terms of "what your mind is saying." Third, validating and normalizing them.

I also, very often, disclose how my mind does similar things to the client's mind: "You know, your mind is a lot like mine. When I'm in new situations outside my comfort zone, my mind says things to me like *I don't think this is going to work.*"

Then, as mentioned above, you can point out how the mind is trying to be helpful; typically it would be trying to help the client avoid something potentially "bad" (painful, unpleasant, scary, risky, and so on). And then you could predict that the mind is likely to keep doing this.

Notice how this is the polar opposite of challenging the thoughts, trying to get rid of them, judging them as dysfunctional, or trying to prove them wrong or false or invalid. And notice how in addition to defusion, it also builds self-acceptance and strengthens therapeutic rapport.

Q: What if clients resist doing exercises?

Russ: When clients express reluctance, first thank them for being honest and genuine with you. This strengthens rapport, instead of pulling you into conflict. Then validate and normalize the reluctance; it's completely understandable. And then reiterate that, as you said earlier (during informed consent), you'll never demand that clients do anything they don't want to. Explain that you'll only ever ask them to try things because you believe it will help, but they are always free to say no.

Below are several strategies that will increase the client's likelihood of doing an exercise.

General Tips for Handling Resistance to Exercises

- Give the client a clear rationale before starting the exercise: What is the point? How will it help?
- Build willingness by explicitly linking it to values and values-congruent goals.

- Carefully titrate it: start with small doses. Test the water. Increase the dosage over time.
- If one technique doesn't work, try another. For example, with self-compassion, you can work on any of the six key "elements" at any time (see chapter 10: Surprising Self-Compassion).
- Dance around the hexaflex. If you get stuck on one process, move to another.
- Don't immediately give up on an exercise because the client says it's weird or uncomfortable or strange or makes her feel nervous. Validate and normalize those reactions. Reframe them as "good signs." For example, you could say, "The fact that you're feeling this way is a good sign. It means you're doing something new, something different—stepping out of your comfort zone. If you felt totally comfortable, that would mean we are just doing the same old stuff that you're familiar and comfortable with, even though we know that's not helping you build a better life." Then remind him of the goals and values this work is in the service of and ask, "Would you be willing, in the service of those goals and values, to persist with the exercise a little longer?"
- Consider if there's an alternative exercise that serves the same purpose but may be a better fit for the client at this time. For example, if your client strongly dislikes anything that resembles meditation, or requires extensive writing, then don't push it; there are so many alternatives available to us in this model. We'll run into problems if we become overly attached to particular exercises.
- Draw up a choice point (chapter 1) for the situation itself. We might say, "Can we just take a moment to map out what's happening here?" At the bottom of the diagram we'd write in the situation ("opportunity to try a new exercise in therapy") and the client's thoughts and feelings ("anxiety"; "I can't do it"). We'd write in some helpers: values and goals that this exercise is linked to ("being a loving mother"). Then we'd ask if doing the exercise is a towards move or an away move. Assuming the client says it's a

towards move, we'd write that in: "doing the exercise," and we'd write "avoiding the exercise" under away moves. (If the client sees doing the exercise as an away move, then the therapist needs to clearly link it to the client's therapy goals.) Then we'd say, "So in order for you to do this exercise, it looks like we're first going to need to do some unhooking from these thoughts and feelings." Then we'd segue into the relevant unhooking skills, such as acceptance of anxiety or further defusion from "It's too hard."

Q: What if clients insist on exploring the past in great depth?

Russ: There's no right or wrong about how much history we gather in ACT, how far back it goes, and how detailed it is. We all do it our own way. Personally, I aim to take a brief history in the first session, spending no more than forty minutes on it, and then I move into active intervention as quickly as possible. I operate on the brief therapy assumption that we can gather more history later if we need it. But other ACT therapists who don't have a brief therapy orientation would probably take a much more in-depth and detailed history up front, before getting into active intervention.

Of course, in trauma-related work, it's important to go as far back in time as is necessary, and often this does involve looking in depth at childhood events. Indeed, for many adult clients, we work with the past through "inner child work," to help them develop self-compassion. Typically, this involves imagery exercises where the client imagines herself (as she is today) traveling back in time to distressing childhood events, where she can comfort, care for, and support the childhood version of herself who is suffering.

An insistence on exploring the past to such an extent that it actually becomes problematic is most likely to be seen in clients who subscribe to traditional psychoanalytic ideas. If a client believes she can only get better through exploring her past in great depth, and that only such exploration will give her the "deep insight" necessary to solve all her problems, then ideally we'd address that up front during the informed consent process (appendix 2). We'd explain that we don't do that kind of therapy. We'd explain what ACT is, and if the client isn't interested in ACT, we'd recommend she find someone who does the sort of therapy she's looking for. But if she is open to ACT, here's a useful metaphor:

The Gearbox Metaphor

When the gearbox in your car is jammed, you can spend a lot of time analyzing all the possible factors that played a role: what materials were used in the gearbox, where was the gearbox made, who has driven the car, what terrain has it been driven over, what were the drivers' skills like, what weather conditions has it been driven in, and so on. And none of that has any effect whatsoever on the gearbox. Nor does it tell you what to do to get the gearbox functioning. The only way to get the gearbox functioning is to have a look at what's jamming it, right here and now, and take action to unjam it.

Q: How does ACT address systemic factors such as relationship issues?

Russ: You'll find systemic factors covered in your ACT Case Formulation worksheet (appendix 1). The third section is titled "EXTERNAL BARRIERS" and reads, "Are there any external barriers (as opposed to psychological barriers) to a rich and full life (e.g., legal, social, medical, financial, occupational problems) that require problem solving and/or skills training?"

All such systemic factors or external barriers are addressed through values-guided committed action. This includes values-guided goal setting, action planning, problem solving, and skills training. (If you're filling in a case formulation worksheet, you will write these down in the brainstorm section at the very end.) So if relationship issues play a role, we'd address them through learning and applying communication skills, assertiveness skills, negotiation skills, intimacy skills, and so on, as outlined in my book on relationship issues: *ACT with Love* (Harris, 2009b).

However, if clients are highly fused and avoidant, this is likely to interfere with taking action to address systemic factors, so we often need to work on unhooking skills such as defusion, acceptance, and grounding first.

Q: How does ACT address readiness to change?

As the ACT model focuses on clarifying values and taking action, how effective would it be for clients who may not be ready to change? And is there any way we can assist in developing clients' insight to assist moving toward change?

Russ: In ACT, readiness for change is rapidly assessed through informed consent (appendix 2) and establishing therapy goals (chapter 3). As we run through these on the first session, we'll get a pretty good idea of client readiness. If clients are "not ready to change," it's usually because of fusion and experiential avoidance, so ACT is ideal for such clients because those are precisely the processes it targets.

But we wouldn't say about a client that he's "not ready to change," as that doesn't give us any useful information to target our interventions; instead we'd explore what's maintaining his unworkable behavior. We'd identify the antecedents for his unworkable behavior (the thoughts, feelings, and situations that trigger it) and the reinforcing consequences (the outcomes of the behavior that maintain it, such as getting to escape or avoid unpleasant feelings or situations). And then we'd target those with relevant ACT processes, such as defusion from self-defeating beliefs like *I can't change* or *It's too hard*, or acceptance of the feelings he's trying to avoid.

As for insight, ACT develops this in every session. For example, the choice point is a great tool for helping people rapidly develop insight into what influences their behavior and what effects their behavior has on their life. Similarly, every time we ask clients to notice their thoughts and feelings, they develop insight into their inner world. And when we get them to notice their actions, and the workability of their actions, they develop further insight into their behavior and its consequences. And when we explore values, they develop insight into what truly matters to them and how they want to live their lives. So mapping out a choice point is probably one of the simplest ways to develop insight and assist moving toward change.

The Wrap-Up

If we set up our sessions well, right from the beginning—which means good informed consent and clear goals for therapy—they will go a lot smoother. Remember, we're always dancing between two questions: "What valued direction does the client want to move in?" and "What's getting in the way?" If clients can't or won't answer the first question, we focus on the second. But often, just taking the time to establish behavioral goals for therapy develops readiness to change. And if clients are extremely fused with reasons why therapy won't work, I recommend the strategy covered in appendix 4: Defusion from Barriers to Therapy.

Finally, keep in mind what I said at the start of this chapter: we want to see our clients as rainbows, not roadblocks. So if therapy stalls because of any of the issues mentioned above, or numerous others we haven't yet touched upon, let's first practice ACT on ourselves: unhook from our unhelpful thoughts, make room for our uncomfortable feelings, reconnect with our values as therapists, and engage fully with the unique human being in front of us.

CHAPTER 5

Freaky Functional Analysis

The whole ACT model rests on a foundation of behavior analysis, BA. Even a little bit of knowledge of BA principles can go a long way to improving your understanding of ACT—and your ability to do it effectively. So in this chapter, we'll cover what is arguably the single most clinically useful tool in BA: the ABCs of functional analysis. If you find after reading it you'd like to learn more about BA, the best beginners-level book I know is The ABCs of Human Behavior (Ramnerö & Törneke, 2008).

Keep in mind, as you read this chapter, no one says YOU HAVE TO KNOW FUNCTIONAL ANALYSIS in order to do ACT well. Nor do you have to teach it to your clients. However, even a little knowledge about this topic can be very helpful, as you'll see shortly.

Discussions in This Chapter:

- The term *behavior* in ACT seems to have a different meaning than in other models. Can you explain it?
- What does the term *context* mean in ACT?
- What is functional analysis of behavior?
- How can functional analysis help us clinically?
- What is a four-term contingency?

- How do we identify triggers for away moves?
- How do we identify payoffs for away moves?
- Do we ever identify punishing consequences?
- Can we do functional analysis with the choice point?

Q: The term *behavior* in ACT seems to have a different meaning than in other models. Can you explain it?

Russ: Yes, the term *behavior* in ACT is a bit different from how it's used in many models. Remember, ACT is based on behavior analysis, BA. And in BA, behavior means anything a whole organism does. The term often refers to overt behaviors, such as eating and drinking and running and sleeping. *Overt behavior* means behavior that other people can potentially observe *directly*; in other words, if observers were present they'd be able to *directly see or hear* the behavior in question.

However, in BA, the term also refers to covert behaviors. *Covert behavior* could never possibly be *directly* observed by others, even if they were present while it was happening. For example, covert behavior includes thinking and sensing and remembering and feeling; these behaviors can be inferred by others, or reported to others, but not directly observed by others. So if I'm silently worrying, that's covert behavior—because no one else can ever *directly observe* the worrying thoughts that I'm having. But if I write those worrying thoughts down in a journal, or I speak them aloud, that's overt behavior—because if observers were present, they'd be able to see what I'm writing or hear what I'm saying.

Q: What does the term *context* mean in ACT?

Russ: All behavior happens within a context. The term *context*, in BA, refers to each and every factor that may influence the behavior in question. This may include:

- Emotions, feelings, moods
- Cognitive events (thoughts, beliefs, attitudes, assumptions, schemas)
- Cognitive processes (attention, memory)
- Interpersonal factors (who else is present, what they are saying and doing, your past relationship history with them)
- Social and cultural events (public holidays, religious festivals, important anniversaries, traditional celebrations and rituals)
- The physical environment (location, furnishings, weather, time of day, temperature, smell in the air)
- Genes and epigenes
- Physiological states such as thirst, hunger, fatigue
- Consumption of drugs, alcohol, food
- Physical health or illness
- Social and cultural status (social class, oppression by others, position and rank, privileges, peer groups)
- Developmental and learning history, including attachment style

Q: What is functional analysis of behavior?

Russ: All behavior occurs amid a vast, ever-changing, nonstop stream of influences, and it's impossible for us to ever know *everything* that's influencing our behavior at a given time. Collectively, these influences are referred to as the context in which the behavior happens. And we can divide this context up into antecedents and consequences. *Antecedents* are factors that precede the behavior in question, and cue or trigger its recurrence. For example, a craving to get high, a feeling of anxiety, a fight with a partner, or seeing other people using drugs at a party all might act as triggers or antecedents to the behavior of taking drugs. With clients, I like to use the term *triggers* rather than *antecedents*.

Consequences are events that follow the behavior and influence whether it's likely to get stronger or weaker in the long term.

If the consequences of a behavior lead to it weakening or reducing over time, we say they are "punishing." For example, if the client takes drugs, has a "bad trip," and therefore uses such drugs less in the future, his "bad trip" was a punishing consequence. If the consequences lead to a behavior strengthening or increasing over time, we say they are "reinforcing." For instance, if the client takes drugs, has an ecstatic "mind-altering experience," and therefore uses drugs more in future, this ecstatic state was a reinforcing consequence. With clients, we usually use the term *payoffs* rather than *reinforcing consequences*.

Loosely speaking, the *function* of a behavior means the effects it has. To analyze the function of a behavior, we need to identify antecedents that trigger it and the consequences that follow it. This process of specifying a behavior and identifying the key antecedents and consequences that either reinforce or punish it is called *functional analysis*. It enables us to figure out the function of the behavior: the effects the behavior has, or what the behavior achieves.

This process of functional analysis is often playfully called *function-spotting*, or identifying *the ABCs of behavior* (ABC: Antecedents => Behavior => Consequences). And the technical term for an ABC analysis is a *three-term contingency*.

Q: How can functional analysis help us clinically?

Russ: I'm so glad you asked! Best way to answer this is with an example. I'm going to use the common clinical issue of self-harming. But you can use the same principles with any problematic behavior.

So suppose you have a client who self-harms by cutting her arms with a razor blade, and she wants to stop. Let's do a quick functional analysis, using the three-term contingency. There are always three questions we explore with our ABC analysis:

- What is the person doing (behavior)?

- What triggers the behavior (antecedents)?
- What outcomes of the behavior strengthen it or weaken it (consequences)?

When we're looking at life-enhancing, workable behaviors that the client has reduced, stopped, or given up, we're going to be interested in the punishing consequences: what outcomes of the behavior lead the client to stop or cut back on doing it? And when we're looking at ineffective, unworkable behaviors that the client continues to do, we're interested in the reinforcing consequences (or "payoffs") that keep it going.

It's often useful to map this out in three columns, as below:

Antecedents (Triggers)	**Behavior**	**Reinforcing Consequences (Payoffs)**
Situation: alone in bedroom after a fight with her mother. Thoughts & Feelings: "Life sucks," "Mom's a bitch," "Why does nothing good ever happen to me?" "I'm such a loser." Anger, sadness, hopelessness Urge to cut	Cuts her forearm with a razor blade	Feeling of relief; painful thoughts, feelings, and urges disappear

In appendix 7, you'll find a Triggers-Behavior-Payoffs worksheet that you can use with clients for this purpose. The next few diagrams highlight the many ways we can intervene, given this information. For example, we may target the antecedent thoughts and feelings with mindfulness skills:

Antecedents (Triggers)	Respond with:
Thoughts & Feelings: "Life sucks," "Mom's a bitch," "Why does nothing good ever happen to me?" "I'm such a loser." Anger, sadness, hopelessness Urge to cut	Dropping anchor (chapter 7) Acknowledging thoughts and feelings Defusion Acceptance Self-compassion Urge surfing

We may target the antecedent situation:

Antecedents (Triggers)	Respond with:
Situation: alone in bedroom after a fight with her mother	Values & committed action

We may look at alternative, more effective values-congruent behavior:

Behavior	Respond with:
Cuts her forearm with a razor blade	Values & committed action Explore alternative, values-congruent behaviors to cutting that the client could do, after mindfully responding to her antecedent thoughts, feelings, and urges with defusion, grounding, and acceptance.

We may target the reinforcing consequences in terms of workability:

Reinforcing Consequences (Payoffs)	**Respond with:**
Feeling of relief; painful thoughts, feelings, and urges disappear	Workability Clarify and validate the payoffs. For example: "In the short term, there are real benefits for you; it gives you a sense of relief, the pain goes away." Compassionately help the client to contact the costs, such as cutting habit worsens, scarring of the forearm, upsetting her mother and creating even more conflict with her.

So hopefully you can see that a good ABC analysis gives us many options for effective intervention. If therapy is successful, something like this will now start happening at home:

Antecedents (Triggers)	**NEW Behavior**	**NEW Reinforcing Consequences (Payoffs)**
Situation: alone in bedroom after a fight with her mother. Thoughts & Feelings: "Life sucks," "Mom's a bitch," "Why does nothing good ever happen to me?" "I'm such a loser." Anger, sadness, hopelessness Urge to cut	Defusion Acceptance Dropping anchor Urge surfing Self-compassion	Painful thoughts, feelings, and urges lose some of their impact and influence; switch off "automatic pilot" & get present; experience a sense of greater self-control, more freedom to choose behavior

This new (covert) behavior has new consequences, and these in turn become antecedents for further new behaviors:

NEW Antecedents (Triggers)	NEW Behavior	NEW Reinforcing Consequences (Payoffs)
Situation: alone in bedroom after a fight with her mother, and now mindfully responding to painful thoughts, feelings, urges with: defusing & accepting surfing urges dropping anchor self-compassion	Connects with values. "This pain reminds me that what I really want is to have a better relationship with Mom; what matters to me is fairness and respect. And really, I want to take care of myself, not harm myself."	Sense of clarity and self-awareness; sense of purpose; making sense of this pain; connecting with importance of self-care

And so it continues. These new behaviors now have new consequences, which in turn are the antecedents for yet more new behaviors:

NEW Antecedents (Triggers)	NEW Behavior	NEW Reinforcing Consequences (Payoffs)
Situation: alone in bedroom after a fight with her mother, and mindfully responding to thoughts and feelings—and now also in touch with values of self-care, and "getting along better with Mom"	Committed action Massages forearm with hand cream, then connects with a friend on Skype.	Feeling of vitality or satisfaction; sense of living by values & moving in a positive life direction

So, this is what we hope will happen after a course of ACT. And you may now be wondering: *But what if after all that, the behavior doesn't change?*

Well, we go through a functional analysis: are there other triggers and reinforcing consequences that we didn't identify?

For example, perhaps the main antecedent to the client's cutting behavior is actually a sense of feeling alone and disconnected; and perhaps the main reinforcer for cutting is a sense of belonging to her peer group (who all look favorably upon cutting) and the sense of satisfaction she gets as she imagines their approval.

Alternatively, maybe when Mom gets upset over the cutting, that reaction is a reinforcer for the client's cutting behavior—perhaps through giving the client a sense of power over her mother.

Or maybe the payoff is that when the client cuts, Mom gives her a lot of attention that she otherwise doesn't get. Or maybe the payoff is that when the client cuts herself, Mom backs down on various demands and expectations and lets her off certain duties, chores, or responsibilities.

We may also consider expanding our analysis from a three-term contingency to a four-term contingency.

Q: What is a four-term contingency?

Russ: We can add a fourth term into the functional analysis of behavior. We can factor in events that don't immediately precede the behavior but do play a role in triggering it. For example, this may include:

- the person's state of health or sickness, physiological states such as thirst or hunger or tiredness, withdrawal or intoxication from a drug
- the physical environment, for example, too hot, cold, dirty, or noisy
- events that happened earlier, such as having a big argument with a loved one, getting a fine, failing a test, or having a bad day at work
- the nature of the day itself, for example, whether it is a Monday or a Friday or a holiday or a religious festival or the anniversary of a loved one's death

- past learning history, such as via a group the person belongs to that advocates, models, or rewards the behavior
- for interpersonal problems: the past interpersonal history with the other(s) involved

This information can help us make sense of a behavior that happens on some occasions or situations but not others, such as a parent who sometimes yells aggressively at the kids when they are taking a long time to get ready for school, but at other times is calm and assertive; or why a teenager cuts herself on some days but not others. It can help us to identify reinforcing or punishing consequences we may have missed initially, and why they are such strong reinforcers or punishers of behavior.

In behavior analysis textbooks these influences on behavior are variously called "setting events," "establishing operations," "motivating operations," or "slow triggers." In everyday language, when people talk about "extenuating circumstances" for a "bad behavior," they are often referring, at least in part, to these setting events. With clients, I usually refer to this extra column as "contributing factors," or the "backdrop" to what happened, or the "circumstances surrounding" what happened.

The Four-Term Contingency

Setting Events (Backdrop)	**Antecedents (Triggers)**	**Behavior**	**Reinforcing Consequences (Payoffs)**
Health Physiological state Physical environment Interpersonal history with other(s) involved Other factors	Situation Thoughts Feelings	Something an organism does	Outcomes of the behavior that maintain or strengthen it

We work with setting events the same way we work with anything else in ACT: we bring in psychological flexibility. We help the client to respond mindfully, guided by her values, to change what can be changed and accept what can't be changed.

Q: How do we identify triggers for away moves?

Russ: A good place to start is with asking the client simple questions such as:

- What happened just before (you started doing that)?
- What were you thinking just before (you started doing that)?
- What were you feeling just before (you started doing that)?
- Immediately before (you started doing that), where were you? What was the situation? Who else was there? What was going on?

Of course, many clients can't readily identify their triggers. In such cases, we attempt to recreate the triggering situation and identify the triggering thoughts and feelings. What follows are a couple of ways we might do this. In the first example, some sort of problematic behavior has just happened in session. After some grounding, the therapist may something like, "Is it okay if we rewind the session to just before you did X (*therapist nonjudgmentally names the problematic behavior that has just occurred in the session*) and see if we can identify what triggered it? The behavior started right after I asked you that question about your values. So if it's okay with you, I'm going to ask you the very same question again, but this time all I want you to do is pause for twenty seconds, notice what thoughts and feelings show up, and see if you have any urge to repeat it."

In the next example, the therapist helps the client to remember the antecedents to behavior that happened outside the session:

"Okay, see if you can remember the last time this happened. Picture the scene as vividly as you can, as if it were happening right now. (*The therapist now asks a string of questions to identify the situation, thoughts, and feelings.*) Where are you?… What are you doing?… What time is it?…

What can you see and hear?… Who's there with you?… What is the other person saying or doing?… How are you feeling?… What are you thinking?" Note how these questions are asked as if the event is happening NOW, in order to make it more vivid, more present ("What are you doing?" as opposed to "What were you doing?"). Another option is to have the client keep a journal or complete a worksheet between sessions. Here she can write in, as soon as possible after it happens, what the behavior was and what the antecedents were.

Of course, clients who don't yet have the skills to notice and name their thoughts and feelings will struggle with this. If so, therapy focuses first on building those basic skills, with lots of active practice on noticing and naming thoughts and feelings that arise throughout the session.

Q: How do we identify payoffs for away moves?

Russ: To identify reinforcing consequences of a behavior, we can ask these questions:

- What happened next (or immediately) after you started doing that?
- What was that like? How did you feel at the time?
- Did you get something you want or avoid something you didn't want?
- Did you feel better in some way, or get rid of some unwanted feelings?

I explain it to clients this way: "Sometimes it's hard to know what our payoffs are for doing this stuff—there could be so many different factors involved—but basically all of our payoffs boil down to just four things: (1) we get away from something we don't want; (2) we get something that we do want; (3) we get to escape unwanted feelings; (4) we get to feel good. Often our payoffs are a mixture of all those things. Do you think any of those apply to you in this case?"

In appendix 7, you'll find a Triggers-Behavior-Payoffs worksheet (available on the free resources page on http://www.ImLearningACT.com). Listed on the right-hand column of the worksheet you'll see this list of common payoffs for unworkable behaviors:

- Escape/avoid people, places, situations, events
- Escape/avoid unwanted thoughts and feelings
- Get your needs met/get what you want
- Feel good
- Feel safe or familiar
- Feel like you deserve it
- Feel like you are right and others are wrong
- Feel powerful or in control
- Gain attention
- Look good to others
- Make sense (of life, the world, yourself, others)

Of course, there are countless other possible reinforcers for any given away move. But this lists the most common ones we'll find in clinical practice. The idea is to show it to the client and ask, "Could any of these things be your payoffs?"

Remember, there will always be reinforcing consequences for any type of away move—otherwise the behavior would cease. So the more entrenched the problematic behavior, the more important it is to raise clients' awareness of these payoffs, and then validate them: "So there are real benefits to you, in the short term, such as…" After that, we can compassionately and respectfully help the client to contact the costs and explore if the behavior is "workable" (in other words, working to give her the life she wants in the long term).

Q: Do we ever identify punishing consequences?

Russ: For sure. Most commonly we'll spend time on this when a client stops or does less of an effective life-enhancing behavior. We want to identify the punishing consequences using questions such as:

- What happened next (or immediately) after you started doing that?
- What was that like? How did you feel at the time?
- Did you lose or miss out on something?
- Did you get something (or come into contact with something) that you don't want?
- Did unwanted thoughts, feelings, emotions, memories show up?

What we hope to do, through ACT, is to help clients develop willingness to make room for all these costs—to accept them, in the service of living their values.

Q: Can we do functional analysis with the choice point?

Russ: We can't *not* do functional analysis with the choice point. The tool immediately identifies some of the most important functions of behavior: whether it functions as an effective, values-guided, life-enhancing behavior (towards move) or an ineffective, self-defeating behavior (away move). And we can easily map an ABC analysis onto the tool, if desired.

For the self-harming example I gave earlier, we'd write the situation, thoughts, and feelings (antecedents to cutting) at the bottom. And the behavior of cutting herself would go on the left side, as an away move. (Remember, away and towards are always defined by the client, not the therapist. If the client sees cutting herself as a towards move, we wouldn't argue with her; we'd write it as a towards move and leave it for the time being. Instead we'd focus on a behavior that the client *does* currently see as an away move. As therapy progresses, we'd expect the client to change her mind and re-class cutting as an away move. But if we started trying to convince her it's an away move, we'd just get into a battle.) Finally, if we wanted to highlight the reinforcing consequences of the behavior, we'd write the word "payoffs" at the top left, above the word "away," and jot them in there.

But note, we don't need to draw out a choice point or fill in a Triggers-Behavior-Payoffs worksheet. These are useful visual aids, but hardly essential. We can run through functional analysis in a purely conversational manner, if preferred.

The Wrap-Up

I hope you can see how the whole ACT model is infused with functional analysis. Again and again we ask clients to notice their behavior, the consequences it has (both positive and negative), and the antecedents to it. And there are so many ways we can use this information to target our interventions or plan our sessions. If a client ever asks, "Why do I keep doing this?" or "Why did I do that?" we can do an ABC analysis to provide a quick and useful answer. This is especially useful for clients who insist, "I need to understand myself; I need to know why I am doing this." The ABC analysis neatly answers the question and gives us multiple pointers for ACT interventions.

CHAPTER 6

Vicious Values

Values, glorious values. What would we do without them? They're the heart and soul of the ACT model. They guide us like a compass. They fuel us through dark nights of despair, and light up the way to a new and better life. They're an endless source of inspiration and motivation for humans of all races and cultures. And yet, getting clients in touch with them creates soooooo many problems. In this chapter we're going to look at both conceptual barriers (misunderstandings about what values are) and clinical barriers (the sorts of blocks that show up in session) to effective work with values.

But first a word of caution: while many clients are fine with the word values, some aren't. For some clients, the word has aversive connotations. And some clients have no idea what it really means. So it's a good idea to have alternative words or phrases you can use instead that convey the concept of living by and acting on values. These may not fully encapsulate the concept, but if they at least convey key elements of it, that's a good start. Examples of phrases you might use are:

- *Doing what matters to you*
- *Behaving like the sort of person do you want to be*
- *Living life your way*
- *Treating yourself or others the way you really want to, deep in your heart*

Some therapists don't even use the word values until later in therapy, once values have actually been identified. There's no right or wrong in this; the main thing is to be flexible. (Come to think of it, that's pretty much the main thing in just about anything and everything we ever do as ACT therapists.)

Discussions in This Chapter:

- Why do some clients say "I don't know" to every question about values?
- How do we work with clients who keep saying "I don't know"?
- Which comes first in therapy: clarifying values or setting goals?
- How many domains should we focus on, and how many values should we identify, at any one time?
- How do you work with destructive values?
- What if a client's value is "to be successful in selling drugs"?
- What if a client's main value is "power"?
- What's the difference between values and rules?
- What if a client's value is "don't trust others"?
- What if chronic pain or illness stops clients from living their values?
- How do we resolve values conflicts?
- What if living by and acting on your values means rejection or hostility from your family, community, or culture?
- What is the Connect and Reflect exercise?
- What are useful questions to get people to open up about values?
- What is "flavoring and savoring"?

Q: Why do some clients say "I don't know" to every question about values?

Russ: Well, it depends. There may be a variety of reasons. So we need to consider what the function of "I don't know" is. (See chapter 5: Freaky Functional Analysis.) For example, is it a request for more information because the client simply doesn't understand what we are talking about? If so, then we'd do some brief psychoeducation (no more than a few minutes' worth) and use a metaphor to explain what values are. We'd explain how they differ from goals and give a few examples to distinguish the difference, such as being loving versus getting married, being reliable and friendly versus getting a great job, being supportive and loving toward your family versus buying a house for them to live in. And then we'd launch into an experiential exercise, of which you'll find many in any ACT textbook, and quite a few in this chapter.

Far more commonly, however, "I don't know" functions as an attempt to avoid an uncomfortable conversation, and the uncomfortable feelings that go with it. In this case, we may take the opportunity to do an ABC functional analysis (A = antecedents, B = behavior, C = consequences) of "I don't know," as outlined in depth in chapter 5. It may go something like this:

A Brief Functional Analysis of "I Don't Know"

- **A—Antecedents (situation, thoughts, feelings):** "Take a moment to notice what's happening here. This is a challenging situation; I'm asking you difficult questions. And I'm guessing that's bringing up some uncomfortable thoughts and feelings. Can I get you to check in and notice what's happening in your body? Where are you feeling it? What's that like? What's your mind saying?" Typically, this line of questioning will reveal anxiety, confusion, urges to change the topic, thoughts such as *I don't know*, and so forth.

- **B—Behavior:** "Given that we're in this challenging situation, and you're feeling X, and your mind is saying Y, it's completely natural that your first answer would be 'I don't know' (or 'I don't have any values')."
- **C—Consequences:** "So let's suppose that we give up, end the conversation, move on to something else. There'd be immediate relief for you; all that anxiety and confusion would be gone, and I'd no longer be bothering you with difficult questions."

Here the therapist has identified the main reinforcing consequence, or payoff, of "I don't know": avoiding discomfort. She can now look at the behavior in terms of workability: acknowledging and validating the payoffs and then compassionately contrasting them with the long-term costs. The therapist may say something like this: "So we can think of this as your mind being overly helpful, trying very hard to help you avoid an uncomfortable situation and some unpleasant feelings. And in the short term, if we go along with your mind's agenda here and give up on finding out your values, then there's a very real payoff for you; you get to escape all that discomfort. But in the long term, therapy grinds to a halt. Because we don't get to find out the essential information we need, in order to help you build a better life. Your life carries on as it is, without any values to guide you, or inspire you, or motivate you, or help you move forward. So in the service of building a better life, would you be willing to…?"

At this point, the therapist segues into one of the four strategies mentioned in the next Q&A.

Q: How do we work with clients who keep saying "I don't know"?

Russ: First, let's validate their response. If they keep saying "I don't know," we might say something like "Yes, right now that's exactly how it is. You don't know what they are." Or if the client says, "I don't have any values," we might reply, "That's right. You are so unaware of them right now, that for all intents and purposes, it's as if you don't have any."

Then we could ask, "So would you like to change that? Would you like to discover some? Right now, they're buried down so deep inside you, you don't even know they're there. Would you like to change that?"

If the client answers no, then check: have you gotten informed consent to do ACT (appendix 2)? If no, get it. If yes, have you established behavioral goals for therapy (chapter 3)? If not, do so.

If, however, the client answers yes—great! We can now launch into action using one of the following approaches.

Four Responses to "I Don't Know"

1. **Sit with the question a bit longer:** "I get that 'I don't know' is your first answer. That's very common. However, often, if you think about it for a minute or two, other answers show up. Would you be willing to close your eyes or fix them on a spot, and I'll ask the question again, but this time, just think about it for a minute or two before answering, and see if any other answers show up?"

2. **Do an experiential exercise:** "Asking you more questions isn't likely to be helpful at this point, I think. So instead, would you be willing to do an exercise with me? I'm going to ask you to close your eyes or fix them on a spot, and think about something." You would then lead into an experiential exercise such as the Connect and Reflect exercise described later this chapter, or numerous others. (Any ACT textbook will give you several different experiential exercises for values clarification.) Alternatively, you can explore artistic, creative ways to access values such as drawing; making collages; taking photos of people, places, objects, and activities that matter; and listening to and discussing themes in the client's favorite music.

3. **Fill in a values worksheet or checklist:** In any ACT textbook you'll find many values worksheets. You can also download values checklists (lists of common values that the client can go through and rate as very important, quite important, or not important)

from the free resources page on http://www.ImLearningACT.com, or use the one in the ACT Companion app (available for all types of smartphones).

4. **Do a values cards sort:** A quick search on Google reveals there are many types of values cards you can purchase. (If you live in Australia, you can get my own set from http://www.actmindfully.com.au.) The client can sort the values cards into piles of very important, quite important, and not important; in doing so, often she connects with and clarifies her own values.

Q: Which comes first in therapy: clarifying values or setting goals?

Russ: We explored this question to some extent in chapter 3, in the Q&A "But don't values come before goals?" However, let's look at it again from a different angle, as it's very important. Values and goals and actions are all on a continuum. At times we use values to set goals and create action plans. At other times we elicit and clarify values by considering what motivates or inspires the client's goals and actions.

If we run through those questions in the "behavioral goals" section of the ACT Case Formulation worksheet (appendix 1), we will likely get a mixed bunch of desired goals, desired actions, and desired qualities of action. The desired qualities of action are what we call *values*.

When it comes to formal goal setting, we can set short-term goals (e.g., join an online dating agency), medium-term goals (e.g., go on lots of dates), and long-term goals (e.g., get married). Then we can look at the actions necessary to increase the chances of achieving those goals.

Values work can come in before, during, or after such goal setting.

Values work before goal setting: We identify values the client wants to live by, then explore how the client would like to act on them.

Values work during goal setting: We may explore questions such as "How do you want to treat yourself and others as you go about pursuing these goals? What qualities do you want to bring to your actions as you do this? What do you want to stand for as you work toward this?"

Values work after clarifying goals: We may explore with the client, "What do these goals tell you about what matters to you, about the sort of person you want to be?" or "What's this goal in the service of?"

When we establish behavioral goals up front in therapy (as in chapter 3), we straddle two core ACT processes: values and committed action. Often to begin with, the values are implicit within these goals and don't become explicit until later in therapy when we start to tease them out. Initially, we are simply trying to get a sense of how the client wants her behavior to change as a result of therapy.

So, for example, if we identify a goal such as to find a partner, get a better job, ride a bike, learn to ski, or go to a party, our next step is to explore what the client would need to start doing differently to increase the likelihood of achieving that goal. How would her behavior need to change?

From there we could explore what values underpin those goals. And once we know them, then we can look for ongoing actions that could be ways to live by those values on a daily basis, and to keep living by them every step of the way—whether the client ultimately achieves the goal or not.

Q: How many domains should we focus on, and how many values should we identify, at any one time?

Russ: We can split life up into as many domains as we like. Some ACT tools divide life up into ten or twelve different domains, but I like the bull's-eye (appendix 3) for its simplicity: it slices life into four broad domains—work, love, play, and health. There are no hard rules about this in ACT, but personally I think it's wise to stick to one domain per session and identify two or three values within it; otherwise it easily gets confusing or overwhelming. Many values will be the same across most or all life domains, but some will differ from domain to domain.

Q: How do you work with destructive values?

Russ: There's a starting assumption in ACT that when people engage in destructive behavior it's usually because they are disconnected from their values (as we use the term in ACT, which is of course very different from other everyday meanings of the term *values*). We assume that destructive behavior usually happens when people have become fused with all sorts of beliefs, ideas, attitudes, assumptions, convictions, and judgments, and that this fusion pulls them away from their values.

Why do we start from this assumption? Well, look at your own behavior; we've all done destructive things at times, to ourselves or to others. So were you mindfully acting on your values when you did this destructive stuff? Or were you hooked and moving away from your values? On the choice point (chapter 1), would you class your destructive behavior as a towards move or an away move?

It's worth noting that ACT is now used in lots of prisons and other forensic settings, and getting good results; and I've never heard of clients in these settings asking for help to be more sadistic or more hateful or identifying core values such as cruelty and prejudice.

The bottom line is, if a client wants help to do some sort of destructive behavior that would compromise the ethics of the therapist, the therapist should say so at once, and address it. And if the client can't be shifted to an agenda that is ACT-congruent and ethical for the therapist, then the therapist should terminate the relationship.

Q: What if a client's value is "to be successful in selling drugs"?

I'm currently seeing a local criminal and his values are to be successful in selling drugs, being very violent if challenged, and being uncaring about anyone who gets in his way. Surprisingly these values work quite well for him and get him most of the things he wants, and he's not interested in looking at an alternative approach. Ethically, should I help him work toward those values?

Russ: A value, as we define it in ACT, is a desired quality of behavior. So "to successfully sell drugs" is a goal, not a value. It describes what you want to achieve; it doesn't describe the qualities you want to bring to your actions on an ongoing moment-to-moment basis.

Now I guess you could argue that "being violent" and "being uncaring" are his values, provided that "deep in his heart" that is how he truly wants to behave. But I'd be wondering—are those truly his core values? Or has he just learned those are qualities of action that meet his needs in the short term?

Certainly it would be unethical for you to help any client do anything self-destructive or destructive to others, and we should always declare ethical conflicts and refuse to do anything that might compromise us ethically. Now regarding this client, what does he want from therapy? Have you done informed consent, and has he agreed to it? And have you then completed the desired behavioral goals section in the second box on your ACT Case Formulation worksheet (appendix 1)?

If you can't ethically agree to work with him on his desired behavioral goals, then refer him on. If you *can* find desired behavioral goals to work with him on (without ethical conflict), then you can come back to the concept of workability: is what he is doing working to help him achieve those behavioral goals?

If he answers yes, you could reply, "So there's no problem, then. How about we focus on something that's a problem for you?"

If he answers no, then you could ask, "So are you open to doing something different?"

If he says yes, it is a problem, but no, he's not open to doing something different, then we want to ask, why is he coming to therapy? What does he want to get from it? (See chapter 3: Ghastly Goals.)

And if he's a mandated client? Well, that's a big topic that I've covered in depth elsewhere (*Getting Unstuck in ACT*; Harris, 2013).

Q: What if a client's main value is "power"?

I work with a lot of successful professionals and often encounter clients who identify values such as "power." This often drives destructive behavior such as being aggressive to others. Any tips?

Russ: I'd reframe it as "influence." We might say, "The word *power* is a term we use to describe your capacity to influence others. The more you can influence the behavior of others, the more power you have." We could then go on to explore the concept of influence. Often, in ACT, we explicitly help clients to influence the behavior of others in the service of pursuing their own goals, but the emphasis is always on *how* do you want to go about influencing others? Do you want to influence them through lying, deceit, manipulation, intimidation, coercion, cruelty, and bullying? Or do you want to influence them in more healthy, constructive ways that build rich and meaningful relationships?

And it's never yet happened (and I don't expect it ever will) that a client said, "Really and truly, deep in my heart, I want to influence others through lying, deceit, manipulation, intimidation, coercion, cruelty, and bullying." But if I ever did have a client say that, I'd declare an ethical conflict: "I can't help you with that because my aim is to help people live better lives, and the research is clear that if you go through life treating others that way, not only will they suffer, but so will you."

Q: What's the difference between values and rules?

Russ: *Values* describe the personal qualities I want to embody in my actions, the sort of person I want to be, the manner in which I want to treat myself, others, and the world around me. So, for example, in the life domain of family, my values might include being loving, kind, honest, and caring. In the life domain of work, my values might include being fair, trustworthy, reliable, and responsible. In the life domain of health, my values might be self-care, self-protection, and self-compassion.

Rules is a term we often use in ACT to describe tightly held, narrow, rigid beliefs—attitudes and assumptions about what you can or can't or should or shouldn't do, or the right or wrong way to do things. So if your thoughts contain words like *should, have to, must, ought, right, wrong, always, never, can't because, won't until, shouldn't unless, this way is right, that way is wrong, must do it like that, mustn't do it like this,* then they're almost certainly rules rather than values.

There are a vast number of ways to live a value, but only a few ways to follow a rule. An example I'm fond of is the famous commandment "Thou shalt not kill!" This is a rule, not a value. It tells you what you can't do (and tells you nothing about what you can do). The values underlying this rule are loving or caring or respecting life; and there are a vast number of ways of living such values, through actions great and small.

Consider *perfectionism*. This is a term we use when clients are fused with rules such as "I must do it perfectly, or there's no point doing it all." So often in ACT, we help clients to defuse from their rules and uncover the values underneath them. Then the aim is to act flexibly on those underlying values.

For another example, suppose the client's rule is "I must do what my parents tell me to do." The value hiding beneath the rule is likely to be "being respectful" or something similar. There are thousands of ways for the client to be respectful to himself and to others. He doesn't have to obey his parents' every demand in order to live the value of being respectful.

And for one last example (I do so love an example; don't you?), suppose your client states she "wants to help the world" as much as possible, and she finds it hard to take time off to rest, relax, and have fun because she always wants to be productive and active, even when resting. There's a lot of fusion with rules here. The values she's mentioned are being helpful, being productive, and being active. And there are many ways to flexibly act on those values, while also balancing them with the value of self-care. Now notice the rule: "always be productive, even when resting." If the client fuses with this rule, then rest, relaxation, and having fun are all off the table. (To help clients unhook from rigid rules, see chapter 9: Dastardly Defusion.)

Q: What if a client's value is "don't trust others"?

Russ: Many clients who have been badly hurt or betrayed by others have trust issues. We especially see this a lot in trauma work: "Don't trust others or you'll get hurt." But note: this isn't a value; it's a rule. So the issue here is about flexibly living values versus rigidly following rules. The rule is "don't trust others." The value is self-protection, and we can explore with clients the million and one ways they can flexibly and adaptively live this value through their words and actions, both great and small. And we can contrast this to the rigid rule of "do not trust others."

Of course, we want to respectfully validate the payoffs of following this rule: it has protected the client from getting hurt by others. And then we want to look at the long-term costs of following this rule: it prevents or interferes with close relationships.

The value of self-protection can motivate or inspire a vast range of different actions, from shooting at the enemy in a war zone to being incredibly trusting of others when your life, health, and well-being depend on it. The rule "do not trust others" is, in comparison, a rigid rule that dramatically narrows one's options. (Again, to help clients unhook from rigid rules, see chapter 9: Dastardly Defusion.)

Q: What if chronic pain or illness stops clients from living their values?

Russ: When clients have chronic pain or illness, or a disability, or the infirmity of old age, they are often unable to do things the way they used to. And they may have to reduce or give up a whole range of activities. However, we can help them find alternative ways of living a rich, full, and meaningful life, adapting to the limitations their physical condition places upon them.

For example, suppose that your client is mad passionate about playing football, but due to his condition, he can no longer play. After validating his pain and encouraging self-compassion, we want to clarify what the values implicit in the activity of playing football are. For example, they may include playfulness and having fun, keeping fit (not technically a value, but aligned to the value of self-care), and teamwork (also not technically a value, but aligned with other values such as cooperation, respect, helpfulness, and supportiveness). Having identified these values, we can then look at other ways to live them, to put them into action, even though football is out of the question.

As I mentioned in chapter 3, there's a great book on this theme: *Tuesdays with Morrie* by Mitch Albom (1997), a true story about Maurice Schwartz's premature death from motor neuron disease. In a truly heartbreaking but inspiring narrative, we get to see that even when his body is totally paralyzed, Morrie is able to live by his values. If you haven't read it, you've got to! (But make sure you have a box of tissues handy.)

Q: How do we resolve values conflicts?

Russ: Most of us have experienced a major values conflict at times, and it's usually pretty stressful. We can easily get caught up in trying to figure out "the right thing to do" and end up spending a lot of time inside our heads, worrying, ruminating, stressing out, or just going over and over the issue, trying to make a decision. These types of conflicts present a major challenge for therapists, coaches, counselors, clients, and...well, just about everyone. And the inconvenient truth is, this is a HUUUUGE topic, so much so, that I considered giving it its own chapter. Well, here goes!

Five-Step Values Conflict Formula

First, I'm going to present you with the outline of my five-step formula for handling values conflicts, then I'll take you through it in depth.

Step 1: The Domain: Identify the main life domain where the values conflict.

Step 2: The Values: Identify the two main values that conflict within that domain.

Step 3: The Globe of the World Metaphor: Introduce this to convey that values are dynamic.

Step 4: Brainstorm: Think of all the different possible ways to live value A by itself, value B by itself, and both values A and B simultaneously, within this domain of life. (It's often best to draw this out on a Venn diagram.)

Step 5: Self-compassion: These conflicts are painful, so be self-compassionate.

Let's now go through this, step by step.

STEP 1: THE DOMAIN

The first step is always to identify *just one* life domain in which the values conflict is occurring, such as work, study, parenting, marriage, health, spirituality, or leisure. If it's occurring in more than one domain, then initially pick just the main one, where it's happening most or creating the greatest problems. This is an important first step because it helps weed out the incredibly common confusion between time-management issues and true values conflicts.

For example, if the client says the conflict is "family versus work," he hasn't identified two conflicting values; he's simply identified two important life domains. And what he's dealing with is probably a time-management issue: how much time does he spend with the family versus how much time does he spend at work?

To make this clear, let's suppose his three most important values in the domain of work are to be reliable, cooperative, and creative. These values will not alter whether he spends ten hours, thirty hours, or sixty hours a week at work. And let's suppose his three most important values in the domain of family are to be loving, kind, and supportive. Again, these values will not alter whether he spends ten hours, thirty hours, or sixty hours a week with his family. In this case, it's a time-management issue, not a values conflict.

If we wish to uncover a true values conflict, we'd need to focus on just one of those domains at a time—either family or work—and then find out *which two values within that one domain* are competing with each other. (We work with only two competing values at a time, or it gets confusing.)

Then, if necessary, we can come back later and work on the other important life domain that the client originally mentioned. For example, we might address values conflict in the domain of family first, and then later address values conflict in the domain of work.

So let's look at how to deal with a true values conflict. Suppose there is something going on at your client's workplace, such as bullying, harassment, victimization, dishonesty, or corruption. And he can't decide whether to speak up about it or keep quiet. The first step is to identify the life domain: work. The next step is...

STEP 2: THE VALUES

Step 2 is to identify the two main values that are in conflict within this domain. In this scenario, it seems that if your client speaks up, he'll be living his value of honesty. However, if he does this, there may well be some very negative repercussions: he may lose his job or become a target himself, which goes against his value of self-care. On the other hand, if he remains silent, he will keep his job and avoid being a target, thus living his value of self-care, but he'll be going against his value of being honest.

As we run through steps 1 and 2 with our clients, we want to respond with great compassion, validating the stress and suffering of being in such a difficult situation. Then we can move to...

STEP 3: THE GLOBE OF THE WORLD METAPHOR

Some clients seem to think of values as static entities, and expect them to line up and stay in position like books in a bookcase. We want to help them see that values are dynamic, continually shifting and moving position, sometimes coming to the foreground and other times fading into the background. My favorite way to do this is with the following metaphor:

> Our values are like the continents on a globe of the world. No matter how fast you spin that globe, you can never see all the continents at once; there are always some at the front, some at the

back. From moment to moment, you get to choose: which values come to the front, and which move to the back?

This then paves the way for the next step…

STEP 4: BRAINSTORM

We now help our client think of all the different ways, in this specific domain of life, that he can live value A by itself, value B by itself, and both values A and B simultaneously. We can include everything from the smallest of actions to the largest of goals.

So in this case, throughout the day at work, your client can live value A—honesty—in many ways:

- honestly expressing his feelings and opinions in situations where there is no personal danger for doing so,
- being honest with himself about how he is feeling and how difficult the situation is, and
- being honest in his dealings with clients, customers, colleagues, and coworkers.

And throughout the day at work, ways he can live value B—self-care—might include

- eating healthy snacks in the morning and afternoon, instead of muffins and biscuits;
- being prudent and cautious about when, where, and with whom he shares his true feelings and opinions; and
- getting some fresh air and exercise with a walk at lunchtime.

And throughout the day at work, ways to live both value A and value B simultaneously include

- combining any of the above options, where practical, and
- practicing self-compassion: this involves being honest with himself about the emotional pain and stress he is suffering while also

treating himself with kindness and caring (such as through saying kind, supportive things to himself or by doing a mindful self-compassion exercise).

After we have completed our brainstorming, we move to the final step...

STEP 5: SELF-COMPASSION

When we resolve our own values conflicts, we tend to experience a sense of liberation; we realize that we can live by our values whichever course of action we pursue. Unfortunately, that may not help us make the decision that we need to make, or solve the problem, or remedy the situation. For example, in the case described above, the client has resolved his values conflict, in that he has found ways to live both values in this important domain of life. However, he still faces the dilemma (or difficult decision, or tough choice—whatever you prefer to call it) of whether to "blow the whistle" or not. In such cases, we can expect ongoing anxiety and other uncomfortable thoughts and feelings. So self-compassion is warranted. Let's acknowledge our pain and suffering and respond to ourselves with kindness. (For more on self-compassion, see chapter 10.)

Other Types of Conflict

Genuine values conflicts are quite rare in therapy. Far more commonly we encounter goal conflicts, mostly around how to allocate time, energy, or money. Goal conflicts might sound like this: "Will I spend my time, energy, and money to do what my partner (or parents or friends or family) wants, or to do what I want? Will I spend it at work, or at home? Will I invest it in hobby A or leisure activity B? Will I do what my religion (or culture) demands, or what I really want to do?"

Values clarification often does not solve such issues. Usually we'll need to use other strategies to resolve these difficult decisions and tough choices. And if the client is struggling with a major dilemma, such as "Do I stay silent or report it?" in the workplace scenario above, then I recommend using my 10 Steps for Any Dilemma worksheet (which you can download from the free resources page on http://www.ImLearningACT.com).

Q: What if living by and acting on your values means rejection or hostility from your family, community, or culture?

Russ: There are no easy answers when clients find themselves in these complex and intensely painful situations. So our starting point is usually lots of validation of their suffering, segueing into self-compassion (chapter 10). After that, we can start teasing out values from rules and looking at ways to live one's values without running the risk of rejection or hostility.

For example, a therapist recently asked me about this case: *I am seeing a client who has identified a core value that she wants to live by: being honest. The thing is, she is gay, and her culture teaches that homosexuality is a sin. She is aware that if she tells friends and family about her sexuality, they will react very negatively. Any tips on how to handle this?*

Our clients present with many variants on this theme: "Should I tell others about my… (religious beliefs, sexuality, political persuasion, plans to leave home, secret boyfriend or girlfriend), knowing that I will probably elicit rejecting or hostile reactions, or endanger my place in the community?" And notice how similar this is to the issue addressed earlier in the Q&A on values conflicts: "Should I speak up about the workplace problems I've witnessed, knowing that it will probably elicit hostile reactions, or endanger my job?"

In all these scenarios, the values conflict is between caring and honesty. The issue boils down to this: "If I am honest, I will get hurt, which conflicts with caring for myself, or I will hurt others, which conflicts with caring for them." And doesn't this "honesty versus caring" conflict play out for most of us in our relationships at times? If we were to be completely honest with the other person about some particular issue—which may be something that we are doing, or something that he is doing, or how we truly think or feel about something—we fear that he will react badly. We fear that either we will hurt him, which seems to conflict with caring, or that his reaction will hurt us, which conflicts with caring for ourselves.

An important piece of dealing with these issues is to help the client see that there are many ways to live the value of being honest without actually revealing whatever it is she's keeping secret. Honesty doesn't mean "I must not keep anything secret; I must reveal all to everybody." For example, the client can be honest with herself through writing a journal, or mindfully acknowledging whatever it is she's keeping secret (and how painful it is to keep it). She can also be honest with her therapist about it, and with anyone else she knows who will not judge her. She can also be honest with others in zillions of little ways that she knows won't upset them. And of course, committed action will often involve building a new social group with people to whom she can safely open up about the things she really wants to; in some cases, this may need to be with people outside of her family, culture, tradition, or religion.

It's often useful to draw a Venn diagram with two overlapping circles, in this case labeled "honesty" and "caring." In the central overlapping region, the client can write in things she can say and do that are both caring and honest. In the nonoverlapping region of the caring circle, she can write down things she can say and do that are caring but have little or nothing to do with honesty. In the nonoverlapping region of the honesty circle she can write down things she can say and do that are honest but have little or nothing to do with caring. This gives the client lots of options to choose either value, or both, throughout the day. We can of course do this with any two values; there will always be things the client can say and do that go into the overlapping region, allowing her to live both values.

Now suppose the client insists on revealing her secret to people from her social group or culture who she knows will disapprove and react negatively. If so, we want to explore whether she is willing to live with the consequences of that action. What matters enough that she'd be willing to do something that she knows will upset people she cares about? Let's do our best to ensure that if she takes such action, it's truly motivated by her values (honesty, courage, authenticity) rather than fusion with a rigid rule like "I must tell them."

It's such a difficult situation to be in, when we know full well that if we say and do the things we really want to, our friends and family or other important members of our social group will disapprove or reject us. And the reality for our clients in these situations is this: there's no way not to choose. Your client will either choose to reveal what she's been keeping secret, or she won't. There's no third option. And both options—speaking up or staying silent—will be painful for her in different ways. So whichever choice she makes, we'll want to work with her on acceptance of the inevitable pain that goes with it, and lots of self-compassion.

Q: What is the Connect and Reflect exercise?

Russ: This is a very simple exercise to get just about anyone in touch with important values in relationships. It often goes down well with adolescents; when you get them thinking about their best friend(s) and what they like to do together, they usually find it energizing and engaging.

Of course, sometimes it will trigger strong, painful emotions—especially if the person they think of is no longer in their life (possibly due to death, separation, or ending the relationship). If this happens, we segue to defusion, acceptance, self-compassion, or grounding, and then return to the exercise later. If you're concerned about this possibility, then specify that it be someone who is still actively in the client's life today.

What follows are the "bare bones" instructions. The idea is that you flesh them out with your own words, your own way of speaking. There are two parts to the exercise.

Connect and Reflect

Part 1

The therapist should go slowly with this exercise, allowing plenty of time for the client to process each instruction. It can be done with eyes open or eyes closed, and it often goes down best if we preface it with a couple of minutes of mindfulness practice. When the therapist asks questions, there is no need for the client to answer; some will speak, others will stay silent, and it doesn't matter either way.

- Think of someone you care about, someone you like to spend quality time with. Remember a time—recent or distant—when you were with each other, doing some sort of activity that you really like.

- Make this memory as vivid as possible.

- Relive it. Feel it emotionally.

- Look out from behind your own eyes onto the scene: Notice where you are... Time of day?... Indoors or outdoors?... Weather? Scenery? Temperature?... What's the air like? What can you see?... What can you hear?... What can you touch...taste...smell?

- Notice the other person: What does he or she look like? What is he or she saying or doing? What's her tone of voice, the expression on his face, her body posture, the way he is moving?

- In this memory, what are you thinking?... And feeling? And doing? What are you doing with your arms...legs...mouth? Are you moving or still? Get into your body (in this memory); what does it feel like?

- Savor the moment. Make the most of it. What's it like? Really appreciate it. (*The therapist allows the client at least a minute or two to savor the memory, then moves on to part 2.*)

Part 2

You can do part 2 as a conversation, or you can do it as an eyes-closed silent exercise, allowing the client plenty of time to process your questions, and then discuss it at the end.

- Now step back and look at the memory as if you're watching it on a TV screen. Focus on yourself. What are you saying and doing? How are you interacting with the other person? How are you treating him or her? How are you responding to him or her?

- What qualities are you showing in this memory? For example, are you being open, engaged, interested, loving, kind, fun-loving, playful, connected, engaged, interested, appreciative, honest, real, courageous, intimate?

- What does this remind you about the sort of person you want to be, the way you want to treat yourself and others, the sort of relationships you want to build, how you want to spend your time?

Debrief

After the exercise, run through these questions and any others that spring to mind:

- What qualities were you showing in this memory?
- (*Prompt as needed*): Were you being open, engaged, interested, loving, kind, fun-loving, playful, connected, engaged, interested, appreciative, honest, real, courageous, intimate? (*If needed, run through a values checklist or a pack of values cards to help with this.*)
- What does this remind you about the sort of person you want to be? About the way you want to treat yourself and others? The sort of relationships you want to build? How you want to spend your time?

Modifications

You can modify this exercise; it doesn't have to focus on relationships. You can ask the client to remember any activity he enjoys or has enjoyed—with others or by himself, at home or at work—and help him to really connect with the memory experientially.

Then reflect on the same or similar questions as those in part 2:

- What qualities were you showing in this memory?
- What does this remind you about the sort of person you want to be? How you want to spend your time? How you want to treat XYZ (objects, people, places involved in the activity)?
- If relevant, also ask: What does this reveal about the way you want to treat yourself and others? The sort of relationships you want to build?

Q: What are useful questions to get people to open up about values?

Russ: There are so many useful questions, answering this question could take up an entire chapter. (Keep in mind many of the questions to elicit goals in chapter 3 also elicit values.) Here are a few of my favorites, divided by category:

Interests, Hobbies, Fun

Ask about, and show genuine interest in, something the client enjoys doing. (This is also a good way to build rapport and engagement with disengaged or reluctant clients). For example, we might ask, "What do you do for fun?" or "What do you like to do on holidays and weekends?" or "What do you really enjoy?" or "What movies/music/books/comics/games do you like?"

After some discussion, we can begin to explore:

- What do you notice you enjoy about that?
- What do you notice about yourself when you're doing this?
- What are you like to be around when you're doing this?

We can usually then go on to unearth qualities of action or skills required to do this activity well or get the most out of it. These are likely to involve values, or overlap with values in important ways.

"Being yourself"

Many clients will at some point talk about "just wanting to be myself." (This seems to be especially common in teenagers.) It's rich ground to explore:

- When are you being yourself? With whom? Doing what?
- What qualities do you bring into play when you are being yourself?
- What would I see and hear on a video of you being yourself?

- What are you like to be around when you are being yourself?
- How do you treat the people you care about when you are being yourself?
- With whom is it easiest to be yourself? How come? What does that person do that makes it easier for you to be yourself?
- What does it feel like when you are being yourself?

Self-Judgment As a Starting Point

If a client is doing a lot of negative self-judgment about his own character, the things he does, and the way he behaves, we can get to values by first commenting on this: "Your mind really likes to give you a hard time here! It's quick to criticize you."

If we've referenced the idea of the mind as an "overly helpful friend" (see the Q&A on caveman mind metaphors in chapter 9: Dastardly Defusion), we can say, "So this is your mind trying to help you. Your mind figures out if it just beats you up enough, you'll stop behaving like this and behave more like the sort of person you want to be."

We could then add, "Thing is, if beating yourself up was a good way to change behavior…wouldn't you be perfect by now? So can we take a different tack? Let's put all the self-judgment to one side for a moment and let's explore. If you weren't behaving that way/doing those things/treating yourself or others that way…

- How would you like to be instead? Doing what? Behaving how? Treating yourself or others how?
- Is there any time in your life when you are actually like that—when you are being the sort of person you want to be? Doing what? When? Where? With whom?

Role Reversal

Last but not least, role reversal questions are often a good way to get to values. For example, we might ask, "Tell me about someone who treats you in a way that really pisses you off. What does that person say? What does he or she do? How does that feel?" (Teenagers often answer these questions with great passion!)

We may then follow up with, "Suppose your roles were reversed—if you were the teacher/father/mother/other kid, and he/she were you, then what would you do differently? What would you say and do that's different from what he/she says and does?"

We can almost always elicit values around how to treat other people from such questions.

Q: What is "flavoring and savoring"?

Russ: *Flavoring and savoring* is a playful term I like to use to convey the idea of bringing values flexibly into your daily routine and mindfully appreciating the benefits of doing so.

I might say to a client,

> When you wake up each morning, pick one or two of your most important values and aim to "flavor" your day with them. See if you can find little ways to "sprinkle" these flavors into whatever you're doing. Suppose you pick kindness and courage; as you go through your day look for little ways to sprinkle those flavors into your interactions with other people, with yourself, with the world around you; into the things you're saying and doing, at home and at work and at play.
>
> And whenever you do this, take a moment to "savor" it. Notice what it's like to be living those values, and whether it's more like the person you want to be, or less. And if it's more like the person you want to be, then really savor that; notice what it's like for you; appreciate it.

This is a good way to set values homework without getting into the nitty-gritty of specific goal setting and action planning. It's especially useful to have up your sleeve as a quick homework task, for those occasions when you're running out of time in the session.

The Wrap-Up

Yup, values can be tricky. But if we slow down and dig them out from all the rules, judgments, goals, morals, beliefs, dilemmas, and other stuff they tend to get buried beneath, they're an incredible resource. In ending this chapter, I want to answer another question I'm often asked: How does ACT address psychological needs?

Addressing psychological needs mostly comes under values and committed action. (After all, needs *is simply another word for important goals, which, as we discussed, can help clarify values and vice versa.) So we aim to help the client identify what his needs are, and then commit to action to get those needs met as effectively as possible—mindfully and skillfully guided by his values. In other words, we want to help him do what's likely to get his needs met in a healthy, life-enhancing way, behaving like the sort of person he wants to be (as opposed to trying to get them met through manipulation, lying, deceiving, threatening, or coercion). We also want to help him learn how to accept the inevitable pain and be self-compassionate if and when his needs aren't met (which will happen, sooner or later). Self-compassion, of course, is the one value that's infused in the whole model and meets many deeper psychological needs.*

CHAPTER 7

Dodgy Dropping Anchor

If you were to ask me, "Russ, what is the single most useful and versatile technique in the whole of ACT?" I'd answer without hesitation, "Buy me a beer, and I'll tell you." Then after you'd bought me a beer, I'd say, "It is, without a doubt, dropping anchor." (Sometimes I also call it "expansive awareness," but dropping anchor sounds catchier). This style of intervention comes under the heading of "contacting the present moment," but it's a world apart from meditative-style mindfulness techniques. It's a great starting point for any client who presents with emotional dysregulation, hypoarousal, hyperarousal, dissociation, flashbacks, panic attacks, overwhelming emotions, and extreme fusion. So if you haven't been using it, I hope you start to as of now. And if you find it even remotely as useful as I do, then you owe me a beer.

Discussions in This Chapter:

- How does extreme fusion tend to manifest?
- How can we help extremely fused clients?
- What's actually involved in dropping anchor?
- Won't clients think it's a way to distract from pain?
- Is dropping anchor a defusion technique?
- How long does dropping anchor go for?

- What if clients don't want to notice or acknowledge their pain?
- How can we practice this with clients if they are feeling good in session?
- What if clients say "it isn't working"?
- What if clients don't like or don't get the metaphor?
- Do clients need to tell us the thoughts and feelings that constitute the storm?

Q: How does extreme fusion tend to manifest?

Russ: Extreme fusion can manifest in a wide variety of ways, depending on the thoughts, images, memories, and emotions that we fuse with. Here are some common ways we might see it (in ourselves or in others):

- When we are overwhelmed by our emotions, we might be crushed with guilt, drowning in shame, swamped with sadness, paralyzed by fear, seething with rage, flooded with grief, or gripped by a "panic attack."
- When we are jerked around by our emotions like a puppet on a string, we may start yelling or acting aggressively when fused with angry thoughts and feelings.
- When we are so caught up in our thoughts and feelings, we may lose touch with all the other important things that are here in the present moment.

Even more extreme fusion can show up when dealing with trauma. For example, the term *flashback* refers to such extreme fusion with a traumatic memory that the person experiences it as vividly reliving the experience over again. Extreme fusion with trauma-related thoughts, feelings, emotions, and memories can render people literally speechless—incapable of talking about their experience. MRI brain scans show that during these experiences, Broca's area of the brain, which is largely responsible for speech, actually starts to "shut down" due to significantly less blood flow to the area (Rauch et al., 1996).

Q: How can we help extremely fused clients?

Russ: When extreme fusion happens during a therapy session, clients are often incapable of speaking about it. They may even be so overwhelmed by their emotions that they just can't talk. And if a therapist responds to this by trying to get the client to talk about what she's thinking or feeling, it's not likely to go well.

On the other hand, sometimes extreme fusion shows up as clients who can't stop talking; they go into angry or anxious tirades, and the therapist can't get a word in edgewise.

In such situations, traditional or commonplace defusion techniques are likely to be highly ineffective. If you ask your client to say, "I'm having the thought that…," or to do a Leaves on the Stream exercise, or to "thank your mind," or to write her thoughts on a card, or to do any of the more-than-a-hundred defusion techniques currently published in ACT textbooks, it's very unlikely to be helpful. (In fact, the chances are, the client will feel invalidated, and fusion will intensify.)

When fusion is extreme, I can't think of any intervention that's more effective than what I like to call *dropping anchor* exercises. I call them this because we are basically learning to drop an anchor (to stay present, aware, and grounded) in the midst of an emotional storm. These exercises don't require any speaking or self-talk, so they are especially useful when people are so overwhelmed that speaking or self-talk is difficult.

Just to be clear, the *emotional storm* refers to all the difficult thoughts, feelings, emotions, memories, urges, and sensation that are present. And *anchors* are anything else here in the present moment that is *not* a part of the storm. Anchors can include what we see, hear, touch, taste, smell; our breathing; our body posture; what we are doing with our arms and our legs; and so on. Basically, anything that can help us to stay present, stay grounded, stay in contact with where we are and what we're doing—drinking a glass of water, stretching our arms out, slowing our breathing, listening to the sound of the air conditioner—can be an anchor in the midst of our emotional storm.

Q: What's actually involved in dropping anchor?

Russ: Dropping anchor exercises are based on two strands of instruction:

A. Expand your awareness of what is here in the present moment.

B. Exert self-control over your physical actions: breathing, physical movement, body posture, and so on.

Let's look at them in more detail:

Expand Awareness

The aim here is to acknowledge the presence of your difficult thoughts and feelings and *at the same time* notice where you are, what you're doing, and what you can see, hear, touch, taste, and smell. This is not to *distract from* pain, but to notice that *in addition to* pain there is a lot happening here in the present moment; there is so much more present than these difficult thoughts and feelings that are currently dominating awareness.

Exert Self-Control over Physical Action

The aim here is to regain a sense of self-control by focusing on what you have most control over when struggling with difficult thoughts and feelings: your physical actions. Move, stretch, change posture, sit upright, stand up, walk, alter your breathing, push your feet into the floor, push your hands into the chair, push your fingertips together, drink water, hug yourself, massage a tense spot, do a yoga or tai chi movement, or make any other physical action.

I'm going to give you a sample script for a dropping anchor exercise, but first, a request: when you do these exercises on yourself or with your clients, *please don't stick to the script*. There are zillions of possible variations on the script that follows, so be flexible and creative. For example, if your client has chronic pain that worsens if he pushes his feet into the floor, then don't ask him to push his feet into the floor! Instead, ask him to wriggle his toes, or tap his fingers, or shrug his shoulders, or press his tongue against the roof of his mouth. Why not set yourself the challenge of varying the exercise with every single client? It's quite possible, and it keeps things fresh. (You can download a copy of this script from the free resources page on http://www.ImLearningACT.com.)

Dropping Anchor: A Script

In the ideal scenario, before starting this exercise, you've asked the client what she's experiencing and she's been able to tell you what thoughts, feelings, emotions, and memories are showing up; this means you can refer to them specifically. You might say, for example, "There's a very painful memory showing up right now, and a lot of sadness and a lot of anger." But if the client is too distressed to speak, or unable or unwilling to say what thoughts and feelings are present, then you can refer to them with nonspecific terms such as pain, or painful thoughts and feelings, or emotional storm, as in the script that follows.

Take your time with this exercise. You should allow a good ten seconds between instructions. And give your voice a kind and calming quality. The therapist should model all the actions for the client, to help reduce the client's self-consciousness.

- There's a lot of emotional pain showing up for you right now. I can see how much you're struggling with it, how difficult it is for you. And I really want to help you handle it. So please would you follow my instructions? Okay. First, just see if you can push your feet hard into the floor. Push them down. That's it. Feel the ground beneath you.

- Now sit forward in your chair, and straighten your back. Feel the chair beneath you; notice your back supporting you.

- Now slowly press your fingertips together, and as you do that, gently move your elbows and your shoulders.

- Feel your arms moving, all the way from your fingers to shoulder blades.

- Take a moment to acknowledge there's a lot of pain here that you're struggling with... You didn't ask for it...but here it is...and it's challenging and it's difficult and you want it to go away, and yet it's not going... Silently acknowledge to yourself what type of pain it is... For example, say to yourself, *Here's sadness* or *Here's anxiety* or *Here's a painful memory. (If the therapist knows what the pain is, he can specifically mention it.)*

- Now notice that as well as this pain, there's also a body around that pain—a body that you can move and control. Straighten your back again, and notice your whole body now—your hands, feet, arms, legs. Gently move them, and feel them moving... Have a good stretch... Notice your muscles stretching... Press your feet down and feel the floor.

- Now also look around the room—up, down, and side to side—and notice five things that you can see.

- And also notice three or four things you can hear—sounds coming from me or you or the room around you.

- And also notice you and me, working here together, as a team.

- So notice, there's something very painful here that you're struggling with, and at the same time see if you can also notice your body in the chair...and gently move that body, have a stretch... that's it, take control of your arms and legs.

- And also notice the room around you.

- And also notice you and me here, working together as a team.

The therapist continues to cycle through the exercise—acknowledging the pain, expanding awareness, establishing control over body movement—until the client is grounded and able to engage in the session. At this point, the therapist brings the exercise to an end by asking these types of debriefing questions:

- Do you notice any difference now? Are you less caught up in the emotional storm? Are you less hooked by these difficult thoughts and feelings? Are you less "swept away" by the storm? Are you less "pushed around" or "jerked around" by these feelings?
- Is it easier for you to engage with me, to be present, to focus?
- Do you have more control over your actions now—over your arms and legs and mouth? Check it out, move your arms and legs, have a stretch; do you notice you have control?

Note: in all these questions, the therapist *never* asks if the storm or the emotional pain has reduced or gone away—because this is not the purpose of the exercise. To ask such questions would send the wrong message: that the aim is to reduce or distract from emotional pain. Of course, this does often happen, but in ACT that's a bonus, not the main aim; and there's plenty of times that it won't happen.

After the exercise is finished, further useful questions to ask include "How could doing this be useful when emotional storms blow up outside this room? When and where could you apply this? With whom, doing what? How might this help you with you X,Y,Z (*where X, Y, Z are therapy goals*)?"

Once the client sees how dropping anchor can be useful outside the therapy room, and relevant to her therapy goals (see chapter 3), we can then ask, "Can we do more of this in our sessions? Would you be willing to practice this between sessions?"

Q: Won't clients think it's a way to distract from pain?

Russ: Yes, if we're not careful. The most common mistake both clients and therapists make with these kinds of exercises is to use them as a distraction technique. Distraction techniques are the very opposite of mindfulness techniques; distraction involves *turning away* from what is unwanted in the present moment, trying to escape or avoid it. Mindfulness skills involve *turning toward* what is here in the present moment—whether it is wanted or not—with openness and curiosity. So, if therapists or clients start using the methods that follow to try to distract from the painful thoughts and feelings that are present, well, it sure ain't mindfulness anymore.

To reduce the risk of this misunderstanding, I often introduce this exercise to clients with the metaphor of an emotional storm: "I can see there's an emotional storm inside you right now, and I want to help you deal with it. While you're being swept away by that storm, there's nothing effective you can do about the issues you're dealing with. So, the first thing you need to do is drop an anchor. The anchor doesn't make the storm go away; the anchor holds you steady until the storm passes. The storm may pass quickly, or it may pass slowly. It may get worse before it gets better. The anchor holds you steady during this time, so the storm doesn't sweep you away."

Also, did you notice in the script how the therapist keeps referring to the pain that is present? If the therapist fails to keep acknowledging the presence of the pain, feelings, or emotional storm, this will almost certainly function as a distraction technique rather than a mindfulness technique.

Here is the formula:

- Acknowledge your pain/feelings/emotional storm.
- And also notice A, B, C.
- Acknowledge your pain/feelings/emotional storm.
- And also notice D, E, F.
- Acknowledge your pain/feelings/emotional storm and A, B, C, D, E, F.

Note that if the therapist deliberately uses dropping anchor to try to stop the client's crying, to distract her from pain, to reduce her anxiety, or the like, this is a misuse. The aim of dropping anchor is to help the client to be present, regain control of her actions, and engage in and focus on what she is doing.

This is a massive difference between ACT and many other models that have grounding and centering techniques that are superficially very similar to dropping anchor. In almost all of these other models, the aim of such grounding techniques is to distract from pain or reduce anxiety and hyperarousal. In ACT, the aim is radically different.

Q: Is dropping anchor a defusion technique?

Russ: These dropping anchor exercises are usually classed under "contacting the present moment" in ACT, but they almost always result in a significant degree of defusion. (This is not surprising, because all four core ACT mindfulness processes are overlapping and interconnected.)

When there is extreme fusion, therapists will usually need to do this kind of nonverbal grounding and centering work before they move on to more conventional defusion exercises. So dropping anchor or expansive awareness will almost always be my first line in targeting the most severe states of fusion. Indeed, these are usually the very first mindfulness techniques I teach to clients who suffer from issues such as emotional dysregulation, panic attacks, overwhelming grief, dissociative states, flashbacks, and "anger management" problems.

Q: How long does dropping anchor go for?

Russ: As long as necessary to ground and center the client, to help him regain control over his physical actions and be present and engaged in the session. This can take anything from thirty seconds to thirty minutes in the extreme case of severe dissociative states. But most of the time, it ranges from one to five minutes. (To give you a sense of the variety, I've recorded a few versions of different lengths that you can download from the free resources page on http://www.ImLearningACT.com.)

We can also repeat these exercises as often as needed. When working with clients who keep dissociating or having flashbacks, we may drop anchor many times in one session.

Typically, as therapy progresses, the exercises get shorter because the client responds more quickly and more dramatically. Also, the debriefing becomes unnecessary after we've done it a few times; the client gets the point, knows the purpose. Also keep in mind that as the client is exposed to more of the ACT model, these exercises tend to evolve into more complex interventions, bringing in other core processes. For example, they often segue into self-compassion exercises, as we'll discuss in chapter 10.

Q: What if clients don't want to notice or acknowledge their pain?

Russ: This is very common when clients are high in experiential avoidance, clinging tightly to the emotional control agenda. It's especially common in clients with anxiety disorders, trauma, and chronic pain. These clients typically don't want to notice their pain because they are desperate to avoid or escape it. If so, we need to turn to creative hopelessness (see chapter 8).

Q: How can we practice this with clients if they are feeling good in session?

Russ: The great thing with these exercises is we can practice them anytime and anywhere, no matter how we are feeling. We don't have to wait until an emotional storm blows up. I explain it to clients this way: "When a boat sails into a harbor, it doesn't matter how calm the sea, how still the wind; if that boat doesn't drop anchor, it will drift back out to sea again. Throughout the day, we 'drift off' repeatedly; we get hooked by thoughts and feelings, pulled out of what we are doing."

At this point, it's good to help the client connect with everyday examples of drifting off, such as driving on autopilot and not remembering the journey, or reading a page in a book and taking in nothing, or having a conversation and suddenly realizing you haven't heard a word the other person's been saying and you don't actually know what he's talking about.

The great thing is, as soon as we realize we've drifted off, we can drop anchor. We acknowledge the thoughts and feelings that hooked us (which may, of course, be pleasant ones), and we also expand awareness to notice where we are, what we are doing, what we can see, hear, touch, taste, smell; and we take control over our physical actions—moving, stretching, breathing—to anchor ourselves firmly in the here and now and engage fully in what we are doing.

So if there is no pain present, the formula for dropping anchor is:

- Notice your thoughts and feelings.
- And also notice A, B, C.
- Notice your thoughts and feelings.
- And also notice D, E, F.
- Notice your thoughts and feelings and A, B, C, D, E, F.

By practicing dropping anchor during times when we're not so fused, or the storms are not so painful, we're more likely to remember to do them when we're extremely fused.

Q: What if clients say "it isn't working"?

Russ: If the client says, "It isn't working" as we do this exercise, we want to always ask, "What do you mean by that?" Ninety-nine percent of the time, the client means "The storm isn't going away. The pain isn't going." This shows he has misunderstood the purpose of the exercise. If we're using the metaphor of the storm and anchor, we can then gently and compassionately remind him, "Dropping an anchor doesn't make the storm go away—it just holds you steady. The storm comes and goes in its own time. The purpose of this exercise isn't to get rid of the storm; it's to hold you steady so the storm doesn't sweep you away."

If the client is confused by that, he probably hasn't understood the purpose of the exercise, in which case it's best to take him through the Hands as Thoughts and Feelings exercise (appendix 5) or the Pushing Away Paper exercise (Appendix 6), or a combination of both.

Q: What if clients don't like or don't get the metaphor?

Russ: You don't have to use the metaphor of storms and anchors. There are many alternatives. (This of course holds true for any metaphor in ACT; we can change, modify, or adapt any of them.) For example, you may prefer to talk about grounding or centering rather than anchoring.

One thing to be wary of if you are using this metaphor is that it only applies to ships and boats that are already in the bay or harbor when a storm blows up. If a vessel is out at sea, it wouldn't drop anchor in the midst of the storm except under very specific circumstances (a very shallow body of water, zero visibility, and going ashore is an immediate threat). Of course, only your nautically-minded clients would know this, but if you wish to prevent an awkward conversation with a sailing aficionado, then don't put anything into the metaphor about "being out at sea."

Q: Do clients need to tell us the thoughts and feelings that constitute the storm?

Russ: If the client is ready and able to speak, it's good to ask her what's showing up, so we have an idea of the thoughts, feelings, and memories she is fusing with. But if your client is so overwhelmed she can't speak (as is not uncommon when working with trauma), then we can do without that information. We don't have to know what specific pain she is struggling with; we can apply dropping anchor to any type, or combined types, of pain.

And if my sense is that the client is so fused that she won't be able to listen to what I'm saying or take on board the storm and anchor metaphor, then I'll just skip it and launch straight into the exercise. Keep in mind we don't have to use this metaphor; we can talk about "pain that you're struggling with" or "difficult thoughts and feeling showing up for you" instead of an "emotional storm." However, I like the metaphor a lot because, as I said above, we can emphasize the fact that dropping an anchor doesn't make the storm go away—it just holds the boat steady.

The Wrap-Up

Dropping anchor exercises are incredibly flexible. We can make them up out of anything that's present, from a crack on the ceiling to a splotch on the floor. We can make them as short or as long as we like, and repeat them as often as needed. We can use them anytime, anywhere—whether we are in the midst of a full-blown emotional storm, or feeling totally calm and relaxed.

And like everything in ACT, we want to apply this to ourselves as well as with our clients. So when you're in the midst of one of those really challenging sessions, where the client is not responding the way you'd like, and you've tried every trick you know and nothing has helped, and your own emotional storm is now raging, then the first thing you want to do, before any other strategy in this book, is drop anchor. Stop talking. Take a few slow breaths. Acknowledge your thoughts and feelings. Push your feet into the floor, sit upright, and refocus on where you are and what you're doing. Engage fully with the client. And go from there. This only takes ten seconds, and it will make a big difference in whatever you do next.

CHAPTER 8

Crummy Creative Hopelessness

Creative hopelessness (CH) is one of the most misunderstood aspects of ACT. It's also one of the most commonly avoided aspects of the model; many therapists are reluctant to use it for fear of upsetting or invalidating their clients. I'm hoping this chapter will clear up any misgivings, misconceptions, misunderstandings, and any other relevant words beginning with "mis," and spur you on to do this kind of work with your clients.

Discussions in This Chapter:

- What's the link between CH and workability?
- Is CH really necessary?
- What's the first step in CH?
- Is there a simple way of doing CH?
- If CH is successful, what next?

Q: What's the link between CH and workability?

Russ: First, it's important to be clear that the aim of CH is to create a sense of hopelessness in the agenda of emotional control. Not hopelessness in one's life, or one's future, but hopelessness in pursuing this agenda of controlling one's thoughts and feelings. (An alternative term in ACT, which I prefer, is *confronting the agenda*.)

There are many CH interventions, and they all hinge on the core ACT concept of workability. They all involve exploring, with openness and curiosity, the agenda of emotional control, and assessing whether clinging tightly to this agenda, letting it guide your actions, works in the long term to build a rich and meaningful life.

Q: Is CH really necessary?

Russ: To answer this question, I think it's useful to consider CH as a "prelude" to acceptance. Sometimes we need that prelude, and sometimes we don't. As mentioned in the previous Q&A, the aim of CH is to open people up to the counterintuitive idea of accepting unwanted thoughts and feelings. We bring it in to therapy if we suspect or know a client is clinging tightly to what ACT calls the *agenda of emotional control*: in order to have a good life, I need to control how I feel; I need to get rid of my unwanted thoughts and feelings, and replace them with more desirable ones.

Clients clinging tightly to this so-called control agenda are high in experiential avoidance (and vice-versa) and therefore likely to resist or misunderstand the *acceptance agenda*: allowing your thoughts and feelings to be as they are in this moment (whether they are pleasant or painful, wanted or unwanted), neither struggling with them nor getting swept away by them, allowing them to come and stay and go in their own good time.

Now keep in mind fusion is the overarching problem in the ACT model. Experiential avoidance is normal, not pathological. And it isn't always a problem. We only target experiential avoidance if and when it becomes so rigid, excessive, or inappropriate that it's significantly interfering with the client's quality of life. Thus, CH is an *optional* part of the ACT model. We certainly don't need it if clients are open to the agenda of acceptance. But we *definitely* need it with clients if both of these criteria are met: (a) experiential avoidance is severe enough to be a significant clinical problem, and (b) the client is resistant to or opposed to acceptance.

As a general rule, if clients present with a disorder that is named after an unwanted, unpleasant private experience, such as "anxiety disorder" or "chronic pain syndrome," we can expect we'll need to do CH upfront, early on in therapy. Why? Because such clients will be coming to therapy primarily to get rid of the aforementioned private experience. They will likely believe that anxiety or pain is the cause of their disorder and therefore must be eliminated in order for them to be "cured."

Q: What's the first step in CH?

Russ: The first step is simply to get clear about the private experiences the client is trying to avoid. Specifically, what thoughts, feelings, emotions, sensations, and urges is she wanting to avoid or get rid of? We start gathering this information in session one as we take a history and establish goals for therapy (see chapter 3).

For example, is the client wanting to get rid of private experiences such as anxiety, sensations of physical pain, sadness, anger, guilt, shame, feeling unworthy, traumatic memories, urges to smoke or drink, withdrawal symptoms, feelings of inadequacy, thoughts about being fat or stupid or ugly or bad or unlovable?

Note that *depression* isn't a thought or a feeling. Nor is *grief*. Nor is *low self-esteem*. So when clients use these terms, we want to deconstruct them: what thoughts, feelings, memories, and sensations are they referring to?

Q: Is there a simple way of doing CH?

Russ: Well, it depends on what you mean by simple. All creative hopelessness exercises are based on some combination of the five steps that I'll outline shortly. Some CH exercises are very short—less than five minutes—and miss out on some of these steps. Some CH exercises are much longer—even lasting an entire session in some protocols—and include all of these steps. So let's go through them one by one. In each case, the letters XYZ refer to any combination of thoughts, feelings, emotions, memories, urges, sensations, and images that the client doesn't want to have.

Step 1: What Have You Tried?

In step 1, we explore "What are some of the main ways you've tried to avoid or get rid of XYZ?" Most clients will need prompting to remember all the different things they've tried. I coined the acronym DOTS to help myself remember the four broad categories of experiential avoidance:

- Distraction
- Opting out
- Thinking
- Substances, self-harm, and other strategies

(You can download a Join the DOTS worksheet from the free resources page on http://www.ImLearningACT.com.)

We can run through these categories with clients to tease out all the strategies they've tried to get rid of XYZ. For example, we could say, "Distraction is one of the most common ways we try to escape unwanted thoughts and feelings. Have you tried distracting yourself from XYZ? What are all the different ways you've tried to distract yourself?"

For any given category, if clients don't mention the common methods used, we can explicitly ask. For example, in the category of distraction, we might ask, "Have you tried computer games, TV, music, books, movies, shopping...?"

Step 2: How Has That Worked?

In step 2, we respectfully and compassionately validate the client's experience: "You've put a lot of time and effort and energy into getting rid of XYZ. And most of those methods you've used give you some short-term relief. For a little while, they've helped you reduce, escape, or get rid of XYZ. But in the long term, has anything you've tried permanently gotten rid of XYZ—so that it never came back?" The client will of course answer no.

We can then go on to ask, "How long do you get relief with these methods, before XYZ returns?" We can pick a few of the client's main strategies and ask the client to "guesstimate" for how long each one provides relief.

After this we can then summarize: "So the amount of relief you get varies—sometimes a few minutes, sometimes hours, occasionally days—but sooner or later, XYZ comes back?"

Note that step 1 can be done simultaneously with step 2. For example, suppose the client says she uses alcohol (step 1). The therapist then asks, "So that gets rid of the anxiety for a little while? How long before it comes back again?"

Step 3: What Has It Cost?

In step 3, we compassionately explore, "What has it cost you, doing all these things to try to get rid of anxiety?"

We want to specifically ask about costs in terms of work, health, time, money, energy, relationships, missing out, and giving up on important things. We especially want to explore the long-term costs.

After identifying the costs, we validate (in our own words) that it's taken a huge toll. We might say, "Doing all this stuff to get rid of XYZ has really cost you. It's taken a huge toll on your health, your relationships, your life. It's cost you in terms of… (*summarize all the costs identified so far*).

We often follow this by asking, "Overall, would you say the amount of time and energy you spend struggling with XYZ has increased or decreased over time?" or "Overall, would you say your life has gotten better or worse over time?" or "Overall, would you say the impact of XYZ on your life and health is getting smaller or greater over time?" Clients will typically answer that life is getting worse, not better, over time.

Step 4: What's That Like?

In step 4, we aim to cultivate a self-compassionate reflection on how clinging to the control agenda is creating more and more suffering in the long term. We might say, very compassionately, "Let's take a moment to reflect on this: you've tried so hard, for so long, to get rid of XYZ… And you've found many ways to get short-term relief, but in the long term, it keeps coming back, and getting worse… And all this stuff you're doing to get rid of XYZ is really taking a toll on your life, your health, your relationships… What's that like for you?" The client is likely to report that it's painful, hurtful, horrible, or some other such response.

Then, as part of this step, we want to add massive doses of validation! We might say, "That's really rough. It's a hard realization. It hurts, right?" We especially want to validate that the client has tried hard: "You've tried really hard here. You've put in a massive effort to get rid of XYZ. No one can call you lazy."

We also want to add that most of what the client has tried is completely reasonable. "It makes perfect sense that you've tried all this stuff. Most of these things you've done are widely recommended by therapists, doctors, psychologists, self-help books, and well-meaning friends. No one can call you stupid."

After this, we again want to gently connect the client with reality: "So in the short term these methods work. They give you a bit of temporary relief. But unfortunately, in the long term, they don't. Your life's getting worse."

At this point, the client will typically be contacting emotional pain. Sadness, anger, fear, and frustration are common at this point. We want to validate these feelings: emphasize they are a normal reaction when we realize that what we've been trying really hard at for a long time just isn't working. It's worth attempting to introduce self-compassion at this point (knowing we won't always be successful). For example, we can experiment with asking the client, "What would you say to someone you love who had been caught in the same trap as you for so long, and was feeling what you are feeling right now?"

Step 5: Are You Open to Something Different?

In step 5, we aim to raise curiosity about a different approach. We might say, "You've been fighting with and running from XYZ for so long. It's taken such a toll on you. The costs have been huge… Are you open to trying something different, that might work better, in terms of building a better life? It's a very different way of dealing with XYZ. It's radically different from everything else you've ever tried."

Q: If CH is successful, what next?

Russ: If the client is now open to a new approach, we can move on to other aspects of the ACT model. Often, the next step is to introduce a metaphor about dropping the struggle (such as Tug of War with a Monster or Floating in Quicksand; Hayes, Strosahl, & Wilson, 1999). My favorite metaphor for this purpose is the Pushing Away Paper exercise, which you'll find in appendix 6.

From there, we usually move to process work around developing willingness to have thoughts and feelings, using a short, simple, nonconfronting exercise based on any of the core ACT mindfulness processes: defusion, acceptance, contacting the present moment, self-as-context, and self-compassion. (I usually start with dropping anchor or "I'm having the thought that" as my first exercise.) However, we'll likely need to cycle back to CH repeatedly throughout therapy because clients easily fall back into the control agenda—hardly surprising when it's been deeply entrenched for many years.

The Wrap-Up

In summary then, creative hopelessness is an optional part of the ACT model that we bring in if and when it's needed to help clients let go of the emotional control agenda and open up to the emotional acceptance agenda. CH interventions can be as short or as long as we like, and usually include most if not all of these five steps:

1. *What have you tried?*
2. *How has that worked?*
3. *What has it cost?*
4. *What's that like?*
5. *Are you open to something different?*

As long as we are compassionate and respectful (as opposed to condescending or righteous), it's unlikely we'll upset or invalidate our clients, especially if we validate their struggles and emphasize that they are not stupid or lazy, as in step 4. So if you've been skipping over this part of the model, no more excuses: go ahead and try it. With our high-end experientially avoidant clients, CH is one of our most powerful allies in therapy.

CHAPTER 9

Dastardly Defusion

Welcome to the longest chapter in the book. The term fusion means that in response to our thoughts and feelings, our behavior becomes narrow, rigid, and inflexible in a way that is ineffective and self-defeating (makes life worse in the long term, impairs health and well-being, pulls us away from our values). Fusion is the overarching problem in the ACT model, so it's not that surprising that this chapter is so looooooooong. But given its inordinate length, I'll keep my introduction really short. So short, in fact, that I'm not even going to complete this sen...

Discussions in This Chapter:

- Is fusion always problematic?
- Can people fuse with both thoughts and feelings?
- What are the "three N"s of defusion?
- Can you give me some useful questions for looking at thoughts functionally?
- Do we target all fusion?
- What are "caveman mind" metaphors and how do they help with defusion?
- Can caveman mind metaphors backfire?
- What should I do when clients get anxious during defusion?

- How can I use defusion to help clients with traumatic thoughts and memories?
- How can I help clients to defuse from others' harsh criticisms?
- How can I help clients defuse from rigid rules?
- What if it really matters to clients whether their thoughts are true or not?
- Why should we "thank our mind" for unhelpful thoughts?
- How can we help clients defuse from deeply entrenched reason-giving?
- What do you mean by "dance in the dark and lead to the light"?
- What techniques work best with extreme fusion?
- Can fusion with certain thoughts and feelings have a payoff?

Q: Is fusion always problematic?

Obviously, sometimes it's helpful to think uplifting, positive thoughts in life. Are there situations where it isn't necessary to defuse from thoughts?

Russ: It depends on how you define fusion. In years gone by, I used to write that fusion isn't always problematic, that it can sometimes be helpful. But I've been steadily updating those earlier writings because in recent times, most authorities in ACT have come to a consensus that the term *fusion* should be used only if the process gives rise to problematic, self-defeating behavior. In other words, if in response to our thoughts and feelings, our behavior becomes narrow, rigid, and inflexible in a way that is ineffective and self-defeating (makes life worse in the long term, impairs health and well-being, pulls us away from our values), then we would use the term *fusion*. But if not, we wouldn't.

For example, if I'm lost in my thoughts in a way that is life-enhancing—such as daydreaming while lying on the beach on vacation, or mentally rehearsing an important speech at an appropriate time—we'd call that *absorption* rather than fusion. But if I'm lost in in my thoughts in a way that's making life worse for me—such as daydreaming or mentally rehearsing a speech while someone I love is trying to open up and share with me something very personal and intimate—then we'd call that *fusion*.

So with that in mind, it's a good idea to be a little defused from all thoughts. (Of course, that's probably not possible for a normal human being, but we can get better at it.)

Now from an ACT perspective there's really no such thing as a "positive" or "negative" thought. In other models, the terms *positive thought* and *negative thought* refer to the content of the thought: the actual words the thought contains, and whether they are positive in tone and outlook, or negative. In ACT, we aren't primarily concerned with the content of the thought; our main interest is in the function of the thought, or the effects it has on behavior.

In ACT, we're interested in questions such as "Does this thought function in a positive (meaning life-enhancing) way if I let it guide my actions?" Even the most "negative" of thoughts (as other models would classify them) can function in positive, life-enhancing ways, and even the most "positive" of thoughts (as other models would classify them) can function in negative, life-worsening ways. So the term *fusion* indicates a problematic narrowing of behavioral repertoire in response to one's thoughts and feelings.

Q: Can people fuse with both thoughts and feelings?

You often talk about fusing with both thoughts and feelings, but isn't fusion short for cognitive fusion? And if so, how can it involve feelings?

Russ: Given that *fusion* is short for *cognitive fusion*, there is often an assumption that it has to do with thoughts only. This misunderstanding is due to a narrow interpretation of the term *cognition*. In many models, cognition basically means thoughts.

When we use the term *cognition* in ACT, it has a much broader meaning than in most other models. ACT is based on a behavioral theory of language and cognition called relational frame theory (RFT). So when we use the term *cognition* in ACT, we don't just mean thoughts; we mean any type of private experience that involves *relational framing*.

"What the hell is relational framing?" I hear you ask. Good question. To avoid getting bogged down in the technical details of RFT, let's say that relational framing can roughly be translated as "symbolic behavior"—that is to say, behavior that involves creating, using, and responding to symbols. These symbols usually take the form of words and pictures. Explore any feeling or emotion and you will find a lot of relational framing going on: a lot of symbolic behavior or cognition. There is no feeling or emotion that doesn't include cognition as a deeply interwoven part of it. Explore sadness, anxiety, anger, or guilt, and there will be a lot of cognition (or relational framing) amid that experience.

For example, suppose someone is feeling anxiety or dread. Just recognizing the experience as "anxiety" or "dread" is cognition. Now, as we explore this emotion, we may encounter all sorts of thoughts, such as worrying or catastrophizing. We may also find memories of similar events from the past, and mental images about what we fear might happen in the future. And if we explore concurrent physical sensations in the body, we may encounter a racing heart. But notice the cognition implicit even in a sensation like this: the client identifies it's her "heart" (cognition) and it's "racing" (cognition) and it's in her "chest" (cognition). Judging the sensation as "bad" or "unpleasant" is cognition.

Furthermore, in neuroanatomical terms, the cerebral cortex is involved in the formation of all emotions. There are no emotions that arise from the limbic system without input from the cerebral cortex. So I like to talk of fusion with (and defusion from) "thoughts and feelings" to help us remember this; to help us let go of the often artificial distinction between them.

The simplest way to defuse from feelings, emotions, and sensations is to notice and name them: "I'm noticing anxiety," "Here is sadness," "I'm having a feeling of anger," "There's that feeling of guilt showing up again," "I'm noticing tightness in my chest," and so on.

Now having said all of the above, there is a convention in ACT that we tend to talk of defusion when dealing with words, memories, and images; whereas for feelings, urges, and sensations we mostly tend to talk of acceptance. Indeed, you will find some ACT trainers and authors who say, "We don't defuse from emotions; we defuse from the cognitive elements of an emotion." But in my mind, that really is an artificial distinction, so I'm sticking to "defusion from thoughts and feelings."

Q: What are the "three Ns" of defusion?

Russ: Many therapists get overwhelmed by the vast and ever-growing number of defusion techniques in ACT. The *three Ns* are my attempt to simplify what we're doing with all these different techniques: Noticing, Naming, and Neutralizing. Let's go through these one by one.

Noticing

All defusion techniques (as well as acceptance techniques) begin with noticing the thoughts and feelings with which we are fused with an attitude of openness and curiosity.

Naming

Most defusion techniques (as well as acceptance techniques) also incorporate some degree of nonjudgmental naming of the thoughts and feelings in question. This ranges from playful and creative names like "radio doom and gloom," "the reason-giving machine," "the fascist dictator," "the judgment factory," "the not-good-enough story," and "the inner critic" to more straightforward names like "the mind" or "the thinking self." It also includes the simple labeling of these private experiences: "thinking," "feeling," "worrying," "reason-giving," "anxiety," "sadness," "I'm having the thought that," "I'm having the feeling of," "abandonment schema," "predicting the worst," "judgment."

Neutralizing

When an explosive device is disarmed, or a military threat is counteracted, we say it is "neutralized." When a country refuses to take sides in a war, we say it is "neutral." So when I talk of *neutralizing*, what I mean is moving the thought and feeling into a radically new context where we are not at war with it and we are not threatened by it; we see it in a new way that neutralizes its power over us.

Neutralizing includes all those playful defusion techniques where we sing thoughts or say them in silly voices; or we imagine them spoken by a cartoon character, or broadcast by a radio, or typed on a computer, or printed on a billboard; or we paint or draw or sculpt them; or simply write them down so we can clearly see them as words.

It also includes meditative-type exercises where we "place" thoughts on clouds, trains, leaves, blackboards, conveyor belts, and the like, or simply observe them coming and going as if they are objects passing by.

And last but not least, it includes all those interventions where we look at thoughts purely in terms of their function, with openness and curiosity, rather than judging, disputing, or invalidating them. We might ask, for example, "If you let this thought push you around, where will it take you: toward or away from the life you want?"

Any defusion technique is going to involve some or all of the three Ns, and all techniques serve the same purpose: to help us respond to our thoughts and feelings with broader, more flexible repertoires of behavior so we are better able to build the lives we want.

Q: Can you give me some useful questions for looking at thoughts functionally?

Russ: Sure. There are many useful questions that can help us to look at clients' thoughts in terms of function (as opposed to getting caught up in their content). Here are some of my favorites:

- If you hold on tightly to this thought, where does it take you? (toward or away?)
- If you let this thought dictate what you do with your arms and legs and mouth, what happens?

- When you get hooked/caught up/pushed around/jerked around by this thought...where do you go/what do you do/what tends to happen?
- If you let this thought guide you/advise you/instruct you/counsel you, does it help you to be the person you want to be/do the things you want to do?
- After you get hooked by that thought, what happens next? What do you say or do?
- How would I know, if I were watching you on a video, that you'd been hooked by that thought? What would I see or hear you doing so that I'd know?

Q: Do we target all fusion?

Russ: Noooooooo! If we tried to target every bit of fusion, we'd soon upset, anger, or invalidate our clients. We target fusion selectively, when it is clearly getting in the way of the client's goals for therapy (chapter 3). If we want a client to learn and practice defusion skills, we need to make it clear how fusion is a barrier to the life he wants; how it pulls him away from being the sort of person he wants to be, doing the things that matter to him. The choice point (chapter 1) is a great tool for making this explicit.

Q: What are "caveman mind" metaphors and how do they help with defusion?

Russ: In ACT, we often talk about how the mind has evolved "to think negatively," or, more accurately, to think in such a way that it naturally creates psychological suffering. There are many variants on this spiel, and I tend to class them all under the heading of "caveman mind" metaphors.

Basically, all these spiels point out how the Stone Age mind was geared toward safety (avoiding threats, steering away from danger, protecting you from harm, ensuring you don't get cut off from the group, preparing for future dangers) as its top priority. Often during this spiel, we ask clients questions such as "What did a caveman have to be on the lookout for, to survive?" "If a cavewoman's mind wasn't good at predicting, spotting, or avoiding danger, what happened to her?" We tease out how the better a caveperson's mind was at doing this job (of spotting, predicting, and avoiding danger), the longer that person lived and the more offspring he or she had (which means the more those "keep yourself safe" genes got passed on to the next generation, and so on).

We then link this idea—that the default setting of the caveman mind was "safety first!" and that we have inherited this from our prehistoric ancestors—to the many unhelpful things that our minds now do in the modern era. We especially point out that our modern mind reacts to difficult thoughts, feelings, and memories the same way a Stone Age mind reacted to dangerous beasts: fight or flight! We then give examples, always linking directly to the client's experience. Here are some examples:

- **Caveman mind**: *Watch out! There might be a bear in that cave. You could get eaten. Watch out! That shadow on the horizon—that could be an enemy from another clan. You could get speared!*
- **Modern mind**: Worrying, catastrophizing, predicting the worst, avoiding anything that scares you.

- **Caveman mind**: *Watch out! There was a saber-toothed tiger on that hill last week. It might come back!*
- **Modern mind**: Projecting the painful past into a scary future: *It happened before so it'll happen again.*

- **Caveman mind**: You survive an encounter with a bear or a wolf, so it's useful to replay it: to go over the events in your mind and remember what you did to survive so that you are better prepared for next time.
- **Modern mind**: We go over and over painful memories, dwelling on them, reliving them, even when there's nothing useful to learn or the lesson has been well learned.

And here's a practical tip for you: after describing the caveman mind, ask, "Does this sound a bit like your mind, at times? After 200,000 years of evolution, our minds are doing this kind of thing all the time!"

Now just for good measure, here are a few more examples:

- **Caveman mind**: As a caveman, you have to fit in with the group. If you are alone, you soon die. The wolves will eat you for breakfast! (If you survive past breakfast, the bears will get you for lunch.) So your mind compares you to others in the group: *Am I fitting in, contributing enough, following the rules? Am I doing anything that might get me thrown out?*

- **Modern mind**: Comparing yourself to others, fear of negative evaluation, fear of judgment, fear of rejection.

- **Caveman mind**: When encountering real physical threats such as dangerous animals, bad weather, treacherous terrain, rival tribes: *Watch out! You might get hurt. Stay away! Take cover!*

- **Modern mind**: When encountering anything that gives rise to discomfort, we respond to it the same ways as cavemen responded to real physical threats. So our minds start reason-giving—coming up with all the reasons why we can't do it, shouldn't do it, shouldn't have to do it. This is our mind trying to protect us from danger.

- **Caveman mind:** Conservation of physical resources is vitally important to a Stone Age person. If this task or challenge involves significant expenditure of time and energy and there's a good chance of failure, then it's safer not to undertake it.

- **Modern mind:** Our modern minds love to conjure up fear of failure. And they readily generate hopelessness (*There's no point; I'll only fail*), especially if there have been failures in the past. This also shows up as your mind telling you to give up if you're not getting quick or easy results. (Note: this is extremely useful for clients who are depressed and fused with helplessness and fear of failure.)

- **Caveman mind:** *You need more food, more water, better weapons, better shelter.* (The cavepeople who thought this way lived longer and had more offspring.)
- **Modern mind**: greed; dissatisfaction; craving; wanting; *it's never enough; I need more, more, more!*

- **Caveman mind**: tells you to avoid physical threats like bears and wolves; this keeps you safe!
- **Modern mind**: treats painful thoughts and feelings the same way as bears and wolves; tells you to avoid them!

These spiels all boil down to the same conclusions we give our clients:

- "Your mind is trying to save you from getting hurt. That's its number one job. So yes, there's all this unhelpful stuff your mind keeps saying to you. But it's not your mind deliberately trying to making life difficult; it's just your mind doing its number one job: trying to keep you safe, trying to save you from pain."
- "Your mind's not defective or abnormal; it's evolved to do this." I especially like to reframe it this way:

The Overly Helpful Friend

"Your mind is like an overly helpful friend—one of those friends who try so hard to help, they end up getting in the way, becoming a nuisance. When your mind says XYZ, it's basically trying to save you from pain in some form or another. That's its job. That's what it evolved to do."

This is usually very validating for clients.

And we can explore this with our client: "How do you think your mind might be trying to help you here?" (Self-criticism and self-judgment is your mind trying to help you improve. Reason-giving is your mind trying to save you from failure or getting hurt. Worrying is your mind trying to prepare you for the future.)

All in all, caveman mind metaphors offer much potential for effective therapy, including:

- Normalization and Validation: "It's normal, not a sign you're defective. All minds do this. Mine too!"
- Acceptance: "Our minds will keep doing this stuff; that's what they've evolved to do. We need to tell ourselves, *It's normal, not a sign I'm defective.*"
- Defusion: "When you catch your caveperson mind or overly helpful friend in action, say, *Aha! Here it is again: caveman mind.* Or, *Thanks mind. I know you're trying to help. It's okay, I've got it covered.* Or *Ah. There goes my overly helpful friend again.*"
- Self-compassion: "Can we acknowledge how our minds create this psychological suffering, against our will and out of our control, as a result of our evolutionary heritage? And recognizing this, can we be kind to ourselves?"

Q: Can caveman mind metaphors backfire?

I wonder if clients might find such metaphors irrelevant or boring, or even threatening, if they don't believe in evolution.

Russ: Yes, anything in ACT can backfire—and sooner or later will. (See chapter 13, Obnoxious Outcomes, for how to handle this). But it's not common. To increase the chances that such metaphors will hit home and be effective, we want to clearly link the metaphor to the client's main issues: fear of failure, rejection, abandonment, looking foolish, being judged, not fitting in, making mistakes...; avoidance of thoughts, feelings, emotions, memories, people, places, events, activities, and so on. And to make sure the link is clear, we can ask the client, "So what's all this talk about cavemen got to do with you?"

To make sure we don't bore the client to death with a long rambling monologue about evolution, we can involve him in cocreating the metaphor. In other words, rather than trotting the metaphor out as a script, we can ask the client questions such as:

- What kinds of things were dangerous to cavemen? What did they have to look out for? What kinds of animals were a threat?
- What happened to a cavewoman if she got kicked out by the group? How long would she last on her own? What would she need to do to make sure the group didn't kick her out?
- What happened to cavemen who weren't good at looking out for danger? Or weren't prepared for it? Or went hunting without their spears?
- If a cavewoman sees a bear, what does she need to do? If she survives, would there be any benefit to her in going over what happened and how she survived?

As clients answer these questions, the metaphor is fleshed out in an engaging, interactive manner.

Finally, if clients don't believe in evolution, skip the metaphor. There's no metaphor (or any other intervention) in ACT that's essential; so if you think or know a client won't respond well, ditch it and find an alternative. One option is simply to leave out all the evolutionary stuff and say, "This is what a human mind naturally tends to do. My mind does it too. And so does the mind of everyone I've ever met." From here it's easy to segue into "Your mind is like an overly helpful friend."

Q: What should I do when clients get anxious during defusion?

Sometimes clients become anxious when a defusion exercise has an initial focus on breathing. Would it be better to change the focus to something else, or to keep going with an emphasis on accepting the anxiety?

Russ: Always, always, always modify and adapt an exercise to suit yourself, the client, the situation. Always. Any exercise from any model can have unexpected consequences. So we need to be flexible. There's no doubt a focus on breathing will sometimes trigger anxiety in certain clients. Indeed, some clients hate any exercise that focuses on the breath; if so, we can leave it out.

There are many different defusion, acceptance, self-compassion, and present moment exercises that have a focus on the breath at the start, but there's no need to ever "stick to the script" for any type of experiential exercise; we can modify and adapt everything and anything.

If any client is having a negative reaction, the first step is to stop the exercise and bring mindfulness to what is happening: to notice the thoughts and feelings that are arising, and to get present. I call this dropping anchor (see chapter 7). We want to find out what is going on for the client: why is he reacting negatively? And then we adapt our response to that.

For example, some people get dizzy when they breathe slowly; this requires a different response than someone who is feeling intense anxiety and is fused with *I hate this feeling.*

If it seems like a good time to do some work on acceptance, we might morph the exercise into working with the feelings of anxiety: noticing where they are in the body and opening up, allowing them. Or we could morph it into a self-compassion exercise, or into a grounding and centering exercise. The possibilities are endless. But the first step is almost always to help the client notice and acknowledge—with openness and curiosity—the thoughts, feelings, memories, emotions, and sensations that are arising in this moment.

Q: How can I use defusion to help clients with traumatic thoughts and memories?

Russ: First things first. In ACT, we always want to know what the client wants from therapy (chapter 3). How is she currently responding to such cognitions? If a client identifies that the way she's currently responding to these cognitions is problematic (in other words, what she typically does when these thoughts and memories arise is getting in the way of the life she wants), we can ask her whether she's open to learning a new way of responding to them, so as to reduce their impact and influence; so that when they arise, they no longer hook her, jerk her around, hold her back. Again, the choice point (chapter 1) provides a simple and practical way to do this very quickly: write the thoughts and memories at the bottom, and the away moves the client currently does when hooked. Then identify the towards moves she'd like to be doing. We'd want to emphasize that these cognitions are likely to keep recurring, and there's no known way of eliminating them. So our work together will need to be about learning how to respond to them differently—to learn how to unhook from them, so it's easier for her to choose towards moves.

Once all that is in place, we can start explicitly working on defusion. Obviously, there are some defusion techniques we wouldn't use due to an extremely high risk of invalidating the client: singing thoughts to Happy Birthday, saying thoughts in silly voices, or "thanking your mind." But there are many others we could effectively use, including the simple noticing and nonjudgmental naming of cognitions ("I'm having a memory of the time I was assaulted.") We'd likely need to combine these with grounding exercises such as dropping anchor (chapter 7).

Hopefully my answer highlights the point that defusion probably won't help any client unless:

A. The degree of fusion with these particular thoughts is, *from the client's own perspective,* significantly impacting her quality of life.

B. The client is able to recognize and acknowledge the above.

C. The client is open to learning a new way of responding so that when these cognitions recur, they will have much less impact or influence.

And it's always so important to address the issue that these thoughts and memories will keep coming back; no one can eliminate them, so there's a real need to learn new ways of responding.

Q: How can I help clients to defuse from others' harsh criticisms?

Russ: A good place to begin is with validating the client's pain and compassionately acknowledging that criticism hurts. And then we want to help the client develop self-compassion: to acknowledge her pain, and make room for it, and be kind, caring, and supportive to herself. (For more on self-compassion, see chapter 10.)

Let's also help our client to acknowledge the inconvenient fact of life that other people *will* judge us and criticize us; it's inevitable. It's very painful, we don't like it, and there's no escaping it (unless we become a recluse).

Once she's acknowledged her pain and responded kindly to herself, our next step is to help her notice and name those painful thoughts: *Here's judgment*, *I'm noticing criticism*, and so on. And note that it doesn't matter if those criticisms originally came from someone else's mouth; the point is, those words are arising in the client's head right now, so let's help her to notice and name them, and reengage in life, here and now.

And keep in mind, it's very important to actually practice doing this, over and over throughout the session: noticing, naming, and reengaging, as in this example: "There's the not-good-enough story again. Did you notice it? How hooked are you? See if you can unhook: come back, refocus, give me your full attention." The more you can practice this in your sessions, the more likely the client will be to practice it outside of sessions.

Also, can we help the client open to the reality that usually there is at least a grain of truth in the judgments and criticisms that others direct toward us? Because we aren't perfect; we all have flaws. So even though it hurts, is there a way to acknowledge whatever truth there may be in the criticism? Is there something to learn from it, if only the importance of self-acceptance? Again, this calls for self-compassion. And of course, if there are interpersonal issues—conflict, discrimination, abuse—we address these through values and committed action.

Q: How can I help clients defuse from rigid rules?

Russ: I'll begin by clarifying something that can easily get lost in translation. Having and following rules to guide us in life is not a problem; it's fusion with these rules that creates suffering. When we obey these rules, cling to them tightly, follow them at all costs, allow them to dictate our lives, restrict our freedom and limit our choices—that's when we suffer. (If you're not sure what we mean by "rules" in ACT, go to chapter 6: Vicious Values, and read the Q&A on "What's the difference between values and rules?") We learn to follow rules from a young age, because it's such a useful way to learn. If Mom says, "Don't play in the road, kids; it's dangerous," and we obey that rule, then we don't get hit by cars. This is much better for us than learning by direct experience: playing in the road and getting hit by a car and learning from that painful event that it's not safe to play in the road. The problem is, as we grow up, we spend more and more of our life guided by our ever-growing list of rules, and less and less of our life learning from direct experience. All too often, we end up ignoring our direct experience (the actual consequences of our behavior) as we automatically follow our mental rules.

Typically, there are many reinforcing consequences for rule following. For example, often following rules

- helps people avoid anxiety or other uncomfortable emotions in the short term;
- helps people get their needs met in the short term;
- gives a sense of safety, security, certainty, or familiarity;
- gives a sense of confidence or "doing it right" or "doing it properly"; and
- gives a sense of coherence: making sense of the world, how it works, our place in it, and what we need to do to make life work.

It's often helpful to explore, illuminate, and validate these payoffs with clients before compassionately looking at the costs, which we do using the following steps.

Six Steps for Defusion from Rules

STEP 1: NOTICE AND NAME THE RULE

The therapist draws the client's attention to the rule and puts it into words: "I'm willing to be wrong about this, but it seems to me that you've got a rule here that goes something like this: 'I must do everything perfectly or there's no point in doing it at all.' Have I got that right?"

Rules often take forms such as *He should* A, *You have to* B, *Others shouldn't* C, *They can't* D, *I won't* E *unless* F, *You shouldn't* G *until* H, *Never do* J, *Always do* K, Z *is the right way to do it,* Q *is the wrong way,* and *If* M *then* P. In naming such a cognition, we can refer to it as a rule, or we can speak of it metaphorically as a law, dictate, commandment, order, or imperative. In later defusion work, we can go further with this way of speaking and introduce the metaphor of an inner judge, tyrant, or dictator laying down all these laws and rules and making threats about what will happen if we disobey them.

STEP 2: TRACK THE CONSEQUENCES OF FOLLOWING THE RULE

We only target fusion if it interferes with the client's goals for therapy (chapter 3). So let's first recap with the client what his goals are: "I'm only mentioning this rule because our aim here is to help you XYZ (*therapist recaps the client's therapy goals*), and it seems to me that when you get hooked by this rule, it pulls you away from those things."

The client's reaction may vary from acknowledgment ("I know") to curiosity ("Really? How?") to opposition ("No it doesn't"). If the reaction is somewhat defensive or oppositional, we could say something like "Well of course, I could have that wrong. Would it be okay if we just explore it for a moment, see if there's anything in it?"

Once the client is open to it, we can gently explore: "What generally happens when you follow that rule? What are the benefits?" As mentioned above, there are likely to be many reinforcing consequences for following the rule, many benefits that the client does not want to lose. So it's very important that we acknowledge and validate these payoffs before we go on to look at the costs (see chapter 5: Freaky Functional Analysis). We can then summarize: "So there are real benefits to you for following this rule, such as JKL." And then we can gently explore the costs: "Have you noticed any downside when you follow this rule? What does it cost you, in the long term, when you let it dictate what you do?" As we do this, we want to help the client contact the reality that in the long term, rigidly following this rule is pulling him away from his therapy goals.

STEP 3: WORKABILITY

Step 2 morphs into step 3. We look at the workability of following the rule. We validate the payoffs ("In the short term, there are real benefits for following this rule, such as ABC"), and we compassionately connect them to the costs ("But in the long term, it's costing you XYZ"). And then we ask, "So overall, in the long term, when you allow that rule to dictate your actions, would you say it tends to take you toward the life you want, or away from it?"

STEP 4: FLEXIBILITY

In step 3, the client contacts the reality that following this rule rigidly takes her away from the life she wants. We can now follow up with questions such as "So, given the costs of living your life based on this rule, are you willing to be more flexible with it? To bend it a little? To hold it less tightly? To follow it sometimes, when doing so is likely to be effective, but not at other times where it's likely to be self-defeating? Are you willing to maybe experiment with bending, breaking, or disobeying it?"

As we do this, we'd want to highlight that following rules is rarely a problem, provided we do so flexibly; it's when we follow them rigidly, all the time, holding on tight and not letting go, that problems tend to occur.

Then from here we'll often segue to teasing out the values beneath the rule, and finding more flexible ways of living by them. (See chapter 6: Vicious Values.)

STEP 5: ACCEPTANCE AND DEFUSION

One of the big payoffs for rigid rule following is that it often reduces anxiety or helps people escape guilt and shame, in the short term. So when people bend, disobey, or break the rules that they've held tightly for a long time, often a lot of anxiety, guilt, shame, or other painful emotions show up. When this happens, we can segue into working with those difficult thoughts and feelings, responding with acceptance, defusion, and self-compassion.

STEP 6: MORE NOTICING AND NAMING

We want to prepare the client for the fact that this rule will probably resurface, over and over again. Each time it comes back, the aim is to notice and name it and then make a conscious choice about whether or not to follow it, bend it, or break it. (The choice point is very useful for mapping this out visually.)

"But Russ," I hear you ask, "What if the client decides rigid rule following *is* workable, *is* a towards move, *is* something he wants to keep doing?" If so, then let's work on self-compassion (chapter 10). If he continues living life this way, it will come with lots of painful consequences, so let's help him to acknowledge those costs, acknowledge his suffering, and respond to himself with kindness, caring, and support.

Q: What if it really matters to clients whether their thoughts are true or not?

For example, a client of mine is ruminating all the time on thoughts about her husband going to a nursing home, and I think she'd be offended if I said it doesn't matter if those thoughts are true or not.

Russ: Discussing whether or not those thoughts are true doesn't seem like it would be much use to your client. The question in this case is not one of true or false, but rather, "If I hold on to these thoughts tightly, does it help me to live my values, be the person I want to be?"

For your client, we want to know, is ruminating helping her to take action, live her values, be the sort of partner she wants to be in the face of this challenge? You want to help her to move from rumination and worrying to living her values: committed action, values-guided problem solving and action planning, standing for something in the face of this crisis. The thoughts she's fused with when ruminating may well be true, but is getting hooked by them helping her to cope effectively? If so, there's no problem—keep ruminating. But if not, would she be interested in learning how to unhook/disentangle/defuse from those thoughts?

When I do explicitly broach the true or false issue, I tend to say something like "In this approach we're not usually interested in whether your thoughts are true or false, 99% of the time, with rare exceptions. What we're mainly interested in is this: when these thoughts show up, if you get all caught up and entangled in them, or if you let them push you around and dictate what you do, will that help you to behave like the sort of person you want to be? Do the things you want to do? Or will it pull you away from them?"

But note, I don't just trot this type of spiel out to every client, every session. I bring it in only when clients are unhelpfully focused on whether their thoughts are true or false ("But it's true! I really am fat/stupid/a bad mother") to justify why they are incapable of doing something life-enhancing.

In the case of your client, the issue of "true or false" might not be relevant at all. I might just say, "So there are all sorts of worrying thoughts showing up for you about your husband, and his situation, and what the future might hold, and the bad things that might happen, and the stresses you have to deal with. And when you get all entangled in these worries, what happens? Does it help you to act effectively? To come up with a strategy or action plan? To cope with the stress?"

Typically, the answer will be no. Then I'd go on to say, "Well, the most useless advice I've ever heard is 'don't worry about it.' If it were that easy to stop worrying, no one would ever worry, because it's very unpleasant. Now I don't know how to stop your mind from generating scary thoughts about bad things that might happen. That's a normal process. And of course, the reality is, many of these things you're worrying about might well happen. So I don't know how to stop your mind from doing that. But would you like to learn how to unhook yourself from those worrying thoughts? How to disentangle from them, so instead of getting caught up in worrying all day long, you can engage in life, take action, live your values?"

So notice in that spiel, there is no mention of whether or not thoughts are true or false. It's not relevant. It comes in most commonly when clients are fused with negative self-judgment: "But I really am *bad*! And here's the evidence to prove it! It's *true*." This is when it's truly liberating to move away from true or false and instead get into workability.

Q: Why should we "thank our mind" for unhelpful thoughts?

Russ: There's no "should" in it. It's a technique, to use if and when it's likely to be helpful. It has the same purpose as any other defusion technique: to reduce the influence of cognition over behavior. And it's only ever to be done with a playfulness, a sense of humor. If we can't do it in this way, if it's done with sarcasm or aggression, then it won't have the intended effect. It's like playfully talking back to someone who tries to insult you, instead of getting into a fight. The aggressor says, "You're an idiot." But if you reply, lightly and playfully, "Thanks for sharing," then you don't get into a quarrel with the other person. So by doing this with our own thoughts, we don't get into a fight with them; we don't get into a debate about whether they're true or false; we don't take them so seriously; and usually we find this reduces their impact and influence.

But like any defusion technique, if it's not helpful, or if you think it might be invalidating for the client, don't do it. For example, I'd strongly caution against using this technique for dealing with traumatic memories or thoughts linked to horrific events from the past; there's such a high risk of invalidation!

Q: How can we help clients defuse from deeply entrenched reason-giving?

Russ: Reason-giving is one of the most problematic categories of fusion we encounter. I like to say to clients, "The human mind is like a reason-giving machine. As soon as we even think about stepping out of our comfort zone, this machine starts cranking out all the reasons why we can't do it, shouldn't do it, or shouldn't even have to do it. And if we get hooked by those reasons, what happens? That's right, we don't do it!"

We want to normalize and validate this cognitive process. Ideally the therapist will do some self-disclosure about how her own mind does this frequently. And it's often valuable to link this cognitive process back to caveman mind metaphors. This is the modern-day equivalent of the caveman mind trying to keep our ancestors safe: *Don't do it! You might fail, get hurt, get harmed!*

We can use any type of defusion technique with reason-giving. One of my favorites is described in detail in appendix 4: Defusion from Barriers to Therapy. Although in the script the focus is on reasons why therapy won't or can't work, the exercise can easily be used with any type of reason-giving.

Another one of my favorite ways to work with these issues is to…

Build A Reason-Giving Machine

Equipment needed: a pen; a pad of small, colorful sticky notes; and a container of some sort. Ideally, you'll have an interesting container—a cool box or case of some sort, but almost any container will do—even just a large envelope. (I use a transparent acrylic box with a clasp lid that originally housed a watch.)

Part 1: Introduce the Machine

In advance of the session, write down some common types of reason-giving you encounter clinically, one thought per sticky note, such as "I'm too tired," "I'm too anxious," "I'm not good enough," "I might fail," "I've failed in the past when I've tried this," "It'll go wrong," "I don't have the confidence," "I'm depressed," and "I shouldn't have to." Ideally have at least twenty to thirty notes.

Put all the sticky notes into the container and close the lid. Keep a few blank ones handy so that if your client comes up with new reasons, you can write them on the spares and add them to the collection.

At the appropriate point in the session (for example when the client is fusing with reasons not to do something that matters to him), we pull out the device, hand it to the client, and ask, "Any idea what this is?"

When the client answers no, we reply, "It's a reason-giving machine. We've all got one of these things inside our head. And as soon as we even think about stepping out of our comfort zone, this machine starts cranking out all the reasons why we can't do it, shouldn't do it, or shouldn't even have to do it."

Ideally we then validate, normalize, self-disclose, and, if we haven't already done so, link this to caveman mind. And then we ask, "Do you want to open it, have a look inside?"

The client now opens the box.

We then say, "So what you'll find in there are a whole stack of the most common reasons that our minds give us not to do things that really matter to us. Have a look through them, and see if your mind says anything like this to you."

Part 2: Sort the Reasons

Now we can ask the client to sort the sticky notes into two piles:

- **Pile 1:** those reasons that his mind is giving him right now—or often gives him—not to go ahead with XYZ (where XYZ = values-congruent goals and actions). As we do this, ask the client if his mind is coming up with other reasons that aren't listed; if so, write each one down on a blank note and add it to pile 1. (By the time you've done this with ten clients, you'll have so many reasons inside your machine, it'll be rare that anyone comes up with a new one.)

- **Pile 2:** other reasons not to go ahead with XYZ that his mind does not usually give him. Almost always, pile 2 is a lot smaller than pile 1.

As the sticky notes tend to stick and clump together, there are many opportunities to talk about "sticky thoughts" and how they often "clump together" or "form teams" or "get together to gang up on you."

Part 3: Next Steps

There are many ways to go from here. Here are a few ideas:

We can use this for more normalizing and validating, and if we haven't already done so, link it to the caveman mind metaphor. And we can normalize further by disclosing how our own mind gives us almost all the same reasons as the client's pile 1 at times (as well as quite a lot in pile 2).

We can segue into any defusion technique we like. An obvious one would be noticing and naming such cognitions whenever they occur: "Ah, there's reason-giving," or "There's the reason-giving machine," or simply, "reason-giving." We can plot reason-giving on the choice point diagram and explore what happens when the client gets hooked by it: away moves he makes, towards moves he misses.

We can also pull out the machine in later sessions when fusion with reason-giving recurs and say, "Have we got that one in here?" (If it isn't in there, we can add it in.)

Q: What do you mean by "dance in the dark and lead to the light"?

Russ: It's a phrase I use to convey a respectful, calm, and patient way of helping highly fused clients to gently defuse. When we see a client lost in the darkness of fusion, most of us want to immediately turn on the lights, to shine forth the bright beams of defusion. There's nothing unusual in that; we can see the client suffering, so naturally we want to help her. But if we leap into defusion prematurely without first empathizing and validating the client's pain, or if we use playful techniques that are inappropriate for such situations (like singing thoughts or thanking the mind), there's a big risk we will invalidate the client and trigger even more fusion.

For example, suppose your client says, "I can't believe she would do this to me. She's supposed to be my best friend, for f###'s sake. She knows he's an asshole; he treated me like shit, he cheated on me, abused me. And now she's going out with him? I mean, where the f### does she get off? Would you do that to your friends? She f###ing betrayed me. And I'm sure he's just lapping it up, laughing his socks off. Asshole. Both of them, complete f###ing assholes. I'm gonna make 'em pay for this. I'm gonna get back at her if it's the last thing do!"

Imagine what would happen if the therapist now launched into, "Aha, there goes your judgment factory, cranking out the judgments," or "Thank your mind for those thoughts." Would not get a good reaction, right?

So if a client is very fused, let's first "dance in the dark" for a while, and then gently and respectfully "lead her to the light." In other words, let's make room for the fusion, instead of going against it; let's take the time to get a sense of what the client is experiencing, to see things from her perspective, to empathize with her predicament and acknowledge how painful it is. Dancing in the dark would involve:

A. Listening with openness and curiosity

B. Empathizing

C. Normalizing and validating

D. Seeing things from the client's perspective

For example, we might say something like "That's really rough. I'd feel furious if someone did that to me. It's especially hurtful, given she's your best friend. It's perfectly natural to want to get back at her. Most of us want revenge when we feel betrayed."

Obviously there's no one right way to do this, no magic set of words and gestures that we can trot out for any situation. We want to be flexible, adapting what we say and do for each unique client: her issues, her personality, her therapy goals, and how much ACT she's already done up to this point in time.

We may spend quite a few minutes dancing in the dark, if necessary. But we don't want to spend an entire session on it because if that's all we do in a session, we are basically just doing supportive counseling. As soon as we have a sense that the client feels heard, understood, and validated, we can then gently start leading her toward the light. In other words, we can guide and encourage the client gently toward any of the core processes of psychological flexibility, all of which can support defusion.

For example, we may segue to values, teasing them out from underneath the fusion. Underneath "betrayal" we're likely to find values such as "trust" and "loyalty"; underneath "revenge" we'll probably find values such as "fairness" and "justice." Or we may move to committed action: explore what the client wants to stand for in the face of this: what actions does she want to take, what would be the likely consequences, how workable are they?

Alternatively, we might move to acceptance and self-compassion; we might help her to notice and name her emotions, acknowledge her suffering, respond to herself with kindness. Or we might move to dropping anchor, especially if we've been actively working on issues of aggression, "anger management," or impulsive behavior.

And of course, we may move directly to defusion. If so, it's often useful to begin by compassionately acknowledging the mind's role: "So when we're in great pain, dealing with difficult situations, our minds often come up with all sorts of stuff that's not that helpful; doesn't really help us to deal with the situation or recover from the blow. Can we take a look at what your mind's doing right now? See if we can figure out what it's got to say that's helpful, and what's not?"

So if you're ever working with a client who is fused, and what you're doing seems to be making the fusion worse, then pause for a moment, and consider: are you trying to shove her forcefully into the light? If so, step back into the dark, and dance for a while. Then, ever so gently, with baby steps, lead to the light.

Q: What techniques work best with extreme fusion?

Russ: There are well over a hundred different defusion techniques written in ACT textbooks and self-help books, and many more that have never been written down. And it's hard to say that any particular one is more effective than another; certainly there's been no research on this. However, with that disclaimer, my own personal experience is that two methods in particular (or the many variants of them) are very effective when it comes to extreme fusion. (But note: others in the ACT community may not agree with me.)

In my opinion, for extreme fusion, nothing beats dropping anchor (chapter 7). Although such exercises are usually thought of as contacting the present moment, almost always they result in significant defusion. (This is not surprising, as all four of the core ACT mindfulness processes—defusion, acceptance, contacting the present moment, and self-as-context—are overlapping and interconnected.) So dropping anchor will almost always be my first line in targeting the most severe states of fusion, while always keeping in mind the key points from the previous Q&A: let's dance in the dark before we lead to the light.

The other method that I discuss here must be done with the utmost of respect, care, concern, empathy, and compassion. If it's done "Dr. Phil style"—with arrogance, dismissiveness, lack of empathy, lack of compassion, failure to validate the client's pain and suffering, failure to acknowledge and validate the very real difficulties and problems in the client's life—then it's likely to offend, invalidate, and upset the client.

This is one reason why informed consent (appendix 2) is essential: because we can later say to the client, "Remember we talked about how this model involves learning new skills to handle difficult thoughts and feelings more effectively? Is it okay if we try one right now?"

Now whatever the client is fusing with, we write those words down and we say, "So this is what your mind is saying" (or some variant thereof, such as "So these are the thoughts currently showing up" or "These are the worries you're having"). We can write these on any old sheet of paper, but the choice point is especially useful for this purpose. As we do this, some clients will now object, "But it's true." Here's how we might respond:

Therapist: So let's write that down too: "But it's true." (*writes on the paper "But it's true."*)

Client: But it really is true!

Therapist: Please understand. I'm not trying to say these thoughts are false. I just want to get them down in black and white. I just want to write down the thoughts your mind is generating in this moment, so we can work on learning new skills to handle them.

Client: They aren't thoughts, they're facts!

Therapist: Okay, we can call them facts. Or we can call them cognitions. I don't mind what we call them. I just want to document the things your mind is telling you right now, so we can work on learning new skills to handle them.

Client: It's not "my mind"—why do you keep saying it's my mind?

Therapist: What word would you prefer me to use? We need a word for the part of you that generates all this stuff.

Client: It's my brain.

Therapist: Okay. So I just want to write down the things your brain is telling you right now. Is that okay? (*points to the paper*) These seem to be the main ones, right?

Once we've written down what the client is fused with, we can then use the "Where Is Your Mind Taking You?" technique. Suppose the client keeps getting fused with a particular theme, such as *My life was so good before the accident* or *My childhood was so bad* or *Things will go wrong* or *I'll get hurt* or *I've got so many other problems, how can I focus on this one?* or *It's X's fault; X is to blame* or *all the reasons why this won't work.*

Having written some of these thoughts down on a sheet of paper, we can then write a title up top that encapsulates the theme, such as "my past life" or "why this won't work" or "reasons to give up" or "others are at fault" or "all the other problems."

We can then put this somewhere prominent—on the couch beside the client or on the floor. If he gets hooked by a thought linked to that theme, we can point over to it: "Your mind is pulling you there—back into that stuff and out of the session. Can you come back here—to you and me, working together as a team, here and now?"

This is especially useful for the client with multiple problems who keeps jumping from problem to problem, never focusing on one for long enough to create an action plan.

Agree on one problem, and to stay on topic long enough to come up with an action plan. The client will typically try to go off topic to other problems; point it out and redirect her back to the task at hand. Each time you do this, point out that she is learning an essential skill: how to stay focused on a problem long enough to come up with an effective action plan.

This is a great way to disrupt rumination, worrying, and obsessive thinking and develop the skill of refocusing attention, as well as to keep the session on track and help the client to get solution oriented.

A powerful variant on this is to hand the paper to the client, along with a pen, and ask her, "Each time your mind tries to hook you into that thought stream, please pause for a moment, take one slow breath, acknowledge your mind is trying to hook you, and place a tick on the paper—so we can keep track of how many times it happens."

Initially, you will probably need to point it out to her: "Looks like your mind is hooking you again. Can you just pause, take a breath, and place another tick there?"

After each pause, breath, and tick, refocus on whatever you were talking about or doing when the hook showed up. Usually this rapidly and effectively builds defusion and refocusing skills. With recurrent thoughts, expect up to twenty or thirty ticks by the end of the session, with progressive defusion as more and more ticks appear.

Q: Can fusion with certain thoughts and feelings have a payoff?

Russ: Yes, all fusion has payoffs, or in behavioral terms, *reinforcing consequences*. For example, fusion with "I'm right, you're wrong" gives us the payoff of a sense of righteousness, which makes us feel powerful. And fusion with anger not only makes us feel powerful but often helps us escape other more painful feelings such as fear, sadness, shame, and guilt. The payoffs of worrying typically include (a) helping us "escape into our heads" and thereby avoid unpleasant feelings of anxiety in our body, (b) helping us (eventually) prepare for the worst, and (c) giving us the sense that we're working on our problems. It's often very useful to highlight the payoffs of fusion with clients, and then gently and kindly contrast those with the costs by looking at them in terms of workability.

The Wrap-Up

Well done! You made it to the end of the longest chapter in the book, and I hope you've found a wealth of ideas for improving your clients' defusion skills. If you only remember one thing from this chapter...that would suggest you haven't been paying attention, so go back and read it again! But seriously folks, what I would like you to take from this chapter, above all else, is the incredible variety of ways to model, instigate, and reinforce defusion in our clients. There's just so much potential for us to be creative and innovative. So if you're getting bored with the same old handful of tired, worn out defusion techniques, why not play around with some new ones? Step out of your comfort zone. Have some fun. And thank your caveman mind when it tries to stop you.

CHAPTER 10

Surprising Self-Compassion

As the title of the great R.E.M. song says, "Everybody Hurts." Life dishes up pain for all of us. We all get to repeatedly experience disappointment, frustration, failure, rejection, illness, injury, conflict, hostility, grief, fear, anxiety, anger, sadness, guilt, loss, loneliness, health issues, financial issues, relationship issues, work issues, and so on. Unfortunately, when we experience great pain, we often don't treat ourselves very well.

Self-compassion involves acknowledging your own suffering and responding kindly—in other words, treating yourself with the same warmth, caring, and kindness that you'd extend to someone you love who was in similar pain. For thousands of years, self-compassion has played a central role in many religious and spiritual practices, and now it is becoming increasingly important in many models of therapy, coaching, and counseling. Indeed, a wealth of research shows the benefits of self-compassion with a wide range of clinical issues, from depression and anxiety disorders to grief, trauma, and addiction. It's hardly surprising then that self-compassion is implicit in every aspect of the ACT model, and we often make it explicit too.

Discussions in This Chapter:

- What is self-compassion?
- What's the difference between self-compassion and acceptance?

- What are the elements of self-compassion, from an ACT perspective?
- Is everyone capable of self-compassion?
- Where's the best place to start with clients who lack self-compassion?
- What if clients react negatively to the term *self-compassion*?
- What if the client has no personal experience of kind and caring relationships with others?
- What are the most common barriers to self-compassion?

Q: What is self-compassion?

Russ: Just as there's not one universally agreed upon definition of mindfulness, there is not one for self-compassion. To my clients, my trainees, and readers of my books, I define it as "acknowledging one's own suffering, and responding with kindness and caring" (Harris, 2012, p. 31).

Kristin Neff, the world's foremost researcher on the topic, describes self-compassion as comprised of three main elements: mindfulness, kindness, and common humanity (the recognition that suffering is something we have in common with all humans; Neff & Vonk, 2009). I used this triad as my starting point for mapping out self-compassion in terms of ACT, but I ended up expanding it to six elements, as you will see shortly.

Q: What's the difference between self-compassion and acceptance?

Russ: For a long time in ACT, the term *acceptance* was used instead of or synonymously with *self-compassion*. Personally, I think while both concepts are intertwined in rich ways, it's useful conceptually to differentiate them.

I see it this way (though others in ACT may not agree). In acceptance work, we turn toward our unwanted thoughts and feelings with openness and curiosity. And we progressively move through what I like to call the *three As*: acknowledging them, allowing them, and accommodating them. Inherent in this process is the acknowledgment of our suffering and an attitude of kindness and caring toward ourselves, so self-compassion is implicit within the ACT concept of acceptance.

However, I see self-compassion as a much larger construct than acceptance; I see acceptance as only one element of this larger construct, as you'll see in the next Q&A.

Q: What are the six elements of self-compassion, from an ACT perspective?

Russ: I thought you'd never ask! Before I get into this, an important disclaimer: I'm not talking for the entire ACT community here. There may be other trainers or authors who disagree with some of what I'm saying here. This is just my take on things, not some official ACT doctrine.

Element #1: Acknowledging Pain

One of the core ACT processes is contacting the present moment, in other words, flexibly noticing, with an attitude of curiosity and openness, what is present: right here, right now. (This is of course a central element in all forms of mindfulness practice.) This process is an essential first step in self-compassion: we consciously and intentionally notice and acknowledge our own pain. We acknowledge, with openness and curiosity, the painful thoughts, feelings, emotions, images, sensations, urges, memories, and so on that are present within us in this moment. This is very different from our default mode of turning away from our pain as fast as possible—trying to suppress it, avoid it, deny it, escape it, or distract from it.

Often, it's useful to express what we have noticed (in nonjudgmental language). For example, we may say, "I'm noticing painful feelings of rejection" or "I'm noticing thoughts about being a loser" or "I'm noticing sadness and anxiety."

Element #2: Defusion from Self-Judgment

Another core ACT process is defusion. Most of us know all too well just how quick our minds are to judge and criticize us. Our minds seem to relish any opportunity to pull out a big stick and give us a whack, to point out our flaws and failures, to label us as "not good enough" in a hundred different ways.

An essential aspect of self-compassion is learning how to defuse from all that harsh self-talk. We can't magically train our minds to stop speaking to us that way. (If you've ever tried, you know what I'm talking about.)

Sure, we can learn to think more positively and practice nonjudgmental awareness, but that won't stop our minds from judging and criticizing us. Caveman mind metaphors (chapter 9) often come in handy at this point: none of us chose to have a mind that does all this unhelpful stuff. We've inherited our modern minds as a result of countless eons of evolution. And there's no way to turn back the clock, to undo all that evolutionary past. This is what modern minds do, and we need to learn how to handle them.

The good news is we can learn to defuse from those harsh self-judgments and "not good enough" stories. We can notice, name, and unhook from those cognitions. We can learn how to see them as nothing more or less than words and pictures, without getting into debates about whether they are true or false. And we can let them come and stay and go in their own good time, without getting caught up in them or pushed around by them.

Element #3: Responding with Kindness

Another two of the core ACT processes are values and committed action. Values are our hearts' deepest desires for how we want to behave on an ongoing basis, how we want to treat ourselves, others, and the world around us. Committed action means skillful flexible action, guided by our core values.

The value that forms the foundation of self-compassion is kindness. All types of self-compassion practice—wherever they may have originated from—revolve around this powerful core value. Indeed, we can think of kindness as the glue that holds together all the other elements of self-compassion. For example, when we consciously acknowledge our pain, this is an act of kindness. And when we defuse from harsh self-criticism, this too is an act of kindness.

So once we acknowledge our pain, the aim is to treat ourselves with kindness. And fortunately there are many, many ways in which we can act kindly toward ourselves. We can use kind self-talk, such as reminding ourselves that we are human, that we are fallible, that everyone makes mistakes, that no one is perfect. We can talk to ourselves in a caring and gentle and understanding way, much as we would speak to a loved one in similar pain. We can use kind imagery, such as loving-kindness meditation, or inner child rescripting, or numerous other practices where we create powerful images to tap into self-kindness. We can use kind self-touch, such as placing a hand gently on our heart or on top of a painful feeling and sending warmth and caring inward through the palm. And we can do kind deeds, such as self-soothing rituals, or self-care activities, or spending quality time with people who treat us well.

Element #4: Acceptance

Another core ACT process is acceptance. This does not mean passively accepting a difficult situation. On the contrary, the committed action process in ACT involves taking effective action, guided by our values, to do everything we can to improve the situation as much as possible. *Acceptance* in ACT refers to accepting our thoughts, feelings, emotions, memories, urges, and sensations. Acceptance means we "open up" and "make room" for our thoughts and feelings; we allow them to flow through us, without fighting them, running from them, or being controlled by them. And we do this as an act of kindness and caring for ourselves.

When pain shows up in our lives, we often try to escape it through activities that tend to make our lives worse in the long term. For example, we may turn to alcohol, junk food, drugs, cigarettes, mindless consumerism, zoning out in front of the TV, dropping out of important activities, social isolation, self-harm, or even suicidality. These are not kind ways to treat ourselves.

So when we practice making room for our painful thoughts, feelings, memories, and sensations (instead of doing self-defeating or life-draining things to avoid them), when we allow them to freely flow through us, neither struggling against them nor getting swept away by them, this is an act of kindness in itself.

Element #5: Validation

All too often, when we are in great pain, we invalidate our own emotional experience. We don't acknowledge our pain as a valid experience—as a normal and natural part of being human. Our minds tell us that we shouldn't feel like this, we shouldn't react like this, we should be able to handle it better, we shouldn't have these thoughts and feelings. Often, our minds belittle us: tell us that we are overreacting, or we're weak, or we have nothing to complain about because there are starving kids in Africa and these are merely "first world problems." Our minds may even tell us to toughen up, suck it up, stop being a crybaby, or be a real man. Obviously, this type of harsh, critical, invalidating attitude is the very opposite of kindness and caring.

One aspect of validating our experience is defusion. Even though we can't stop them from arising, we can learn to defuse (unhook, detach) from these harsh self-judgments, unrealistic expectations, and unkind comparisons to others.

The other aspect is to actively validate our experience through self-talk. We can remind ourselves, in a warm, caring inner voice, that it is normal and natural for humans to have painful thoughts and feelings when life is difficult, when we make mistakes, when we get rejected, or when we experience any kind of reality gap (a gap between the reality you want and the reality you've got).

And when our minds compare our emotional reactions unfavorably with those of others, we can remind ourselves that we are unique. After all, if anybody else on the planet had your unique DNA, your unique childhood, your unique life history, and your unique physical body, that person would respond exactly the same way that you respond (because that person would, in fact, be you!).

Element #6: Connectedness

Often when we are in great pain, our minds generate thoughts along the lines of *I am the only one going through this, I'm the only one who feels this way, No one else knows what this is like, No one cares, Everyone else is happy, Everyone else is better off than me,* and *Why me?* Thoughts like these are commonplace and completely natural. Most of us have experienced such thoughts at times, and there's no known way to stop our minds from saying them.

However, the problem is not *having* such thoughts. The problem is fusing with them. If we fuse with these thoughts—get all caught up in them, buy in to them—then this creates a sense of disconnection. We feel cut off, disconnected from others; we are on our own, the odd one out, no longer a part of the group. And our pain is all the more difficult because we are suffering alone.

If, on the other hand, we develop a sense of connectedness with others, this can help us with our pain. One way to develop such connectedness is to actively defuse from thoughts such as those above.

Another way is to spend time with people who care about us and treat us kindly, to actively engage with them, to be fully present with them. Often, it's useful to let these people know that we are in pain, and to accept their kindness and caring, if it's forthcoming.

And yet a third way is to actively reflect on how our pain is something we have in common with all human beings. Our pain tells us that we have a heart, that we care deeply, that some things really matter to us. Our pain tells us that we are facing a reality gap. Pain is what all living, caring human beings feel, whenever they meet a reality gap. And the bigger that reality gap, the greater the pain that arises. So, our pain is not a sign of weakness or defectiveness or mental illness; it's a sign that we, like all humans, are living, caring beings.

Q: Is everyone capable of self-compassion?

Russ: I don't know if *everyone* is capable, but most people are. Of course, many people have little or no experience of self-compassion, and some may find it threatening or overwhelming or just "too hard!" This is especially likely if they leap headfirst into an intensive exercise such as a traditional self-compassion meditation.

Luckily, though, we can build self-compassion through baby steps, so it's not threatening, overwhelming, or "too hard." We can start with any one of the six basic building blocks of self-compassion—ideally, whichever one we find easiest—and we can work on that for a while. Then, once we've made some progress with that element, we can start experimenting with another.

In this way, going gently, step-by-step, we can build our self-compassion skills over time. As we develop more building blocks, we can learn how to stack them on top of each other, to build taller and more stable towers. There is no need for people to meditate, or to follow some religious practice, although they can if they want to, of course. The ACT model gives us a vast range of incredibly flexible ways to develop self-compassion in a secular, science-based manner, in just about anybody. (Having said that, though, it's worth noting that quite a few ACT protocols do borrow self-compassion practices from Buddhism, including formal meditations such as Tonglen and loving-kindness. However, where this occurs, these are not introduced as religious or spiritual practices.)

Q: Where's the best place to start with clients who lack self-compassion?

Russ: I don't think there *is* one best place. The main thing is to go slowly. Go gently. Ease into it. Don't throw your client in at the deep end; he'll likely get overwhelmed. We can start with any one of the six elements above—whichever we find easiest or think is most likely to be well-received by the client—and work on that for a while. (For most people, acknowledging the pain is probably the simplest starting point, followed by validating it.) Once we've made some progress with that initial element, we can then start bringing in another, and then another, gently building self-compassion skills step by step.

Q: What if clients react negatively to the term *self-compassion*?

Russ: We always want to modify our language to suit our clients. If we think or know our clients will react negatively to talk of self-compassion, it's a good idea not to use it. For example, when I work with tough male clients from the armed forces or emergency services, I start from the assumption that they would not respond well to the term *self-compassion*. (This assumption could of course be wrong; it's very much based on stereotyping. But so far, it's been working well for me.)

So instead I use the following metaphor:

The Two Friends Metaphor

Suppose you're going through a rough patch, a really hard time in your life. There are all sorts of problems and difficulties, and just about everything that can go wrong has gone wrong. In other words, life is pretty shitty. Now as you're going through this, what kind of friend would you like by your side?

Would you like the sort of friend who says, "Ah, shut up. Stop your whining. I don't want to hear about it. What the hell have you got to complain about? There are people out there a lot worse off than you. You're just a big wimpy kid. Suck it up and get on with it"?

Or would you like the sort of friend who says, "This is really rough. With what you're going through right now, anyone would be struggling. So I want you to know, I'm here for you buddy. I've got your back. We're in this together. I'm with you every step of the way"?

Clients will always choose the second over the first. We can then say, "Of course you would. Who'd want the first sort of friend? He'd just make everything worse than it already is, right? So the question is, what kind of friend are you being to yourself, as you go through this?"

I'm sure you can see how this readily segues into self-compassion, but without ever needing to use the word itself. We can talk about support and caring and other qualities of a good friend, and then help to put these values into action: to become a good friend to himself.

Q: What if the client has no personal experience of kind and caring relationships with others?

Russ: In such cases, self-compassion will likely seem like it's something from another planet. This certainly presents a big challenge (for both therapist and client), but it's not insurmountable. A major thrust of therapy would be to help the client gain such experience, through building or developing such relationships. And of course the therapeutic relationship itself will ideally be a wellspring of such experience. There are also many contemplative, meditative, and visualization practices that involve vivid imagination of a kind, caring, connection with others, ranging from religious figures such as Jesus, Mohammed, and Buddha to a future self or a past self, or even to a symbolic animal or fantasy creature. Practiced regularly, such exercises help the client to gain a sense of that loving connection with others, even if it hasn't happened much in real life.

Q: What are the most common barriers to self-compassion?

Russ: Good question. Helping our clients to develop self-compassion isn't always easy. It's especially difficult with people who have suffered from complex trauma or who have no personal experience of kind and caring relationships with others. In addition to these two issues, here are four more common barriers we'll encounter:

1. **Fusion with unworthiness:** The client fuses with self-narratives such as *I'm unworthy* or *I don't deserve kindness.* This usually requires skillful defusion (chapter 9).

2. **Overwhelming emotions:** The client becomes overwhelmed by emotions such as anxiety, sadness, guilt, or shame. This usually requires dropping anchor (chapter 7).

3. **Prejudice:** The client judges self-compassion harshly, as something "wishy-washy" or "new age," as something "religious," as a sign of weakness, or, in men, as something effeminate. We can deal with this by modifying our language and using the two friends metaphor (or a variant), as in the previous Q&A.

4. **Pointlessness:** The client fails to see the point of self-compassion: "How's this going to help me?" One simple way to address this is with a choice point (chapter 1). First, we identify self-hating or self-judgmental thoughts, and write them at the bottom. Then we identify the self-neglecting, self-defeating, or self-destructive behaviors that the client does when hooked, and we ask him if these are towards or away moves. He will almost certainly answer "away moves," so we can write those in at the top left. And now we can "sell" self-compassion as an unhooking skill, or we can identify it as a towards move, or both. (Of course, there are many other ways to clarify the purpose of self-compassion and make it relevant to the client's issues; again, the two friends metaphor is really useful for this.)

The Wrap-Up

Self-compassion—acknowledging our own suffering and responding with kindness and caring—is at the very heart of the ACT model, permeating all the other processes. And if we think of it in terms of six elements—acknowledging our pain, defusion from self-judgment, responding with kindness, acceptance, validation, and connectedness—then we can pretty much find a way to work with at least one or two of those elements in almost every session. This makes self-compassion a great starting point for therapy, a great end point for therapy, and a great ally whenever clients get stuck.

CHAPTER 11

Sticky Structure

Ever had one of those sessions where you just seemed to go round in circles, without getting anywhere? Where you did lots of talking but no skills building? Of course you have; we all have! When we structure our sessions effectively, with an explicit focus on working experientially, such unproductive sessions are much less likely.

Discussions in This Chapter:

- How can we structure our sessions to be more effective?
- Is it important to set an agenda for ACT sessions?
- What if clients dislike or resist an agenda?
- How do we set an agenda in ACT?
- How important is it to establish a DSM diagnosis?
- What if we have dual-diagnosis clients?
- How do we make our sessions more experiential?
- Can you clarify the distinction between talking and experiential work?
- What if the client just wants insight?
- Should we explain the purpose of exercises to clients?

Q: How can we structure our sessions to be more effective?

My sessions often feel a bit "all over the place." Any tips on how to structure a session for more impact, more process work?

Russ: There is no standard formula or structure for an ACT session. You are free to create your own, to do ACT as you like to do it. I personally am very flexible with how I structure my sessions. For some clients, they are very structured; for others, very free-flowing. However, the more chaotic, unfocused, distracted, unmotivated, or stuck the client is, the more structured my sessions get. That's because these types of clients *need* that structure, and so does the therapist if she wants to work effectively. So if you are ever stuck with your client, if he is not making progress, it's likely to help if you make your sessions more structured. I tend to (loosely) use the following format:

- Begin with a brief mindfulness exercise: usually five minutes or fewer. (I don't insist on this, though; if the client isn't keen on it, I don't do it. See chapter 2.)
- Do a quick inquiry about last session's homework and any between-session changes: usually five minutes max. If there were difficulties, put this on the agenda.
- Set an agenda for the session: usually five minutes or fewer. (Sometimes I do this step right from the outset instead.)
- Work through as many items on the agenda as possible.
- Finish with setting homework: usually five minutes or fewer.

Keep in mind that this is not an "official" ACT session structure. It's just one way of doing it. And I must admit, I vary enormously in the extent that I follow it.

Q: Is it important to set an agenda for ACT sessions?

Russ: There are no hard and fast rules on this. Some clients are very focused and motivated and come in to each session with a very specific agenda for what they want to work on. This makes our work much easier. However, many clients are vague about their concerns or have "no idea" what they want to work on. With them, it's very useful to spend a few minutes setting up an agenda near the start of the session (see the loose format listed in the above Q&A).

Agenda setting is also very useful for clients who just want to talk about their worries, their issues, their feelings, how bad life is, or how bad they feel, session after session, without any clearly defined purpose of such talk and without making any significant behavioral changes between sessions. Likewise, setting an agenda is crucial for clients with multiple problems who jump from problem to problem all session long, without ever formulating a constructive course of action. It also often goes down well with corporate or armed services clients; they tend to like the structure and the sense of efficiency and predictability it brings. So, although we don't *need* to formally set an agenda, it is very often useful to do so.

Q: What if clients dislike or resist an agenda?

Russ: We don't want to impose or insist on an agenda. We want to offer it in the service of making therapy more effective. Here's a simple script for you to modify. (Make sure you adapt and modify all the language to suit your way of speaking and your clientele.)

"Are you okay if we take a few minutes at the start of each session to establish a focus or an agenda for the session? To pick one important problem or area of life that you'd like to improve, so we can make that the main focus of the session? The reason for this is it makes our work much more efficient. If we are trying to deal with several different problems at once, it's very hard to deal effectively with any of them."

Often, clients have a very positive response, but if they seem unsure or adverse to it, we need to clarify for the client how setting an agenda makes the sessions more efficient.

For example, you might repeat, "As I said, if we are trying to deal with several different problems at once, it's very hard to deal effectively with any of them," and then ask, "So can we focus on just one today, so we can stay with it long enough to come up with a constructive course of action?"

Or: "If we don't have a clear agenda for the session—if we don't get clear about what we are wanting to achieve from it—the session will probably turn out like the last one; we'll do a lot of talking, but you won't leave here with anything practical to do to make your life better."

Q: How do we set an agenda in ACT?

Russ: One of the easiest ways is to use the bull's-eye (appendix 3). I often say something like "If we could focus in on just one of these quadrants for today's session, so we can really focus our time and energy on improving this area of your life, which one would you pick?"

Alternatively, we could ask the client to nominate a single problem, goal, or aspect of life to focus on (or in some cases, a specific skill to develop further). Often, clients will want to work on more than one thing and we will need to prioritize. This is how I typically prioritize (but feel free to modify this; there is no official or standard ACT protocol for this):

#1 Suicidality: If the client is actively suicidal, that obviously must take priority over everything else.

#2 Barriers to in-session therapy: Is the client doing anything in session that interferes with therapy (e.g., aggressive behavior, changing the topic, severe dissociation)?

#3 Follow-up to last session's commitment: What did the client commit to doing last session? Did she follow through? If so, what happened—both positive and negative outcomes? (Note: I usually do at least a five-minute review of this before we actually set the agenda, typically immediately after the opening mindfulness exercise. If there have been difficulties, we agree to put those on the agenda.)

#4 Barriers to between-session change: If the client didn't follow through, what stopped her? Identify the barriers (e.g., fusion, avoidance, remoteness from values, skills deficits) and address them.

#5 Main topic for today: There isn't always time, after all the above, but often there is. So let's establish the number one issue the client wants to address, after dealing with the other stuff.

#6 Additional topics for today: If there is time, after all the above, what are other important issues to address?

Q: How important is it to establish a DSM diagnosis?

I can see that diagnosing is pathologizing... AND, I can also see that a diagnosis can help us understand what is going on with a client. (And, of course, at least here in the USA, insurance demands the diagnosis.)

Russ: ACT is a transdiagnostic approach that utilizes the same core processes across a wide range of *DSM-5* (APA, 2013) disorders. From an ACT perspective, a DSM label is useful in a context where it functions to make life richer, fuller, more meaningful. (Indeed, the same goes for any type of label.) Having said that, just about the only context I can think of where a DSM label does actually enhance life is when it gives you access to effective treatment. Outside of that, it's hard (for me at least) to see much utility for it.

In fact, one of the biggest criticisms of DSM labels is that they have little or no treatment utility; the label does not actively guide us as to what we need to do in a therapy session.

And often such labels cause fusion in therapists. (For example, what thoughts and feelings arise in you when you are referred a client with a label such as "borderline personality disorder"? What assumptions do you make about therapy with this client? Diagnosing a client as borderline runs the real risk of triggering therapist hopelessness: "I can't help her. This client won't change; she's borderline.")

In ACT, if the label has granted the client access to effective treatment, it has served its purpose. Thereafter, we aim to help clients defuse from the label so that it doesn't become yet another part of a rigid, inflexible self-concept or yet another reason for why change is impossible.

With this in mind, I say to clients, "The label on the jam jar is not the jam. Let's put the label to one side; let's have a look at the jam." Then we can map out the core issues with a choice point (chapter 1), or a case formulation worksheet (appendix 1), or numerous other ACT tools. And once we've identified the fusion, avoidance, unworkable action, and so on (the "jam"), we can go in and target it effectively.

Q: What if we have dual-diagnosis clients?

These clients tend to have many problems in almost every aspect of life. How do we prioritize which DSM disorder to work on?

Russ: There's no standardized approach to this. From my own experience, I recommend a few basic first steps. A good starting point is to get informed consent (appendix 2) and establish rapport (chapter 4). Then after the first session, print out and work through an ACT Case Formulation worksheet (appendix 1) and conceptualize the entire presentation in terms of ACT.

Of course, you can establish a DSM diagnosis too, but to do ACT well, you'll want to put that to one side. Instead of looking at the client's issues in terms of treating two (or more) disorders, consider what you see in terms of overarching processes that cut across all disorders: fusion, avoidance, unworkable action, inflexible attention. This will immediately bring some clarity to the "mess."

In addition, establish behavioral goals for therapy as soon as possible (chapter 3). Explore with the client what she'll be doing differently in the future that will show you both that therapy has been successful.

Once all that's in place, my next step would be to establish an agenda at the start of every session (see Q&A on how to set an agenda, earlier in this chapter) to keep the work focused and realistic.

In terms of prioritizing which DSM diagnosis to work with first, we can start either with what's simplest and easiest (so we can make some rapid progress) or with what's most important to the client. For example, suppose the client is depressed and alcoholic. If the depression is the most important issue for him, I'd start there; then I'd deal with the alcohol problems as they show up or interfere with the work on depression. Note that the core ACT skills will cut across both disorders. If we teach defusion skills, they'll be useful with both thoughts that trigger depressive behaviors and thoughts that trigger drinking behaviors.

Q: How do we make our sessions more experiential?

Many ACT textbooks and trainers highlight the dangers of talking about ACT instead of working experientially with the core processes. Any tips on how to work more experientially?

Russ: Many therapists struggle with this. I know I did. Here are the approaches I recommend (after the first step, these can be done in any order):

- First, identify your own barriers to doing experiential work. Consider what stories you are fusing with; perhaps it's "The client won't like it or will think it's weird," "I'll screw it up," "I'm too tired," or "I'll start next time." Also consider what feelings you are unwilling to have: maybe fear, self-doubt, anxiety. Unwillingness to make room for anxiety is likely the number one thing holding most therapists back.

- Rehearse experiential moves in private, working with an imaginary client. I recommend you actually "say your lines" aloud, like an actor preparing for a role. (If you hate that idea, then silent mental rehearsal is a good fall-back option, but it's not as powerful in terms of preparation.) Of course, in session we don't want to be slavishly sticking to a formulaic script; we want to be flexible, improvising and adapting and innovating, and taking the work where it needs to go. However, doing this kind of rehearsal in private prepares you to work experientially in your session.

- Tell clients that you'd like to do more of this type of work because it's the most effective way to help them achieve their therapy goals—and get their consent to do it.
- Set an agenda at the start of each session and include in it a skill or process that you'll actively work on in the session.
- Get consent for, and then actually start sessions with, a mindfulness exercise, for example, a three-minute dropping anchor to set the tone (see chapter 2, Miserable Mindfulness).
- Find a colleague to practice with, and hold each other to working experientially. (Or better still, join an ACT peer supervision group.)

Q: Can you clarify the distinction between talking and experiential work?

This distinction is blurred at times for me. When giving the client a metaphor to work through, for example, for me, it's both talking and experiential. What is the distinction?

Russ: All experiential work involves talking. The distinction isn't experiential versus talking; it's experiential versus nonexperiential. *Experiential work* basically means actively building core ACT skills during the session. As a rough guide (to be held very lightly), you could think about it this way: if what you do in session is similar to the kind of heart-to-heart conversation you'd have with a close friend going through a rough patch, then it's probably not experiential; it's probably closer to typical supportive counseling.

But if what you do in session is quite different from the kind of heart-to-heart conversation you'd have with a close friend going through a rough patch, then it probably *is* experiential.

For example, with your close friend you'd likely be doing lots of validating, empathizing, normalizing, questioning, and then maybe some problem solving or strategizing. You probably wouldn't be asking her to notice what her mind is saying, to unhook, to check in and notice what's happening in her body, and to explore her values. This is only a very rough guide—there are lots of exceptions—but I hope it gives you something to go on. Ask yourself: are we having a chat, or are we building a skill?

Q: What if the client just wants insight?

Russ: It depends on what you mean by "insight." Some clients, when asked what they want from therapy, reply, "I want to understand myself" or "I want to understand why I keep doing this." My reply is, "That's a given. This work will give you a lot of insight into yourself, a lot of understanding as to why you think and feel and act the way you do. So, what else do you want to get from our work together?"

Now some clients have little or no insight into (or awareness and understanding of) their own thoughts, feelings, and actions when they first come to therapy. We'd expect such clients to develop this quite rapidly as we work through the ACT model. We can think of "lacking insight" as a skills deficit rather than a fixed trait. As clients develop their mindfulness skills, this leads to self-awareness, other-awareness, awareness of consequences of their actions, and awareness of their own thoughts and feelings—all of which leads to "insight."

Q: Should we explain the purpose of exercises to clients?

Russ: I'm so glad you asked. I think sometimes there is pressure in ACT trainings to be overly experiential, to the detriment of psychoeducation. I think it's important to explain what a new skill or exercise involves before doing it, to make sure the client understands its purpose—how it's relevant to and potentially useful for achieving his therapy goals. Without such psychoeducation, we can expect confusion about or resistance to experiential work with clients.

For example, many therapists take clients into mindful breathing exercises without clarifying the purpose, without specifying what they are hoping will happen and how it links to the client's behavioral goals for therapy. When this happens, the client is almost always going to assume it's a relaxation technique, and the purpose of it is to reduce anxiety and feel calm—which of course is not the aim at all in an ACT approach. Indeed, relaxation often happens, but in ACT, that's a bonus, not the main aim. (See chapter 2: Miserable Mindfulness.)

So I recommend that we be crystal clear about the purpose of the exercise up front: What's the aim of it? How's it relevant to the specific problem or issue the client wants to address? What do we hope will happen?

We don't want to explain the purpose in great detail. Just enough to (a) make it clear what the purpose is, and (b) show how it's relevant to the client's therapy goals. Here's an example: "You said you wanted to be a better mom, and you've identified that means being more attentive and caring toward your children. And you've found when you get hooked by anxious thoughts and feelings, that's hard for you to do. So this exercise is to help you learn to unhook from those anxious thoughts and feelings and refocus your attention on what is most important to you. It's not a relaxation technique to get rid of the anxiety; it's a way of learning how to act well in the presence of anxiety: how to let the anxiety come and stay and go in its own good time, without struggling with it—so you can focus your attention and energy on what matters most to you."

We really need to be careful with our language, so clients don't get the wrong idea. For example, many therapists will say things like, "This is about letting go of your thoughts." Unfortunately, clients will almost always interpret "letting them go" as "making them go away." So "letting go" is a phrase I rarely use, and when I do use it, I modify it to "letting them come and stay and go in their own good time, without struggling with them and without getting swept away by them." It's a good habit to get into this way of speaking—not just about thoughts, but feelings, emotions, memories, urges, and sensations.

The Wrap-Up

Notice how in chapter after chapter, I keep coming back to three basics that so many therapists skip over: informed consent, establishing goals for therapy, and clarity about the purpose of exercises. In addition to these fundamentals, it's really worth taking the time to structure your sessions effectively. They'll be far more productive for your clients, and far more fulfilling for you.

CHAPTER 12

Measly Motivation

We all know how challenging it is to work with unmotivated clients. (And how much easier it is to work with the highly motivated.) The more stuck the client is, the more deeply entrenched in his unworkable behavior, the more we tend to struggle. We may experience difficult emotions such as guilt, anxiety, or hopelessness, or fuse with all sorts of unhelpful judgments about the client. And we commonly feel frustration, irritation, or anger. (Have you ever wanted to shake a client? I know I have!) At times like this, it's so important to practice ACT on ourselves: to unhook, get present, and appreciate our clients as if they are rainbows, not roadblocks.

Discussions in This Chapter:

- How do we motivate unmotivated clients who won't "do any work"?
- How do we motivate clients to do "homework"?
- How do we help clients sustain new behaviors?
- How can we help clients who keep forgetting to do "homework"?
- What if clients say, "I know what to do, but I just don't do it"?
- What if clients say, "I have no motivation"?

Q: How do we motivate unmotivated clients who won't "do any work"?

Russ: First we want to deconstruct the lack of motivation. What's underpinning it? Fusion with hopelessness, helplessness, *it's too hard*, fear of failure? Experiential avoidance of anxiety, shame, other uncomfortable emotions? Remoteness from values? Unclear therapy goals? Insufficient skills to take action? Deficits in problem solving? Then we want to target those factors with relevant ACT processes.

A great place to start is by putting in place all the basics for making sessions effective: making sure we have informed consent to do ACT (appendix 2), establishing behavioral goals for therapy (chapter 3), structuring our sessions and establishing a clear agenda (chapter 11), and helping our clients defuse from all their reasons why therapy can't or won't work (appendix 4). Most of the time, this will get our clients motivated to "do the work."

Q: How do we motivate clients to do "homework"?

Often, clients come back to the next session without having done their homework. How do we get them to follow through?

Russ: Well, first off, never use the word *homework*, because most clients hate it. Use alternative terms like *experiment, play around with it, try it out, practice it, give it a go and see what happens, try it on for size.*

Second, make sure the client sees the point of it. Ask her: "Do you see how this could be useful for you with XYZ?" (XYZ = the behavioral goals you've established for therapy; chapter 3). If the client answers no, it's essential to make this clear. Otherwise, why would she bother to do these new things, especially if they bring up discomfort?

Third, here's a lovely tip I picked up from ACT pioneer Kirk Strosahl. Ask the client to scale, from zero to ten, "How likely does it seem to you right now that you will actually do this? Ten means 'Yes, I'll definitely do it. Nothing will stop me.' And zero means 'There's no way I'm going to actually do this. I'm just kidding myself.'"

If the client answers seven or higher, that's a good sign. But if she scores six or lower, I'd say, "Hmmm, only a six? That doesn't sound too promising. Let's see if we can come up with something you can be more confident about." Then make the goal smaller and simpler and easier—or maybe even change it altogether—until the client can score at least a seven. Finally, link it all to values: "When you are doing this, will that be a towards move?" or "Will this be moving toward the bull's-eye?" or "What values will this be living each time you do this?"

Q: How do we help clients sustain new behaviors?

I often find clients start making behavioral changes but soon give up and fall back into their old behaviors. How can we help them (a) remember to do their new behaviors and (b) keep them going?

Russ: That's a big question, so it's going to require a big answer. The simple fact is, it's a lot easier to start some new type of life-enhancing behavior than it is to keep it going. How can we sustain new patterns of behavior, until we've done them for so long they become habitual? Well, there are hundreds, if not thousands, of tools out there to help our clients, and of course ourselves, with this challenge, but we can pretty much bundle them all into what I like to call the *seven Rs*: Reminders, Records, Rewards, Routines, Relationships, Reflecting, and Restructuring. Let's take a look at each.

A. *Reminders*

We can create all sorts of simple tools to help remind us of the new behavior we wish to persist with. For example, we might create a pop-up or a screen saver on our computer or mobile phone with an important word, phrase, or symbol that reminds us to act mindfully or to utilize a particular value. We might use the old favorite of writing a message on a card and sticking it on the fridge or propping it against the bathroom mirror or taping it to the car dashboard. Or we might write something in a diary or calendar or in the notes app of a smartphone. We might write just one word, like "Breathe" or "Pause" or "Patience," or we might use an acronym like "A.C.T." or "S.T.O.P.," or a phrase like "Letting go" or "Caring and compassionate." Alternatively, we might put a brightly colored sticker on the strap of our wristwatch or the back of our smartphone or the keyboard of our computer, so that every time we use these devices, the sticker reminds us to do the new behavior.

B. *Records*

We can keep a record of our behavior throughout the day, writing down when and where we do the new behavior, and what the benefits are; and also when and where we do the old behavior, and what the costs are. Any diary or notebook, on paper or on a computer screen, can serve this purpose.

C. *Rewards*

When we do some form of new behavior that involves mindfully acting on our values, hopefully that will be rewarding in its own right. However, we can help to reinforce the new behavior with additional rewards. One form of reward is kind, encouraging self-talk, such as saying to yourself, "Well done. You did it!" Another form of reward is sharing your success and progress with a loved one who you know will respond positively. On the other hand, you might prefer more material rewards. For example, if you sustain this new behavior for a whole week, you buy or do something that you really like, such as get a massage or buy some new music.

D. *Routines*

If you get up every morning at the same time to meditate or exercise or do yoga, over time that will become habitual. In other words, you won't have to think so hard about doing it; it will start to come naturally; it will require less "willpower"; it will become a part of your regular routine. So experiment: see if you can find some way to build a regular routine or ritual around your new behavior, so it starts to become part of your way of life. For example, if you drive home from work, then every night, just before you get out of your car, you might do two minutes of mindful breathing, and reflect on what values you want to live by when you walk through the front door into your home.

E. *Relationships*

It's easier to study if you have a study buddy, easier to exercise if you have an exercise buddy. In Alcoholics Anonymous programs, they team you up with a sponsor who is there to help you stay sober when the going gets tough. So can you find a kind, caring, encouraging person who can help support you with your new behavior? Maybe you can check in with this person on a regular basis and share how well you are doing, as mentioned in Rewards. Or maybe you can email your support person the Records you've been keeping. Or maybe you can use the other person as a Reminder; ask him to remind you to do the new behavior, if and when that would be useful. For example, you might say to your partner, "When you see me worrying, can you please remind me to do some mindful breathing?"

F. *Reflecting*

Regularly take time to reflect on how you are behaving, and what effect it is having on your life. You can do this via writing it down (Records) or in discussion with another person (Relationships). Or you can do this as a mental exercise throughout the day, or just before you go to bed, or just as you're waking up in the morning.

You simply take a few moments to reflect on questions such as *How am I doing? What am I doing that's working? What am I doing that's not working? What can I do more of, or less of, or differently?* Make sure you also reflect on the times that you *stop* doing the new behavior and fall back into the old one. Notice what triggers those relapses and setbacks, and notice what it costs you—for instance, how do you suffer?—when that happens. This doesn't mean beat yourself up! This means nonjudgmentally reflect on the genuine costs to your health and well-being of falling back into old habits, and use your awareness of the suffering this causes you to help motivate yourself to get back on track.

G. *Restructuring*

We can often restructure our environment to make our new behavior easier and therefore more likely to be sustained. For example, if the new behavior is healthy eating, we can restructure the kitchen to make that easier: get rid of or hide the junk food, and stock the fridge and pantry with the healthy stuff. If we want to go to the gym in the morning, we could pack up our sports gear in our gym bag and place it by the side of the bed or somewhere else obvious and convenient, so it's all ready to go as soon as we get up. (And of course, when we see our gym bag lying there, it acts as a Reminder.)

So there you have it. The idea is to first introduce your clients to *the seven Rs: Reminders, Records, Rewards, Routines, Relationships, Reflecting, and Restructuring.* And then, you can invite them to be creative; they can mix and match these methods to their heart's content, to create their own set of tools for lasting change. Good luck with it!

Q: How can we help clients who keep forgetting to do "homework"?

Russ: First, let's normalize it. I say to clients, "You are so like me! So often I say, 'I'm going to do this, that, and the other'...and then I completely forget to do it!"

If the client looks anxious, worried, guilty, or ashamed, we might explore this: "You look a bit concerned. What are you feeling in your body right now? What's your mind telling you?" We can segue into defusion from self-criticism, and acceptance and self-compassion in response to guilt, shame, or anxiety.

After that, we should check the relevance of the homework task: does the client see it as useful and relevant to her established behavioral goals for therapy? Is it truly important to the client? Aligned with her values?

Finally, we can collaboratively help the client to generate a plan to help her remember next time. We can use any combination of the seven Rs mentioned in the previous Q&A.

Q: What if clients say, "I know what to do, but I just don't do it"?

For example, some clients say things like, "Oh yes, I know I need to unhook myself and drop anchor, but I just don't manage to do that."

Russ: I've had many such clients. It's generally good to begin with validating and normalizing: "That's so normal, and so commonplace. I've had that issue myself, many times. This stuff is simple, but not easy."

After that, my next step is often asking, "Can we do it right now?"

We then run through the skill and spend a few minutes actively practicing it.

The next step is to ask, "So how is this relevant to the issues that have brought you here?" (See the Q&A "Should we explain the purpose of exercises to clients?" in chapter 11.)

Once the client has made those links, we could ask, "Is it okay if we practice doing more of this kind of thing throughout our sessions—so you can get better at it, and it comes more naturally to you? That way you're more likely to remember to do it between sessions."

Of course, all of this should be infused with self-acceptance and self-compassion; we are all human, we all forget to do this stuff.

The next step, then, is to schedule time to practice, and make full use of the seven Rs to maximize the chances of following through.

And the final step: validate that one of the hardest things about any newly learned behavior is remembering to actually do it.

Q: What if clients say, "I have no motivation"?

Russ: The first thing to consider is, what's the function of that behavior? What's triggering it, and what's reinforcing it? For example, is she fused with hopelessness? If so, defusion is required. On the other hand, is she completely disconnected from her values? If so, values clarification is required, followed by the explicit linking of those values to the desired behavioral changes. Or is her aim to avoid the anxiety that goes with trying new behaviors? If so, acceptance of anxious thoughts and feelings is needed.

On top of that, we want to unpack the term *motivation* itself. Because almost always, when people say "I don't have the motivation," this boils down to "I don't *feel* like doing it." The underlying story is "When I *feel* like doing it—when I *feel* energized, enthusiastic, happy, calm, confident, excited, in the mood—then I will do it. And until I feel that way, I won't do it." You can see how this is yet another manifestation of the emotional control agenda: *I need to control how I feel before I can do what matters.* If the client is deeply attached to this agenda, we'll need to bring in creative hopelessness (chapter 8) to undermine it.

The Wrap-Up

We've focused a lot on the "I've got no motivation" story in this chapter. In wrapping up, I'd like to briefly mention its two close relatives: "I've got no discipline" and "I've got no willpower." Our minds can easily hook us with these stories and turn them into self-fulfilling prophecies. The fantasy our minds conjure up is that there is something called discipline or willpower, and once we possess this thing, we'll be able to start doing what really matters. This fantasy is reinforced by everyday language: when we hear, "It takes discipline to get up early in the morning and go to the gym," it sounds like there is some magic potion called discipline, and until we have this magic potion, we can't get up early and go to the gym.

Unfortunately, if we buy into this notion, then we encounter one of two problems:

> *Problem one: we go off in search of the magic potion—reading books or taking courses to try and develop more willpower or discipline—instead of committing to action here and now.*
>
> *Problem two: we decide the magic potion is unobtainable, and we give up on doing what matters because we "don't have enough" discipline or willpower.*

So we want to be clear with our clients: there is no chemical, hormone, gene, or part of the brain called discipline or willpower. These words are merely descriptive labels; they are ways of describing a pattern of committed action. When we say someone has discipline or willpower, all we mean is this: this person consistently commits to acting on his values and doing what is required to achieve his goals—even when he doesn't feel like doing it. Does this sound familiar at all? I'll bet it does. We all fall into these language traps at times. But the good news is we can all use ACT to escape them.

CHAPTER 13

Obnoxious Outcomes

Therapists often ask me questions that begin with "Is it possible a client might react like this…" The answer to such questions is always yes. As the saying goes, "Whatever can go wrong, will go wrong." Sooner or later even our most tried and trusted interventions will backfire, fail miserably, or have the opposite results of those intended. (Of course, this happens in every model of therapy—nothing unique about ACT there!)

Defusion techniques can sometimes cause fusion. Acceptance exercises can sometimes get clients struggling even more with their pain than before. Mindfulness exercises can put people to sleep. Values exercises can trigger an outburst of anger or fusion with shame. These negative outcomes don't happen that often (luckily for us!), but sooner or later, they will. So the aim of this chapter is to prepare yourself in advance for such eventualities. After all, there's another saying that goes, "Forewarned is forearmed."

Discussions in This Chapter:

- How can we reduce the risk of exercises failing or going wrong?
- What can we do when ACT interventions don't go well?
- Should we give up or persist with an exercise if a client reacts negatively?

Q: How can we reduce the risk of exercises failing or going wrong?

Some of my clients have had negative reactions to various experiential ACT exercises, and that's really knocked my confidence.

Russ: This kind of thing happens to all ACT therapists sooner or later; it's inevitable. But we certainly can reduce the risk by laying those basic foundations I keep mentioning: getting informed consent (appendix 2), establishing behavioral goals (chapter 3) and being very clear about the purpose of exercises and how they are relevant to and helpful for the client's issues.

In addition to all that, it's really useful to use the language of "experiments." We can repeatedly come back to the notion that we never know for sure what the outcome will be of any exercise, technique, or practice. For example, we might say prior to an exercise, "I'm asking you to try this because I think it will be helpful. However, there's no way for us to know for sure what will happen; it's always an experiment. Can we give it a go, see what happens?" This facilitates an open, curious mindset (in both client and therapist). Unexpected results are always easier to handle if we've been liberally using the language of "experiments."

Q: What can we do when ACT interventions don't go well?

Russ: Some general advice: when anything in a therapy session fails, goes wrong, or backfires (in any model of therapy, not just ACT), stay calm! We won't *feel* calm, of course. But we can *act* calmly. We may feel anxious, sad, frustrated, guilty, fearful, or angry; we may have all sorts of unhelpful thoughts about ourselves, the client, the exercise, or even the ACT model itself. But even with all those thoughts and feelings present, we can still *act calmly*.

In other words, let's use ACT on ourselves in these situations: defuse from our thoughts about screwing it up, accept our feelings of anxiety, drop anchor, and get fully present. And even though we don't *feel* calm, we can model the quality of calmness through our voice, our words, our body posture, and our actions.

Of course, not only do we drop anchor for ourselves, we also help our clients to do the same.

If the client is upset or fused or struggling in any way—sad, angry, frightened, shaken, disappointed, frustrated, dissociated, overwhelmed—then a good first step is to help him drop anchor, using any of the methods we've previously practiced in sessions (see chapter 7). And if we haven't yet taken the client experientially through dropping anchor, or some other mindfulness-based grounding exercise, then now is the ideal time to do so.

Having grounded the client (and ourselves), we want to model openness and curiosity as we explore what just happened. This is much easier to do if we first set the exercise up as an experiment, as mentioned in the previous Q&A. For example, we could say something like "Gosh. Well that experiment didn't go as I'd hoped. I'm so sorry; I can see you've had a bad reaction. This wasn't what I expected at all."

From there we'd want to explore what actually did happen, with the aim of finding something useful in the experience: either something directly relevant to the client's therapy goals or something more generally useful for developing psychological flexibility. Useful questions could include:

- What happened just then?
- What thoughts, feelings, memories showed up?
- What did your mind hook you with?
- What feelings are showing up for you now?
- What's your mind saying now?

We also want to consider: is an apology warranted? If so, let's be quick and genuine. For example, we might say, "I'm sorry. I didn't expect that to happen. I can see that you're upset. I hope this hasn't put you off working this way."

It's generally useful at this point to remind the client of the rationale for the exercise. For example, "I'm sorry. As I said to you before we started the exercise, I was hoping it would help you unhook from difficult thoughts, but unfortunately, it looks like you ended up more hooked than before." Or "I'm sorry. I was hoping that exercise would help you stop struggling with difficult feelings, but it looks like you actually ended up struggling even more than before."

After all that, we can now say something like "I didn't want or expect this to happen, but given it has happened, can we look at this as a learning opportunity?"

Among other things, we can learn

- more of the many different ways your mind can hook you,
- more of the many different ways you can get pulled into a struggle with thoughts and feelings, and
- how our minds easily make life difficult for us—and can interfere with anything we try to do.

Q: Should we give up or persist with an exercise if a client reacts negatively?

Russ: It depends. At times, the best thing to do, after we have run through the strategy outlined in the previous Q&A, is to say something like "I'd hate to give up on this important part of our work here. Can we try something different, that hopefully will work better for you?" Then—again emphasizing that *it's an experiment*, and again *clarifying the rationale* for doing it—try something different. This might just be a variation on the same exercise, intervention, or technique, or it might be a radically different one that serves the same purpose.

However, at times, rather than doing something different, it's a good idea to come back to where we were before the exercise backfired. For example, suppose we've been using "noticing and naming" for defusion, but on this occasion it backfired and the client got more fused. Then we might say, "So notice, now your mind has hooked you with something fresh. So this is a good challenge—let's see if you can unhook from this new stuff. See if you can step back and notice what these new thoughts are; notice how they're hooking you, pulling you in. Can I get you to try naming these thoughts?"

Then we can guide the client through naming: "I'm having thoughts that this doesn't work" or "Here's my mind finding new ways to beat me up." (And if this still doesn't work, we can go back to dropping anchor.)

Likewise, if we were working on values or goal setting immediately prior to the unexpected reaction, we might say, "Well, your mind kind of hooked us there, pulled us off track. Is it okay if we get back to where we were?"

And if we've already introduced "the part that notices" or the "observing self" (chapter 14: Slippery Self-as-Context), we can now use this as an intervention to help with any or all of the aforementioned responses. For example, we can ask the client to "use that part of you that notices" to:

- Drop an anchor (contacting the present: excellent for grounding and a useful first step in defusion or acceptance)
- Step back and notice the thoughts that just hooked you (often a useful first step in defusion)
- Step back and notice the feelings you're struggling with (often a useful first step in acceptance)

The Wrap-Up

Things can and will go wrong in therapy, and there's no getting past it. But if we stay calm, respond compassionately, and model openness and curiosity, we can usually turn these happenings into positive learning experiences. Naturally when our interventions have crummy consequences, this triggers a lot of anxiety and self-doubt in us, so we really do need to practice ACT on ourselves: drop anchor, unhook from the "lousy therapist" story, and hold ourselves kindly.

CHAPTER 14

Slippery Self-as-Context

Self-as-context (SAC) *is arguably the single most confusing and tricky part of the ACT model. It baffles and bothers many ACT therapists—even those with advanced training. And it certainly freaked me out when I first started ACT; I didn't have a clue about what to do with it or how to make it relevant to clients.*

At least one major part of the confusion about SAC is that the term has two different meanings in ACT. They're both interlinked, but they're also significantly different from each other. Most of the time in ACT, when people use the term self-as-context, they mean it as a synonym for the observing self: that transcendent aspect of a human being that underpins all noticing and observing of one's inner and outer world. You could call this "meta-awareness" or "pure awareness" or even "pure consciousness" if you prefer, because it's the awareness of one's awareness, or the noticing of one's noticing, or the consciousness of one's consciousness. (Note: To call it a "self" or a "part" or an "aspect" is to speak metaphorically; technically, it's a repertoire of behavior.)

Less commonly, SAC is used to mean "flexible perspective taking." Flexible perspective taking underlies many ACT skills, including defusion, acceptance, contacting the present moment, self-awareness, empathy, compassion, theory of mind, and mental projection into the future or past.

Pretty significant difference, huh? No wonder there's so much bafflement! For the rest of this chapter, when we talk of SAC, I will be using the first meaning given above (the observing self), as this is the one you'll find in most ACT textbooks.

Discussions in This Chapter:

- Is SAC implicit in all mindfulness?
- Do we have to make SAC explicit in therapy?
- But is it essential that clients experience a transcendent sense of self?
- So can clients ever develop a transcendent sense of self without explicit SAC work?
- Are there ways to gently ease into SAC without plunging in the deep end?
- How can we talk about SAC without making it weird or mystical?
- What's the link between SAC and wandering attention?
- What are the most effective metaphors for SAC?
- How do we help clients who "get the metaphor" intellectually but still don't experience SAC?
- How can we respond when clients say, "What's the point of this?"
- How can we respond when clients say, "I don't get it"?

Q: Is SAC implicit in all mindfulness?

I've read that SAC is implicit in the other three core mindfulness skills of ACT: defusion, acceptance, and contacting the present moment. But I don't quite understand what that means. Can you clarify?

Russ: Sure. If you're noticing thoughts, feelings, actions, your body, and the world around you, then it's implicit that there's a part of you, or an aspect of you, doing the noticing; and that part or aspect of you is what we call SAC or observing self.

Sometimes I explain this to clients like this: "It's a bit like this: if you're eating chocolate, you're using a part of you that we call the mouth, and if you're smelling roses, you're using a part of you that we call the nose. But when you're doing all this noticing stuff, well, we don't have a word in everyday language for the part of you that does that. Are you okay if we call it…(*therapist picks an appropriate term*)?"

Q: Do we have to make SAC explicit in therapy?

If SAC is already implicit in defusion, acceptance, and contacting the present moment, why would we bother to make it explicit? Do we really need to? I often feel like I'm making SAC explicit without a clear reason for it, other than it's a part of ACT, so I should do it.

Russ: That's an incredibly common experience in ACT. I can remember doing the same thing myself. I'd think, *Oh, suppose I should do some self-as-context now* and start shoehorning it into the session without really knowing why I was doing it.

So let's be clear. We definitely don't *have to* make SAC explicit to do ACT effectively. There are five main indications for making SAC explicit:

A. To facilitate defusion—especially from the conceptualized self

B. To facilitate acceptance

C. To facilitate flexible contact with the present moment

D. To access a stable sense of self

E. To access a transcendent sense of self

Explicit work with SAC can enhance the other three mindfulness skills: defusion, acceptance, and contacting the present moment—points a, b, and c. But it's certainly not necessary to do SAC work for those purposes. We can help clients develop really good skills in defusion, acceptance, and contacting the present moment and readily defuse from the conceptualized self without ever making SAC explicit. So for the purposes of a, b, and c, we can consider explicit SAC work as an optional extra.

But what about when it comes to accessing a stable sense of self? A client may have an *un*stable sense of self for a variety of reasons, including change in employment (new job, promotion, unemployment, retirement), change in role (becoming a parent, or grown-up kids leaving home), change in health (illness, sickness, aging, disability), change in financial status (major increase or decrease in wealth), dissociative states (with the extreme of dissociative identity disorder), and fusion with rapidly changing self-judgments (with the extreme being the moment-to-moment changes common in borderline personality disorder: one moment *I'm a good mom* and the next, *I'm a terrible mom*).

Explicit SAC work can help the client to access a stable sense of self—a "calm center" from which she can notice her changing thoughts and feelings, her changing roles and circumstances, her changing self-judgments and self-narratives, her changing body and health, and so on. Now this calm center can be developed without SAC, but SAC does seem to build a more stable sense of self in many people.

So that leaves us with the fifth indication for explicit SAC work: to access a transcendent sense of self. Some ACT exercises are specifically designed to instigate and reinforce this experience; they highlight that there is more to you than your body, thoughts, feelings, and memories; more to you than the roles you play and the actions you take; that all these things are continually changing throughout your life, but the aspect of you that notices them all is unchanging and always available. Unlike a, b, c, and d, experiencing this transcendent self is only likely to happen through explicit SAC work.

Q: But is it essential that clients experience a transcendent sense of self?

Russ: No, it's not. Often, it's useful. But it's not essential. It's arguably most useful for survivors of trauma, disaster, severe illness or injury, or other "life-shattering" events: a "part of you" transcended those events and came through unharmed (even if your body was physically harmed).

Q: So can clients ever develop a transcendent sense of self without explicit SAC work?

Russ: For sure. It will almost certainly take a lot longer, but, for example, many formal mindfulness meditation practices facilitate this experience over time.

So, bringing this right back to the earlier question: no, we don't have to make SAC explicit. And if we're going to do so, first let's be clear in our own mind: for what purpose are we doing this? What do we hope to achieve by making it explicit? Is it really necessary? Is it the best or easiest way to achieve what we are hoping for? Especially consider these last two questions if your main intention is one of options a, b, c, or d mentioned above.

Q: Are there ways to gently ease into SAC, without plunging in the deep end?

I often hesitate to bring in big SAC metaphors like the chessboard and pieces (Hayes et al., 1999), or long SAC exercises like the Continuous You exercise (Hayes et al., 1999). Are there easier, smaller, gentler ways of bringing SAC explicitly into a session?

Russ: Yes, for sure. We can start planting the seeds for explicit SAC work early on, without making a big deal out of it. We can then water these seeds in later sessions, when we want them to sprout (for the specific purposes, a–e, outlined in the earlier Q&A).

The way I like to plant these seeds early on in therapy is by mentioning SAC in the form of a passing comment, as part of some other intervention. For example, as I'm doing the first dropping anchor exercise with a client, after I've asked her to "notice X, notice Y, notice Z," I'll casually mention, "So there's a part of you that can notice everything."

I'll often then add, "And we're going to be using that part of you throughout our work together…to help you in various ways."

The client will usually nod or say "uh-huh." On occasion, she may look blank or confused, but I don't mind; at this point, I'm not wanting to explore

SAC, I'm just planting seeds for later work. So unless the client protests, "I don't know what you mean!" or something like that, I won't try to clarify; I'll just carry on with whatever exercise we are in the midst of doing.

We can easily plant SAC seeds while doing any type of mindfulness exercise, whether it's defusion, acceptance, or contacting the present moment, by using phrases like these:

- "As you notice X, be aware you're noticing."
- "There's X and there's a part of you noticing X."

For example, during mindful breathing, we may say, "There's your breath, coming and going—and there's a part of you noticing the breath." Or during Leaves on a Stream (Hayes et al., 1999), we may say, "So there's a part of you that's creating thoughts and putting them on leaves—and another part of you that's noticing them come and go."

Or if we want to go into a bit more detail: "Notice there are two parts of you involved in this. There's your thinking self (or "your mind") that's doing a few different things: creating imagery of the stream and the leaves, creating thoughts, putting those thoughts onto the leaves, and probably creating judgments or other thoughts about the exercise itself and how you're doing with it. And there's another part of you that's noticing all of that."

Or we may say, while debriefing an exercise, "So were there times you got hooked—pulled into your thoughts, lost track of the exercise? And then you noticed that had happened? And then you kind of unhooked yourself, and got back into the exercise—started noticing XYZ again? See, I find that really interesting. There's this part of you that's able to notice when you are hooked, and not only that, but also help you get unhooked, and refocus on what you're doing."

Q: How can we talk about SAC without making it weird or mystical?

A lot of the time, scripts for SAC exercises and metaphors seem to be highly abstract or veering on the mystical. Are there any more down-to-earth ways of speaking about it?

Russ: For sure. Rather than making SAC out to be some weird or mystical experience, we want to link it to everyday experiences the client can readily relate to. For example, in any type of mindfulness training it's common to highlight the way that our attention wanders so readily and the importance of refocusing, of bringing our attention back. On the hexaflex, this comes under "contacting the present moment." Now if we want to make self-as-context explicit, a simple way to do so is by pointing out *there's a part of you that notices your attention has wandered.* So, for instance, we might say something like this:

> Have you ever been watching TV/reading a book/chatting to someone/listening to your teacher…and suddenly you realized you were so caught up in your thoughts that you have no idea what just happened on the TV show/not taken in a word you've been reading/no idea what the other person has been talking about/no idea what the teacher just said? So there's a part of you that's able to notice when you're caught up in your thoughts (or distracted, or lost) and bring you back again—help you to refocus on where you are, what's going on, what you need to do.

If we decide the time is right to go further (and we're clear about the purpose of doing so), then we can readily segue into SAC from comments like those mentioned above by saying, "And you know what? There is no word in everyday language for this part of you. We just don't have one. I like to call it…"

The therapist can now introduce her preferred term, such as "part that notices," "noticing self," or "observing self."

With many clients, I usually focus on SAC explicitly only after we've done a fair bit of practice in session of defusion, acceptance, and contacting the present moment skills (not counting those "seed-planting" interventions in earlier sessions). As these three skills all involve noticing, we can then easily segue into explicit SAC work at this point by asking, "So I've been encouraging you to do a whole heap of noticing. Noticing your body, your breathing, your actions, your thoughts, feelings, emotions, memories, the raisin/piece of chocolate you're eating. So what is this aspect of you that's been doing all the noticing? Can we take a few moments to explore it? Did you know that there is no word in everyday language for this part of you? We just don't have one. I like to call it..."

We can also make SAC explicit with the choice point (chapter 1). We can point to the diagram and say, "So there's a lot of noticing going on here: noticing your thoughts and feelings, noticing the situations you find difficult, noticing when and where you get hooked, noticing your towards and away moves, noticing what you care about, and who matters to you, and so on. So what is this part of you that does all the noticing?"

Q: What's the link between SAC and wandering attention?

I like the example you gave above about linking SAC to wandering attention, but I'm not fully getting it. Can you say more about this?

Russ: There are many ways of highlighting SAC through the concept of attention wandering. You can use these with any sport, hobby, or activity the client is interested in. If a client isn't into anything specific, I often use a generic version based on tennis.

The Tennis Metaphor

You're playing tennis, and the ball is coming toward you... Where does your attention need to be? That's right, on the ball! But hey, at the side of the tennis court, there's someone wearing really bizarre clothes, and someone else playing a radio annoyingly loud, and there's your mom/dad/friend watching you, and OMG, they're filming you on their phone! And now your attention is no longer on the ball. And what happens? That's right. You miss the shot. But if you're very lucky, you can notice this with enough time to correct it; you notice your attention has wandered away from the ball, and you bring it back again, in time to hit it.

It's great to flesh out such metaphors by adding in various thoughts as sources of distraction: "Your mind starts whirring, *Will I hit the ball? Will I miss it? Why's Mom filming me? Do I look silly? Am I holding my racket correctly? Where should my feet be? Who's that person with the radio?* And the more attention you give to all those thoughts, the less attention you're giving to the tennis ball!"

Hopefully you can see how to modify this metaphor to any activity your client enjoys—from painting and drawing to football to dancing to playing the saxophone. Start off by clarifying: "In order to do this well, where does your attention need to be?" Then introduce sources of distraction, which may be external, such as people watching or annoying sounds, or internal, such as the mind's commentary or feelings in the body.

Finally, ask something like "So what is this part of you that notices your attention has wandered and helps you to bring it back again?"

Q: What are the most effective metaphors for SAC?

There are so many metaphors for SAC, I get overwhelmed. Can you tell me which are the best ones?

Russ: Well, it depends on what we're aiming to achieve. In other words, the best or most effective metaphors for what purpose? As you said, there are many metaphors available to us, and they all have strengths and weaknesses. (Technical note: even when referring to SAC as "observing self" or "noticing self" or "a part of you" or "aspect of you," we are speaking metaphorically. It's not literally a self or a part or an aspect; it's a repertoire of psychological behavior.)

My number one preferred metaphor for SAC is the stage show metaphor (Harris, 2009a): "Life is like a stage show; and on that stage are all your thoughts and feelings, and everything you can see, hear, touch, taste, and smell. And that show is changing all the time. And there's a part of you that can step back and watch the show, zoom in and take in the details, or zoom out and take in the big picture."

One class of metaphors illustrates SAC in terms of flexible attention. For example, Turrell and Bell (2016) like to use the metaphor of a sports commentator watching a match, keeping a curious eye on all the players and action. Other options include a teacher on yard duty, a general watching his troops on a battlefield, or a security guard watching a set of TV monitors.

Another class of SAC metaphors is about shifting your viewpoint to gain more information or see things from a new perspective, such as standing in the middle of a busy playground versus watching from a second-story window, viewing a scene from the ground versus from a balcony, or standing in the middle of the football field versus watching from the sidelines. SAC is the part of you that enables these shifts in viewpoints.

A third class of metaphors compares SAC to a "safe place" inside you where you can open up and make room for difficult thoughts and feelings, or watch them flowing by without getting swept away. This aspect of SAC is often highlighted in the classic metaphors that go back to the earliest days of ACT: the chessboard (this part of you is like the chessboard; thoughts and feelings are like the pieces) and the sky and the weather (this part of you is like the sky; thoughts and feelings are like the weather). If we want to highlight the transcendent self or stable self, we'd emphasize that the chess pieces (or weather) constantly change(s), but the board (or sky) doesn't.

Q: How do we help clients who "get the metaphor" intellectually but still don't experience SAC?

Russ: This is not uncommon. If and when we decide to make SAC explicit, we want to watch out for the common therapist trap of staying too intellectual or metaphorical. If we want clients to actually experience a stable sense of self or transcendent sense of self, we are unlikely to achieve this purely through the use of SAC metaphors. So we need to get experiential: to actively develop SAC skills. In addition to the metaphors, we need to do experiential exercises where people get to actually experience the "psychological space" of SAC.

For example, we may do any of the brief SAC experiential exercises, or "notice your noticing" exercises, that I've described elsewhere (Harris,

2009a). Or we can take any mindfulness exercise and modify it to include lots and lots of instructions, such as these:

Four Instructions to Make Self-as-Context Explicit

We can add these explicit SAC instructions into any other mindfulness exercise (e.g., breathing, body scan, eating a raisin, walking, leaves on a stream, physicalizing, mindfulness of the hand). The idea is to use them liberally; the more the merrier.

- "As you notice X, be aware you're noticing."
- "There's X and there's a part of you noticing X."
  To highlight the continuous, unchanging aspects of SAC:
- "X changes all the time, coming and going, but the part of you that notices X is always there."

And with private experiences—thoughts, feelings, memories, sensations, urges:

- "X is a part of you, but it's nowhere near the whole of you; there's so much more to you than X."

The fourth instruction is very powerful for defusion from self-concept: All these thoughts about who you are, all these judgments, all these stories—all these thoughts are a part of you, but there's so much more to you than these thoughts.

Q: How can we respond when clients say, "What's the point of this?"

Sometimes I've had clients say things like "What's the point?" or "Why are you telling me this?" or "So what?" This always throws me.

Russ: This is a good reminder that we first need to be clear in ourselves on why we are doing this, so we can answer effectively if the client asks, "Why are we talking about this/doing this?" "What's the point?" "How's this relevant?" "How will this help?" "What's this got to do with my depression/anxiety?" (If you don't think you could answer these questions clearly, I recommend you practice doing so until you've got a good spiel ready.)

My first answer is generally along the lines of "I'm highlighting this because it's a powerful resource inside you, and it can help you do all sorts of things, but most people don't know about it." (I've had a couple of clients playfully remark, "Oh, you mean I have super powers?") Then I refer back to whatever defusion, acceptance, or present moment we've done before: "This is the part of you that does all that noticing/makes room for your feelings/drops that anchor/brings up the lights on the stage show/notices what your mind is telling you."

I then make my underlying intention clear (which is why we need to know what it is): "So I want to now help you explore this aspect of yourself further in order to..."

And then I go on to specify my intention:

- discover a safe place/calm center inside you, a bit like the eye in the center of the storm
- unhook from all those labels your mind sticks on you/judgments it makes about who you are
- experience a more powerful/higher/different sense of yourself
- build on all those other skills I just mentioned, make them stronger

Q: How can we respond when clients say, "I don't get it"?

Sometimes after doing a SAC exercise, I've had client say things like "I just don't get it," or look at me blankly, or otherwise express confusion. What's a good option when that happens?

Russ: It really depends on the context. For example, is this a first session or a tenth session? What's the function of the client's behavior: is this experiential avoidance, or does the client feel strong if he manages to throw off the therapist with unexpected responses, or is it genuine confusion and the client wants help understanding? Obviously, these would need to be addressed differently, responding to the unique demands of the situation.

For the sake of simplicity, let's suppose the context is one in which

A. we have a willing client (not trying to undermine the therapist or derail the session),

B. the therapist has clearly specified the purpose of the exercise and linked it to the client's therapy goals (the therapist's failure to do this almost guarantees confusion), and

C. the therapist took the client through an actual experiential exercise on SAC, as opposed to just discussing a metaphor.

In such a context, if the client is expressing confusion, my inclination would be to keep working experientially, as follows:

Client: I don't get it.

Therapist: You're confused?

Client: Yeah.

Therapist: Can you notice your confusion?

Client: Yeah.

Therapist: Can you notice your mind trying to make sense of this?

Client: Yeah.

Therapist: Can you notice yourself saying "yeah"?

Client: Yeah (*smiles*).

Therapist: Can you notice me asking all these annoying questions?

Client: Yeah.

Therapist: Can you notice your irritation as I keep asking these questions?

Client: Yeah (*smiles*).

Therapist: Can you notice yourself nodding your head?

Client: Yeah.

Therapist: Can you notice your feet on the floor?

Client: Yeah.

Therapist: So there's a part of you noticing everything.

This experiential way to help the client "get it" will be a lot more effective than trying to explain it didactically or presenting further metaphors.

The Wrap-Up

Self-as-context is a fascinating part of the ACT model, and potentially very confusing (for both clients and therapists). However, a lot of the confusion is due to overcomplicating it as a concept, failure to clarify how it's relevant to the client's goals, or relying on metaphors without doing the experiential work. The take-home message: keep it simple, make it relevant, and do it experientially.

CHAPTER 15

Exasperating Exposure

Exposure is a hot topic in ACT. You'll encounter this word in most ACT textbooks, and you'll often hear trainers say, "ACT is an exposure-based model." And yet, the concept is often skimmed over. So if you're wondering what exposure actually means, and in what sense ACT is based on it, or how it's different in ACT from in other models, then you've come to the right place. It's a massive topic, but the good news is even a little bit of knowledge about exposure goes a long way to helping us understand what we are doing in ACT.

Discussions in This Chapter:

- What is exposure, and how is it different in ACT?
- What is values-guided exposure?
- What can we measure in ACT-style exposure, if not SUDS?
- What if clients resist exposure?
- Do we have to create exposure hierarchies?

Q: What is exposure, and how is it different in ACT?

Russ: There is not one universally agreed-upon definition of exposure. However, in most models, exposure is defined something like this: "organized contact with fear-evoking stimuli for the purpose of habituation." *Habituation* basically means getting used to a stimulus so that it has less influence over behavior. Now, although the aim of exposure in these models is stated as habituation, the degree of habituation is almost always measured in terms of a drop in anxiety levels or SUDS (subjective units of distress scores). The implicit message is that higher habituation equals lower anxiety levels (or lower SUDS). Thus, in practice, most models—whether they acknowledge it or not—do exposure with the primary aim of reducing anxiety.

In ACT, we define exposure somewhat differently: "organized contact with repertoire-narrowing stimuli for the purpose of increasing emotional flexibility, cognitive flexibility, and behavioral flexibility" (S. Hayes, personal communication, 2015). Let's break that down.

Repertoire-narrowing basically means that behavior becomes rigid, inflexible, and limited—narrowing down to a small range of ineffective behavioral responses. Now, behavioral repertoires may be narrowed by all sorts of stimuli, not just by those that are fear evoking. For example, emotions such as guilt and anger and sadness can all be repertoire-narrowing stimuli; so can cognitions such as *I'm not good enough* or painful memories. Likewise, a substance that one finds tempting, such as drugs, alcohol, cigarettes, or chocolate, can be a repertoire-narrowing stimulus, as can any situation, event, or activity that one finds challenging.

Basically, whatever you write at the bottom of the choice point (chapter 1) is a repertoire-narrowing stimulus; the term *hooked* means that behavior has narrowed to such an extent (in response to the stimulus) that it's become self-defeating (an "away move"). Thus, the purpose of exposure in ACT is not to reduce anxiety or lower a SUDS score (although these are both common outcomes of ACT-based exposure). The purpose is to develop *emotional flexibility, cognitive flexibility,* and *behavioral flexibility* (collectively known as *psychological flexibility*) in response to the stimulus.

Q: What is values-guided exposure?

Russ: In ACT, exposure is always done in the service of living our values. We take action, deliberately exposing ourselves to (or making contact with) people, places, situations, objects, activities, and events to which we would normally respond with rigid, ineffective behavioral repertoires, and we learn to respond more flexibly to these stimuli. For example, a client who has been avoiding social situations may, in the service of values such as intimacy, openness, and connectedness, start deliberately going to social events. In other words, when we expose ourselves to repertoire-narrowing stimuli "outside our skin," the primary aim is always to help us live our values and pursue values-congruent goals (not to reduce anxiety levels or SUDS scores).

In the service of living our values, we also expose ourselves to repertoire-narrowing stimuli "inside our skin": thoughts, memories, feelings, emotions, sensations. Defusion, acceptance, self-as-context, and contacting the present moment all function as exposure when they involve consciously turning toward and responding flexibly to thoughts and feelings that usually trigger away moves. And of course, in ACT, the aim of developing and using these skills is to enable values-based living.

You may find it useful then to think that much of what we do in terms of defusion and acceptance is exposure to the world inside the skin, and much of what we do in terms of committed action is exposure to the world outside the skin. (But do keep in mind, these are artificial distinctions.)

Q: What can we measure in ACT-style exposure, if not SUDS?

Russ: In most models outside of ACT, the aim of exposure is primarily to reduce anxiety or emotional distress. So naturally in those models, there's a major emphasis on measuring anxiety levels or SUDS and making sure that they drop. But in recent years, a wealth of research (e.g., Craske et al., 2008) shows there is *no correlation* between the drop in anxiety levels or SUDS during in-session exposure and the long-term behavioral outcomes of exposure.

Furthermore, this emphasis in other models on lowering anxiety or reducing SUDS easily feeds into the agenda of experiential avoidance: it conveys the message that our anxiety or emotional distress is the problem, and we need to reduce it in order to have a good life. So in ACT, instead of measuring SUDS or anxiety levels, it would arguably be wiser to create simple 0–10 scales to measure aspects of psychological flexibility such as degree of acceptance versus avoidance, degree of fusion versus defusion, degree of engagement, degree of control over actions, and degree of connection with values. For example, in the midst of active exposure, we might say to a client, "Right now, how much control do you have over your actions? Ten means you have complete control over your actions, zero means no control at all. Move your body, your arms, legs, hands, feet; check it out." Or we might ask, "Right now, how much are you struggling with this emotion? Ten means you're doing everything possible to avoid it, get rid of it, push it away, or distract yourself from it. Zero means you're not investing even the tiniest bit of energy into trying to escape or avoid it; you're just allowing it to be there."

For other ideas of questions to ask during exposure, see appendix 8, the Exposure Crib Sheet.

Q: What if clients resist exposure?

Russ: We want to find out what's motivating the resistance. For example, is it fusion with the emotional control agenda? If so, creative hopelessness is probably warranted (chapter 8). Or is it that the exposure task is too challenging and needs to be stripped down to something smaller, simpler, easier—something lower down the exposure hierarchy? In supervision, the most common reason I encounter for resistance to exposure is that the client doesn't understand the point of it because the therapist has not made it clear. The therapist must ensure the client understands how exposure will help him to achieve his therapy goals (chapter 3).

The choice point provides a simple way to do this; the client can readily see that his typical ways of responding to the repertoire-narrowing stimuli at the bottom of the diagram are not working for him. For example, suppose a client suffering from post-traumatic stress disorder writes "memories of the assault" at the bottom, and her away moves when these memories arise are taking drugs, social withdrawal, and self-harming. Exposure to those memories would then be an unhooking skill: learning a new way to respond differently to these memories so that when they arise in future, the client can choose towards moves as an alternative to her typical away moves.

Likewise, if exposure involves making contact with the outer world—people, places, events, activities—this would go on the right side of the diagram as towards moves clearly link to the client's therapy goals.

By the way, I never use the word *exposure* with clients (unless they use it first). If it's exposure to the inner world, I'd use words such as *unhooking, noticing, being present, opening up,* or *making room.* And if it's exposure to the outer world, I'd talk about *away moves,* or *taking action,* or *pursuing goals,* or *living values,* or *doing what matters.*

Q: Do we have to create exposure hierarchies?

Russ: Traditional methods of exposure emphasize the need for an exposure hierarchy. This involves creating a step-by-step plan to progressively increase the degree of challenge in the exposure work. For a classic example, suppose we are helping a client to overcome a spider phobia. One possible exposure hierarchy might look like this, starting with the lowest level of difficulty, and steadily increasing:

Talking about spiders

Imagining spiders

Looking at drawings of spiders

Looking at photos of spiders

Looking at videos of spiders

Looking at real dead spiders in glass jars

Looking at real living spiders in glass jars

Looking at real living spiders outside of glass jars

Now in ACT, we can—if we wish—do a formal exposure hierarchy. Indeed, this is commonly done when working with clients with anxiety disorders and chronic pain syndrome. But we certainly don't *have to* do it this way. We can instead work flexibly, spontaneously, fluidly, with whatever repertoire-narrowing stimuli are showing up for the client in this moment of the session.

Generally, though, we do tend to do *graded exposure* with most clients: that is, step-by-step, incrementally increasing the degree of difficulty of the exposure task. For example, often when goal setting, we ask something like "What's the smallest, simplest, easiest step you can take to begin with?" If this step is going to put the client in contact with repertoire-narrowing stimuli, such as a challenging situation or an uncomfortable feeling, we can think of it as exposure, starting at a low level of difficulty.

When clients are able to respond flexibly (i.e., to unhook and do towards moves) to stimuli that are typically repertoire narrowing (i.e., that usually trigger away moves), we can say that exposure has been successful.

The Wrap-Up

Because of the way we define exposure in ACT, we can be incredibly flexible with the way we do it—arguably far more so than in any other exposure-based model. I hope you'll reflect on this chapter and consider how exposure plays out in every session of ACT you ever do, and how it's at the core of both acceptance and committed action. See if you can recognize ways in which you've already been doing exposure, without even realizing it. And why not see if you can come up with your own methods, techniques, adaptations, and modifications for doing it? And last but not least, recognize where you have been doing traditional exposure (primarily to lower anxiety levels or reduce SUDS) and adapt or modify those methods so they become more ACT-congruent (primarily to increase cognitive, emotional, and behavioral flexibility).

CHAPTER 16

Awkward Acceptance

Well, here we are at the final chapter. It's only a short one, because we've already touched on acceptance quite a lot throughout this book. We've looked at undermining the emotional control agenda (chapter 8); we've looked at noticing and naming (chapter 9) and dropping anchor (chapter 7), which are often the first steps in acceptance; we've looked at the overlap between exposure and acceptance (chapter 15); and we've looked at self-compassion (chapter 10), which includes, facilitates, and deepens acceptance.

Now before we go any further, a quick reminder that acceptance is short for experiential acceptance—that is, acceptance of one's private experiences (thoughts, feelings, memories, emotions). It doesn't mean passively accepting a situation that is clearly making life worse. In such circumstances, ACT advocates committed action guided by values to actively improve the situation as much as possible, or to leave it, whichever is most likely to be effective.

Also, one thing to keep in mind as you read on: many clients don't react well to the word acceptance. They often think it means tolerance, resignation, putting up with it, sucking it up, gritting your teeth, white-knuckling it, giving in, or giving up. Or they think it means liking, wanting, or approving of it. And certainly, none of that is what we mean in ACT by acceptance. So, I'd recommend that (at least in early sessions) you don't use the word. Much better alternatives include making room, opening up, making space, allowing, expansion, dropping the struggle, sitting with it, holding it gently or lightly, breathing into it, and leaning into it. And I often like to use this phrase: "allowing these thoughts and feelings to freely flow through you, to come and go in their own good time, neither struggling against them, nor being swept away by them." Later, once clients know what it is and how to do it, it's pretty safe to bring in the "a" word.

Discussions in This Chapter:

- What is willingness?
- Should we target all experiential avoidance?
- What if clients insist, "But I hate this feeling"?
- What if clients ask, "Why should I accept it?"
- Does acceptance preclude medication?
- Does ACT change inner experience?

Q: What is willingness?

Russ: The term *willingness* seems to create a lot of confusion in ACT. Basically, it refers to a quality of behavior: being ready or prepared to do something (even if you don't want to do it). Willingness can refer to both overt and covert behavior. With overt behavior, we may talk of taking action willingly, as opposed to taking action resentfully or halfheartedly. With covert behavior, we may talk of willingness to make room for difficult thoughts and feelings—which is, of course, synonymous with acceptance—as opposed to doing so resentfully or halfheartedly, which is more like tolerance or "putting up with it."

Q: Should we target all experiential avoidance?

Russ: Nooooooo! Experiential avoidance is normal, not pathological. We only target experiential avoidance when it's so extensive or inappropriate that it's interfering with the client's life and getting in the way of his therapy goals (chapter 3). If we start targeting every little bit of experiential avoidance, we'll soon upset or invalidate our clients.

Q: What if clients insist, "But I hate this feeling"?

Russ: We validate that response. We might say something like, "Of course you do. Who wouldn't, when it's having such a huge negative impact on your life? It seems like whenever you *get hooked by* this feeling, it jerks you around, it brings you down, and it pulls you into all manner of away moves. That's a lot of suffering." Note my use of italics in that response. The idea is to subtly reframe the problem: it's not the feeling itself that creates so much suffering; it's *getting hooked by* the feeling that causes all the problems. We might then go on to say, "So would you be interested in learning how to unhook from this feeling? How to take its power away, so it doesn't jerk you around like that?"

If the client says yes, we can then move into unhooking skills, typically progressing from contacting the present moment (dropping anchor) to defusion (noticing and naming) to acceptance. If the client says, "No. I don't want to *unhook* from it, I want to get rid of it," then we'd segue into creative hopelessness (chapter 8). For example, we may say, "You want to get rid of it? Okay, well let's see what's possible. What have you tried doing so far to get rid of it?"

Q: What if clients ask, "Why should I accept it?"

Russ: That's golden feedback for us; it means we haven't clarified the link between acceptance and values. Remember, we'd never encourage a client to accept anything in ACT, unless it were in the service of living her values, pursuing values-congruent goals. For example, we might respond, "Are you willing to make room for these difficult thoughts and feelings, in order to be the sort of partner you want to be?" or "Are you willing to have this tight chest and racing heart, these knots in your stomach, this scary voice in your head, if that's what you need to allow in order to live your values of intimacy and connectedness?" If a client doesn't see how accepting painful thoughts and feelings will help her to live her values (chapter 6) or achieve her therapy goals (chapter 3), confusion or resistance is likely.

Q: Does acceptance preclude medication?

Russ: No, acceptance does not preclude medication. Remember the core ACT construct of workability: if medication works to make life richer and fuller in the long term, and the benefits outweigh the costs, there's no issue. ACT is neither pro nor anti medication; workability is the ultimate arbiter.

Remember, too, we don't always advocate acceptance in ACT; we don't want to turn into mindfulness fascists. There are times when alleviating unpleasant thoughts and feelings is workable, and medication can, in the right context, be an effective way to help with that. For example, if I get a headache, I rarely put up with it; I usually take aspirin if it doesn't ease off quickly. We target experiential avoidance only if and when it is creating significant problems.

Q: Does ACT change inner experience?

Sometimes it seems there is a contradiction in ACT. On the one hand, ACT advocates accepting our inner experience. On the other hand, ACT advocates working with mindfulness to lessen the impact of thoughts and feelings; isn't this an attempt at changing inner experience?

Russ: Yes, ACT does change inner experience—profoundly. When we respond to thoughts and feelings with mindfulness, they change. Sadness in a context of acceptance changes dramatically from sadness in a context of avoidance. When we add the phrase "I'm having the thought that," it changes the original thought. Same if we sing the thought or say it in a silly voice. When we turn toward anxiety with openness and curiosity, or we link it to living our values, the experience of anxiety changes. But the big difference between ACT and many other models is that ACT changes inner experience through values and mindfulness—not through trying to avoid and get rid of the inner experience.

Any inner experience will change significantly—from avoidance to acceptance, or fusion to defusion, or self-hatred to self-compassion, or values remoteness to values connectedness—when the context in which it arises alters. This is one of the lovely paradoxes of ACT: acceptance is change!

The Wrap-Up

So here we are, at the end of the book. I'm feeling a bit sad about that, and I'm accepting it. (And, truth be told, I'm also feeling a bit relieved.) I hope you've found these pages useful in your continuing journey to master ACT. Though, to be honest, I don't think anyone ever truly masters ACT; we can get better at it, for sure, but there's always room for improvement. (At this point, a reminder: if you're feeling really stuck and you just don't know what to do next, then you can always turn to appendix 9: A Clinician's Guide to Getting Unstuck from Just About Anything.)

The reality is, no matter how good we do get, no matter how skillful and knowledgeable we become, there will always be times we screw up and make mistakes. It's inevitable. (I wish I'd made a video compilation of all the most painful mistakes I've made in learning ACT—but if I had, it'd go for days on end. I feel so sorry for all those poor clients I experimented on.)

So the challenge is, when we do make mistakes, can we accept ourselves? And can we be compassionate to ourselves, unhook from the "I'm a lousy therapist" story, acknowledge our pain, and treat ourselves kindly? And can we turn with openness and curiosity toward those mistakes, so that we can learn from them: What worked? What didn't work? And what can we do differently next time around?

I'm going to finish up with one of my favorite quotes, which I hope will inspire your ongoing journey with ACT:

> *The most beautiful people we have known are those who have known defeat, known suffering, known struggle, known loss, and have found their way out of the depths. These persons have an appreciation, a sensitivity, and an understanding of life that fills them with compassion, gentleness, and a deep loving concern. Beautiful people do not just happen.*–Elisabeth Kübler-Ross (1975)

Acknowledgments

As always, I'd like to give vast warehouses full of gratitude to Steve Hayes, Kelly Wilson, and Kirk Strosahl, the cocreators of ACT. They've been an incredible source of help, knowledge, guidance, and inspiration throughout my ACT journey. Also, a huge thank you to the broader ACBS (Association for Contextual Behavioral Science) community, which is always so supportive and helpful; it really is an amazing network of people. And another huge round of thanks to all my trainees over the years, from whom I always learn so much. Last but not least, I am deeply grateful to the whole team at New Harbinger, especially the editorial team of Tesilya Hanauer, Jasmin Star, Georgia Kolias, Clancy Drake, Vicraj Gill, Georg Eifert, and Nicola Skidmore, who did an amazing job of trimming down my original flabby manuscript and turning it into something so much better than I could ever have done alone; and a special extra dose of thanks to my own specially assigned editor, Rona Bernstein, who did a truly whizz-bang job on shaping and polishing the whole thing.

APPENDIX 1

ACT Case Formulation Worksheet

What does the client describe as the main problem(s)?
What does the client want from therapy/coaching? *Emotional Goals:* What thoughts, images, feelings, emotions, sensations, memories, urges would he like to have less of? (*Note: We convert these to behavioral goals with the reframe: "So we'll be learning new skills to handle these difficult thoughts and feelings more effectively, so they have less impact and influence over you."*) *Behavioral Goals:* What would the client like to stop/start; do more/less of? How would she like to treat himself, others, the world differently? What goals would she like to pursue? What activities/skills would she like to start, resume, develop? What people, places, events, activities, challenges would she like to approach rather than avoid? What relationships does she want to improve, and how? What life problems does he want to solve?
EXTERNAL BARRIERS: Are there any external barriers (as opposed to psychological barriers) to a rich and full life (e.g., legal, social, medical, financial, occupational problems) that require problem solving and/or skills training?
UNWORKABLE ACTION: What is the client doing that makes life worse, keeps her stuck, worsens problems, inhibits growth, prevents healthy solutions, impairs health, damages relationships, etc.? (What would we see and/or hear on a video?) What IMPORTANT or MEANINGFUL people, places, events, activities, situations, goals, problems, and challenges is the client avoiding or escaping (e.g., withdrawing from, quitting, procrastinating, giving up on, or staying away from)?

FUSION: (Include examples of specific thoughts, as well as of processes such as "worrying")

PAST & FUTURE: (rumination, worrying, fantasizing, blaming, predicting the worst, reliving old hurts, idealizing the past or the future, flashbacks, "if only...," "why did it happen?," catastrophizing, resentment, regrets, etc.)

SELF-DESCRIPTION: (self-judgments, self-limiting ideas about "who I am" or "what I can and can't do," self-labels)

REASONS: (reasons the client gives for why she can't, won't, or shouldn't change, or why her life can't be improved)

RULES: (about how I, others, and life should be: look for key words such as *should, have to, must, ought, right, wrong, always, never, can't because, won't until, shouldn't unless*, etc.)

JUDGMENTS: (mostly these will be negative, but sometimes positive; may be about anyone or anything: other people, oneself, one's job, one's body, one's thoughts and feelings, the past, the future, or even life itself)

OTHER:

EXPERIENTIAL AVOIDANCE: (Private experiences the client is trying to avoid or get rid of, or is unwilling to have)

THOUGHTS, IMAGES, MEMORIES, EMOTIONS, FEELINGS, SENSATIONS, URGES, CRAVINGS, WITHDRAWAL SYMPTOMS:

LOSS OF CONTACTING THE PRESENT MOMENT:

The 4 Ds: Distractibility, Disengagement, Disconnection, Dissociation?

Deficits in ability to narrow focus, broaden focus, sustain focus, or shift focus?

VALUES & COMMITTED ACTION:

IMPORTANT LIFE DOMAINS: What life domains and what people does the client care about (e.g., work, study, health, parenting, marriage or other intimate relationship, friends, family, spirituality, community, environment)?

VALUES: What values seem important within those domains?

GOALS & ACTIONS: What values-congruent goals and activities does he (a) already have, and (b) want to pursue?

NEED FOR SKILLS TRAINING: What important skills does the client lack or fail to use (e.g., problem solving, goal setting, self-soothing, assertiveness, communication, conflict resolution, relaxation, empathy)?

RESOURCES: What strengths, skills, and other personal resources does the client have that could be utilized? What external resources could be accessed? Who can the client turn to for help and support?

MY PERSONAL BARRIERS: What difficult thoughts and feelings show up for me regarding this client?

BRAINSTORM: What questions, exercises, worksheets, metaphors, tools, techniques, and strategies can I use in the next session? What skills training may be required? Is values-based problem solving required for external barriers?

APPENDIX 2

Informed Consent

It's essential that we get informed consent from our clients to do ACT—to explain the model, let the client know what to expect, and elicit agreement. Without it, we can expect problems. The brief guide that follows will help you approach this important task.

Key Points

At the bare minimum, I recommend you include the following points when obtaining consent (modifying the language to suit your way of speaking and your clientele):

- The name "acceptance and commitment therapy" reflects a key message: accept what is out of your personal control, and commit to action that improves your life.
- It's a very active form of therapy/coaching. It's not just talking about your problems and feelings. Our aim here is to work together as a team, to help you be the sort of person you want to be and build the sort of life you want to live.
- Part of this approach involves learning skills to handle difficult thoughts and feelings more effectively, so they have less impact and influence over you. When we introduce these skills, I'll ask you to practice them between sessions. You don't have to do that, of course, but it's like learning to play a guitar or drive a care: the more practice you do, the better you get.

- ACT also involves clarifying your values: finding out what matters to you, what you want to stand for in life, what strengths and qualities you want to develop, how you want to treat yourself and others. And it also involves taking action to solve your problems, face your challenges, and do things that make life better.

- I want you to leave here after each session with an action plan: something practical to take away and use to actively improve your life.

Consider adding the following:

- At times, therapy may seem like a roller-coaster ride, but I'll be there in the roller-coaster car with you.

- I will ask you at times to try new things that may pull you out of your comfort zone—like learning new skills to handle difficult thoughts and feelings—but you never have to do them. You are always free to say no to anything I suggest.

Press Pause

This isn't essential, but I highly recommend you run through this in your first session because it will give you a very powerful way to interrupt problematic behavior and reinforce workable behavior as it arises in session.

- Can I have permission to "press pause" from time to time, so if I see you doing something that looks like it might be really helpful or useful, in terms of dealing with your problems and improving your life, I can just slow the session down and get you to really notice what you are doing?

- For example, I may ask you to pause or slow down, take a couple of breaths, and notice what you're thinking or feeling or saying or doing. That way, you'll be able to see more clearly what you're doing, and we can look at ways you can use it outside of this room. Is that okay?

- And can I also press pause if I see you doing something that looks like it may be contributing to your problems or making them worse, so we can address it?
- And of course, this goes both ways—you can also press pause on me, any time you like.

APPENDIX 3

The Bull's-Eye

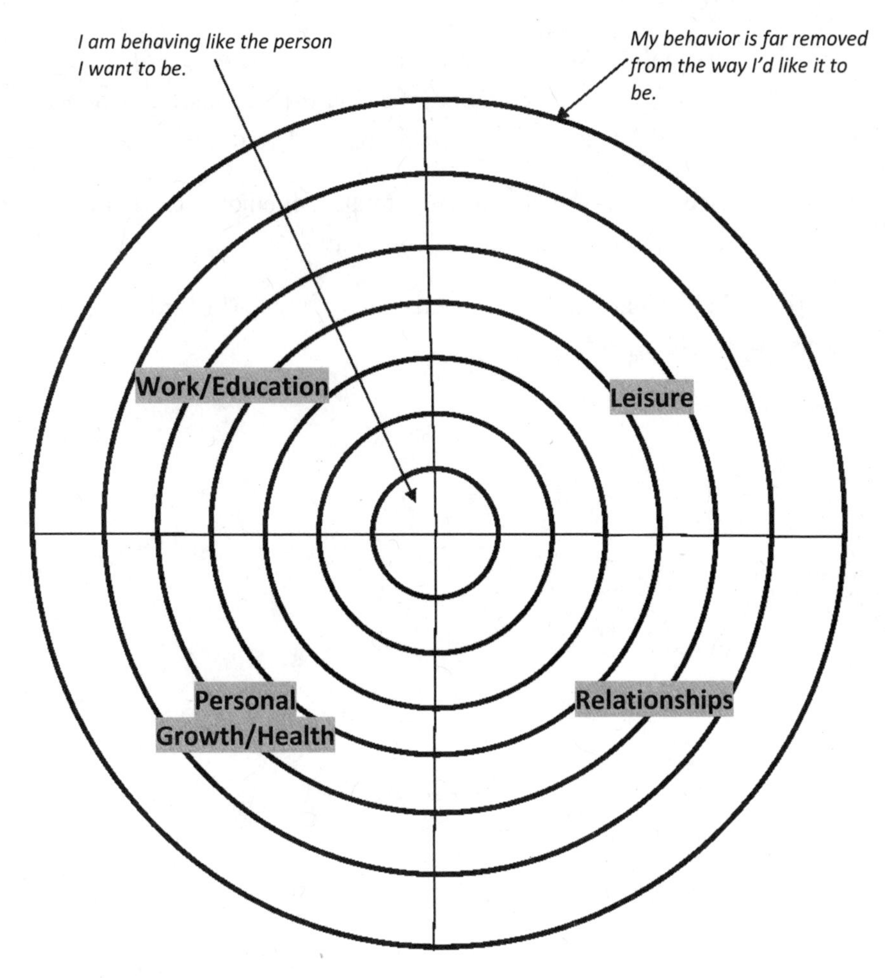

Adapted from *Living Beyond Your Pain* by J. Dahl and T. Lundren, 2006, by permission of New Harbinger Publications (Oakland, CA), http://www.newharbinger.com.

YOUR VALUES: *What really matters to you, deep in your heart? What do you want to do with your time on this planet? What sort of person do you want to be? What personal strengths or qualities do you want to develop?*

1. **Work/Education:** includes workplace, career, education, and skills development.

2. **Relationships:** includes your partner, children, parents, relatives, friends, coworkers, and other social contacts.

3. **Personal Growth/Health:** may include religion, spirituality, creativity, life skills, meditation, yoga, nature; exercise, nutrition, and health risk factors such as smoking, alcohol, drugs, or overeating.

4. **Leisure:** how you play, relax, stimulate, or enjoy yourself; activities for rest, recreation, fun, and creativity.

THE BULL'S-EYE: make an X in each area of the dart board to represent where you stand today.

APPENDIX 4

Defusion from Barriers to Therapy

Many clients naturally come up with all sorts of reasons why therapy won't or can't work for them: I've tried before, I can't do it, it's too hard, this is bullshit, I've always been this way, this is who I am, I'm too depressed, I'm too anxious, I'm an addict, I've been diagnosed with X, my life is Y, other people are Z, I'm too A, I'm not B enough, therapy is useless, this won't work, you can't help me because of CDE, I have disorder FGH, I've got no motivation (or energy, or willpower, or discipline), I've been permanently damaged by IJK and can never recover, and so on.

Luckily, in ACT, we don't get into challenging the content or validity of cognitions by assessing whether they are true or false, valid or invalid, positive or negative, right or wrong, appropriate or inappropriate, warranted or unwarranted. If we had to try to convince clients that their doubts about therapy are false, invalid, or unwarranted, we'd be in trouble! Doubts about therapy are perfectly natural, and only to be expected. However, if clients (or their therapists) fuse with these doubts, it will get in the way of effective work. Thus, such cognitions are good candidates for defusion, right from the word go. So let's take a look at how we can make this happen.

I aim to create, as fast as possible, a context of defusion: a space where we can allow unhelpful cognitions to be present, and see them for what they are. I also want to facilitate a context of acceptance, where there is no fighting with or challenging of thoughts, no trying to invalidate or get rid of them.

My first step is generally to use the simple but effective strategy of *noticing and naming*: noticing the presence of cognitions, and nonjudgmentally naming them. For example, I might say, "I can see there's a bunch of thoughts (or concerns, worries, doubts, fears, objections, and so forth) showing up for you right now about why this won't work for you."

Validate

As therapists, it's vital that we validate such cognitions. They are commonplace—among both clients that are new to therapy and those who have experienced a lot of it. And they are completely normal and natural thoughts to have.

So I tend to say something like, "Those are all very common thoughts (or concerns, worries, doubts, fears, objections, and so forth). Many of my clients have similar thoughts when we first start working. It's perfectly natural. And to be honest, I expect they'll crop up again and again."

A big part of both defusion and acceptance in ACT is helping clients to understand that their mind is not irrational, weird, or defective; it's basically just trying to help. This is both normalizing and validating for clients.

I tend to say something like "These thoughts are basically your mind trying to look out for you, do you a favor. It's basically trying to save you from something that might fail or go wrong or be unpleasant. What your mind is saying is: *Hey, are you sure you want to do this? You might just be wasting your time, money, and energy. This might even make things even worse for you.*"

I continue: "And you know, the truth is, there's probably nothing I can say that will stop your mind from doing that. It's just doing its job—just trying to protect you."

I then, quite often, say something like this: "You know, there's a part of me that really wants to reassure you, to say, 'Hey! This will work for you!' But the truth is, I can't guarantee that it will work. And if you ever go to any type of health professional who guarantees you 'This will work!'—my advice would be don't go back, because that person is either lying or deluded. Because no one can ever guarantee that. I mean, sure, I could show you all the research. I mean, there are over a thousand papers published on the ACT model; it's helped hundreds of thousands of people around the world. But that wouldn't guarantee it will work for you. And I could tell you about all my other clients it's helped, but again that won't guarantee it will work for you.

"But there are two things I will guarantee. I guarantee I'll do my best to help you. And I guarantee, if we give up because your mind has doubts, we won't get anywhere. So even though your mind will keep coming up with reasons as to why this can't or won't work for you—can we go ahead with it anyway?"

By this point, many clients will be unhooking from their doubts, concerns, objections, and other barriers to therapy. But what if this isn't happening? What if the client continues to insist that therapy can't or won't help? Well, before we go any further, there are three important cautions to keep in mind:

First, the therapist must be compassionate, respectful, and incredibly validating of the client's experience. If the techniques described in this document are delivered in a dismissive, impatient, uncaring, or otherwise-invalidating manner, this will obviously offend or upset the client. (And of course, this holds true for any type of intervention in any model of therapy!)

My second caution is about language. Please: don't stick to the script! The idea is to modify and adapt everything in ACT to suit your own way of speaking and working. The words I like to use may be vastly different from the words you'd prefer to use; if so, please change them! Mix, match, adapt, modify, add more, or cut back. In other words, make ACT your own; do it in your own way, true to your own personality and your own manner of speaking.

My third caution is that there is not one intervention in any model of therapy that works predictably and favorably with all clients. So if you apply anything from this book (or from any other material I have written) and it's not having the effect intended, then be flexible. Consider: Do you need to modify what you're doing in some way? Or are you better to cease doing it, and do something else instead?

Write It Down

Now, if the previously mentioned strategies fail to help the client unhook from her objections, doubts, concerns, or other thoughts that act as barriers to therapy, my next step is very often to write those thoughts down. Doing this usually makes it a whole lot easier for any of us to take a step back and "look at" our thoughts—instead of getting caught up in them.

Typically, I ask for permission to write the thoughts down: "So you have some real and valid concerns about whether this will work for you. And I think we need to address these concerns right now, or we're not going to get anywhere. So is it okay if, as a first step, I quickly jot them all down, so I can make sure we address them all?"

And now I write the thoughts down—every objection or concern the client has about why this won't work: I've tried before, I can't do it, it's too hard, this is bullshit, I've got diagnosis ABC, I'm too depressed, my life is V, other people are X, I'm too Y, I'm not Z enough, and so on.

And as I'm doing this, I'll repeat some or all of my previous comments: "I just want to reiterate, these are all very common…"; "Many of my clients have similar thoughts when we first start working…"; "It's perfectly natural—your mind is trying to help, to save you from something that might be unpleasant…"; "So really, we can expect these kinds of thoughts to keep cropping up, again and again."

I often then say, "You know, I don't think I'll be able to persuade you or convince you that this approach is the right for one you, that it's going to work for you. In fact, my guess is, the harder I try to convince you, the more those thoughts are going to show up. What do you think?"

At this point, most clients will reply along the lines of "Yeah, I guess you're right." (And often there's a hint of amusement in this response, which is usually indicative of some defusion.) The door is now wide open to usher in the concept of workability.

Following the previous step, I usually say something like "So here's the thing. These thoughts (pointing to the thoughts written on the paper) are going to show up again and again and again as we do this work together. I have no idea how to stop that from happening. And each time they do, we have a choice to make about how we respond to them.

"One choice is: we give up. We let your mind call the shots. Your mind says *This won't work*, so we go along with that, we call it a day, and we pack it in.

"A second choice is: we get into a debate. I try hard to convince your mind to stop thinking this way; I try to prove your thoughts are false and to convince you that this approach will work. The problem is, that kind of debating will eat up our valuable session time, and I can pretty much guarantee your mind will win the debate anyway—so we won't be any better off.

"A third choice is: we can let your mind say this stuff, and we can just carry on…we just keep on working together as a team…working away here, to help you build a better life…and even though your mind will keep saying all this (pointing to the thoughts on the paper), we just keep on working."

Finally, I ask, "So which of those options would you prefer?"

If our client now agrees to option three, well, that's defusion, right there: the thoughts are present, but they are no longer dominating the client's behavior in self-defeating ways. And the client is also consciously allowing the thoughts to be present: a gentle first step toward acceptance of unwanted thoughts.

If our client now comes up with more objections, we can add them to the list, and then repeat the same three choices. If our client tries to debate, we can notice and name it: "So it seems like you want me to debate this with you. But there's just no point. I won't win. I won't convince your mind. So we really have just two choices here: give up and pack it in, or let your mind say this stuff and carry on." If the client now agrees to option three—again, that's defusion, right there!

I've only ever twice had a client choose option one. Both times, I replied, "Okay. I get that's the choice you'd like to make. But given that you're already here, it seems a shame to give up now. Can we at least finish this one session, given you're here? And for this one session, can we not get into a debate about these thoughts? Can we just let your mind say this stuff, and carry on?" Both times, the client agreed. (Obviously, this strategy may not work with a mandated client, but that's a different issue.)

Ongoing Defusion

The therapist can now use this for ongoing defusion and acceptance throughout the session. For example, when new objections occur, the therapist can write them down and again ask the client to choose how to respond.

If the same objections recur, the therapist can respectfully and compassionately acknowledge it and point to the paper: "We've got that one down already. So again, there's a choice to make here..."

An alternative to the above is to give the sheet to the client with a pen, and ask her to tick each thought as it recurs. The therapist can respectfully and compassionately acknowledge it each time. "Keeps showing up. So do we give up, or waste time debating, or do we acknowledge the thought just popped up again and carry on?"

One option is for the therapist to keep the paper, and on the next session, present it to the client: "I expect these will all show up again today. Any of them showing up right now? Most of them? Cool. Can we let them be there, and carry on? Great. And let's see if your mind comes up with any new ones today."

Reason-Giving

Note that the strategies outlined above fit very neatly with the metaphor of the reason-giving machine. (Our mind is like a reason-giving machine. As soon as we even think about stepping out of our comfort zone into a challenging situation, the reason-giving machine starts cranking out all the reasons why we can't do it, shouldn't do it, or shouldn't even have to do it...)

Reason-giving (coming up with reasons why we can't or shouldn't change our behavior) is one of the main categories of problematic fusion we encounter in ACT. So in using the strategies above, the therapist is already helping the client to notice reason-giving and defuse from it. And we can of course use this strategy with any type of reason-giving that occurs later in therapy. It's also a great way for helping clients defuse from helplessness and hopelessness.

Finally, note just how much we've covered here in terms of defusion. We now have a wealth of strategies to draw on repeatedly and develop further in subsequent sessions. And note too that all of this could be done in the very first session, even as we're getting to know the client: taking our initial history and formulating a treatment plan.

APPENDIX 5

The Hands as Thoughts and Feelings Exercise

This exercise is predominantly a metaphor for defusion, although it references all six core ACT processes. It's evolved from my earlier Hands as Thoughts exercise (Harris, 2009a), and the instructions overlap a lot with the Pushing Away Paper exercise detailed in appendix 6. It's very useful to help clients understand the rationale for and benefits of developing defusion skills, and to explicitly link these to the client's therapy goals. However, it's only a metaphor; it won't give clients the ability to defuse. We need to follow it up with active training of defusion skills, in session.

The script that follows is a generic version, suitable for just about anyone. It's much more powerful if we can make it specific to each unique client, so that instead of saying things like "all the people you care about," we'd say, for example, "your husband, Michael, and your teenage daughter, Sarah."

When I do this, I usually carry my chair over to the client, and we both sit side by side, with our backs to the wall, facing the room, and we both do all the actions simultaneously. You don't have to do it this way, of course; like any exercise in ACT, you can modify and adapt it freely to suit yourself; I've just found it more powerful to do so. I also like to do two lovely variants on this exercise. One option is to write down some relevant thoughts and feelings on a sheet of paper, and use this instead of one's hands; and yet another option is to write them down with an indelible all-surface marker on something thin, flexible, and transparent such as bubble wrap, acetate, or cellophane.

Therapist: (*sitting side by side with the client, both facing the room*) Imagine that out there in front of you (*gesturing to the contents of the room and the far wall*) is everything that really matters to you, deep in your heart; everything that makes your life meaningful (or used to, in the past); all the people, places, and activities you love; all your favorite foods and drinks and music and books and movies; all the things you like to do; and all the people you care about and want to spend time with.

But that's not all. Also over there are all the problems and challenges you need to deal with in your life today, such as…(*therapist gives some examples based on the client's history, such as "your conflict with your son," "your financial issues," "your health problems," "your court case," "your search for a job," "your chemotherapy for your cancer"*).

And also over there are all the tasks you need to do on a regular basis to make your life work: shopping, cooking, cleaning, driving, doing your tax return, and so on.

Now please copy me as we do this exercise. Let's imagine that our hands are our thoughts and feelings, and let's put them together like this. (*Therapist places his hands together, side by side, palms upward, as if they are the pages of a book. The client copies him.*) Now, let's see what happens when we get hooked by our thoughts. (*The therapist slowly raises his hands toward his face, until they are covering his eyes. The client copies him. Both keep their hands over their eyes as the next section of the exercise unfolds.*)

Now notice three things. First, how much are you missing out on right now? How disconnected and disengaged are you from the people and things that matter? If the person you love were right there in front of you, how disconnected would you be? If your favorite movie were playing on a screen over there, how much would you miss out on?

Second, notice how difficult it is to focus your attention on what you need to do. If there's an important task in front of you right now, how hard is it to focus on it? If there's a problem you need to address or a challenge you need to tackle, how hard is it to give it your full attention?

Third, notice how difficult it is, like this, to take action, to do the things that make your life work, such as...(*therapist gives some examples based on the client's history, such as "to cook dinner," "to drive your car," "to cuddle your baby," "to type on your computer," "to hug the person you love"*). So notice how difficult life is when we're hooked. We're missing out, we're cut off and disconnected, it's hard to focus, and it's hard to do the things that make life work.

Now, let's see what happens as we unhook from our thoughts and feelings. (*Therapist now slowly removes his hands from his face, and lowers them until they drop into his lap. The client copies him.*) So notice what happens as we unhook. What's your view of the room like now? How much easier is it to engage and connect? If your favorite person were in front of you right now, how much more connected would you be? If your favorite movie were playing, how much more would you enjoy it? If there were a task you needed to do or a problem you needed to address, how much easier would it be to focus on it, like this? Now move your arms and hands about—(*therapist gently shakes his arms and hands around; client copies*). How much easier is it now to take action: to drive a car, cuddle a baby, cook dinner, type on a computer, hug the person you love? (*Therapist mimes these activities as he says them; the client usually will not copy this part, but that doesn't matter.*)

Now notice these things (*therapist indicates his hands, now once more resting in his lap*) haven't disappeared. We haven't chopped them off and gotten rid of them. They're still here. So if there's something useful we can do with them, we can use them. You see, even really painful thoughts and feelings often have useful information that can help us, even if it's just pointing us toward problems we need to address or things we need to do differently, or simply reminding us to be kinder to ourselves. And if there's nothing useful we can do with them, we just let them sit there.

APPENDIX 6

Pushing Away Paper Exercise

This exercise is predominantly a metaphor for acceptance and experiential avoidance, although it references all six core ACT processes. It's evolved from my earlier Pushing the Clipboard exercise (Harris, 2009a), and the instructions overlap a lot with the Hands as Thoughts and Feelings exercise detailed in appendix 5. "Pushing away paper" is a very useful metaphor to help clients understand the rationale for and benefits of developing acceptance skills, and to explicitly link this to the client's therapy goals.

However, it's only a metaphor; it won't give clients the ability to accept. We need to follow it up with active training of acceptance skills, in session.

The script that follows is a generic version, suitable for just about anyone. It's much more powerful if we can make it specific to each unique client, so that instead of saying things like "all the people you care about," we'd say, for example, "your husband, Michael, and your teenage daughter, Sarah."

When I do this, I usually carry my chair over to the client, and we both sit side by side, each with a sheet of paper. Our chairs back up to the wall, we both face toward the room, and we both do all the actions simultaneously. You don't have to do it this way, of course; like any exercise in ACT, you can modify and adapt it freely to suit yourself. The exercise is more powerful if we first write down on the paper the specific thoughts, feelings, emotions, memories, urges, cravings, and sensations that the client is trying to avoid or escape.

A word of warning: this exercise is quite strenuous for most people, so don't ever do this with clients who have painful neck, spine, and shoulder conditions!

Therapist: (*sitting side by side with the client, both facing the room, both holding sheets of paper*) Imagine that out there in front of you (*gesturing to the contents of the room and the far wall*) is everything that really matters to you, deep in your heart; everything that makes your life meaningful (or used to, in the past); all the people, places, and activities you love; all your favorite foods and drinks and music and books and movies; all the things you like to do; and all the people you care about and want to spend time with.

But that's not all. Also over there are all the problems and challenges you need to deal with in your life today, such as…(*therapist gives some examples based on the client's history, such as "your conflict with your son," "your financial issues," "your health problems," "your court case," "your search for a job," "your chemotherapy for your cancer"*).

And also over there are all the tasks you need to do on a regular basis to make your life work: shopping, cooking, cleaning, driving, doing your tax return, and so on.

Now please copy me as we do this exercise. Let's imagine that this sheet of paper is all those difficult thoughts, feelings, emotions, and memories that you'd like to get rid of. Now hold it tightly at the edges like this, and push it as far away from you as you possibly can. (*Therapist holds the paper tightly at the edges with both hands, and stretches his arms out, pushing the paper as far away as possible. The client copies him.*) This is what your culture tells you to do—get these thoughts and feelings away from you. Friends tell you to do this, doctors, therapists, counselors, women's magazines; everyone. Right? But hey (*therapist says this next part humorously*), it looks like we aren't really trying very hard here; let's push harder. Push as hard as you possibly can. Straighten those elbows, dislocate those shoulders; let's get these thoughts and feelings as far away as possible. (*The therapist and client maintain this posture for the next section of the exercise: holding the paper tightly by the edges, arms straight, holding it as far from the chest as possible.*)

Now notice three things. First, how tiring is this? We've only been going for less than a minute, and already it's tiring. Imagine doing this all day; how much energy it would consume?

Second, notice how distracting it is. If the person you love were right there in front of you, how hard would it be to give her your full attention? If your favorite movie were playing on a screen over there, how much would you miss out on? If there's an important task in front of you right now or a problem you need to address or a challenge you need to tackle, how hard is it to focus on it?

Third, notice while all your effort and energy is going into doing this, how hard it is to take action, to do the things that make your life work, such as (*therapist gives some examples based on the client's history, such as "to cook dinner," "to drive your car," "to cuddle your baby," "to type on your computer," "to hug the person you love"*). So notice how difficult life is when we're struggling with our thoughts and feelings like this. We're distracted, we're missing out on life, it's hard to focus, we're exhausted, and it's so hard to do the things that make life work.

Now, let's see what happens when we drop the struggle with our thoughts and feelings. (*Therapist now relaxes his arms, drops the paper into his lap. The client copies him. Typically the client will express a sigh of relief "Ahh—that's better".*) Big difference, huh? How much less tiring is this? How much more energy do you have now? How much easier is it to engage with and focus on what's in front of you? If your favorite person were in front of you right now, how much more connected would you be? If your favorite movie were playing, how much more would you enjoy it? If there were a task you needed to do or a problem you needed to address, how much easier would it be to focus on it? Now move your arms and hands about—(*therapist gently shakes his arms and hands around; client copies*). How much easier is it now to take action: to drive a car, cuddle a baby, cook dinner, type on a computer, hug the person you love? (*Therapist mimes these activities as he says them; the client usually will not copy this part, but that doesn't matter.*)

Now notice these things (*therapist indicates the paper in his lap*) haven't disappeared. We haven't gotten rid of them. They're still here. But we've got a new way of responding to them. We're handling them differently.

They're no longer holding us back, or bringing us down, or jerking us around. And if there's something useful we can do with them, we can use them. You see, even really painful thoughts and feelings often have useful information that can help us, even if it's just pointing us toward problems we need to address or things we need to do differently, or simply reminding us to be kinder to ourselves. And if there's nothing useful we can do with them, we just let them sit there.

APPENDIX 7

Triggers-Behavior-Payoffs Worksheet

Triggers *(situation, thoughts, and feelings that immediately precede the behavior)*	**Behavior** *(what you do)*	**Payoffs** *(outcomes of the behavior that keep it going)*
		Common payoffs include: *Escape/avoid people, places, situations, events* *Escape/avoid unwanted thoughts & feelings* *Get your needs met/get what you want* *Feel good* *Feel safe or familiar* *Feel like you deserve it* *Feel like you are right and others are wrong* *Feel powerful or in control* *Gain attention* *Look good to others* *Make sense (of life, the world, yourself, others)*

Triggers *(situation, thoughts, and feelings that immediately precede the behavior)*	**Behavior** *(what you do)*	**Payoffs** *(outcomes of the behavior that keep it going)*

APPENDIX 8

Exposure Crib Sheet

ACT Exposure Crib Sheet

Contacting the Present Moment
Dropping anchor, Expansive awareness,
Mindful stretching, breathing, moving
0–10, how present are you right now?
Notice you and me, working together, as a team

Acceptance
Notice & Name
Open up, allow
Let it flow through you
Hold yourself kindly
0–10, how much are you fighting this?
Are you willing to make room for this?

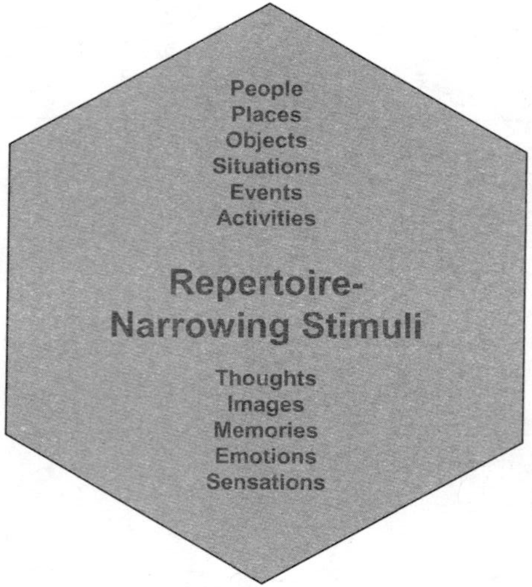

Repertoire-Narrowing Stimuli
People
Places
Objects
Situations
Events
Activities

Thoughts
Images
Memories
Emotions
Sensations

Values
What's this work in the service of?
What matters enough that you are willing to do this?
What values are you living, simply in doing this challenging work?
0–10, how in touch with those values are you right now?

Defusion
Notice & Name difficult thoughts & memories
I'm having a memory of:
Notice size, shape, location, movement
0–10, how hooked are you?

Committed Action
What goals will this help you with?
0–10, how much control do you have over your actions right now?
Mindfully move your arms, legs, body
Are we okay to keep going with this?

Self-as-Context
There's a part of you noticing everything
T.I.M.E.S. change – and this part of you can step back and notice it happening
Use this part to bring up the lights on the stage show

APPENDIX 9

A Clinician's Guide to Getting Unstuck from Just About Anything

ACT practitioners will all get stuck at times, no matter how experienced and knowledgeable they may be. In this appendix, I'll recap the strategies that I have found to be the most useful for helping therapists to get themselves and their clients unstuck. And I'll remind you where you can find them within this book. Any time you find yourself confused, stuck, worried, frustrated, or hopeless about how to work with a client, I encourage you to run through this guide, step by step, and actively apply it. I'm confident that if you do, you'll find something useful.

Case Formulation

Whenever you are stuck with a client, take at least ten to fifteen minutes to fill out an ACT Case Formulation worksheet (appendix 1). This will usually (a) give you a wealth of ideas for where you can intervene, and (b) highlight important areas of information you are missing. When doing this, we always want to ensure that we complete the section on our own personal barriers and apply ACT to ourselves to deal with our own fusion and avoidance. After all, the more fused and avoidant we are in session, the less effective we'll be with our clients.

The Choice Point

The choice point (chapter 1: Playing with the Choice Point) is a great tool for quickly plotting out any issue or problematic behavior, from suicidality and aggression to addiction and anorexia, and generating an action plan to deal with it. It will help you to identify the difficult thoughts and feelings that "trigger" the behavior, which you'll then target with *unhooking skills* (defusion, acceptance, present moment, self-compassion, self-as-context). It will enable you to pinpoint difficult situations and problems that you'll target with values-guided problem solving and committed action. And it'll aid you in identifying alternative, values-congruent behaviors to replace the *away moves.*

Even if you don't use the choice point overtly in session with your client, it can be very useful for you to draw one out as part of your own case formulation: either as a broad snapshot of all the client's problems, or as a detailed map of one specific client behavior.

Informed Consent and Behavioral Goals

By far the most common issues I encounter in supervision are due to omission by the therapist of these two essential steps: obtaining informed consent to do ACT (appendix 2) and establishing behavioral goals for therapy (chapter 3: Ghastly Goals). If you've skipped over either or both of these fundamentals, your client may want something completely different from therapy than what you are offering, in which case you can expect confusion, resistance, or sessions without any sense of direction. Remember, if you don't establish behavioral goals (what the client wants *to do*), your client will almost always have emotional goals (what the client wants *to feel*), and if so, he will assume that the purpose of therapy is to get rid of unpleasant thoughts and feelings and replace them with pleasant ones.

So ask yourself:

- Have I obtained informed consent for ACT? (If yes, has the client forgotten or misunderstood? Do I need to obtain it again?)

- Have I clearly established behavioral goals (as opposed to emotional goals) for therapy?

Press Pause

In session, is your client behaving in ways that interfere with therapy? If so, get permission to "press pause" (appendix 2) and start using this as an active intervention. Use "press pause" to interrupt the behavior as it occurs, then respectfully and compassionately explore it. Bring openness and curiosity to the behavior, and look at it in terms of workability. Explore whether it is towards or an away move. Does it help you and the client work together as a team? Does it help the client move toward or away from the behavioral goals established for therapy (chapter 3: Ghastly Goals)? Once the client agrees that the therapy-interfering behavior is an away move or is getting in the way of working together effectively, one option is to plot the behavior itself on a choice point diagram. This enables you to identify the antecedent thoughts and feelings that trigger the behavior, target them with unhooking skills, and generate more effective behaviors.

Setting an Agenda

If you're not getting much accomplished in a session, then you'd be wise to set an agenda at the start of each session (chapter 11: Sticky Structure). Agree on an area of life to work on, or a skill to practice, or a quadrant of the bull's-eye or an aspect of the choice point to focus on. Use the agenda itself to train focusing, refocusing, and commitment: every time the client goes off track, respectfully notice and name it, and gently and respectfully guide him back to the agenda.

Creative Hopelessness

When a client is fixated on feeling good or getting rid of unwanted thoughts, feelings, sensations, memories, and so on, we will need to introduce (or reintroduce) creative hopelessness (chapter 8: Crummy Creative Hopelessness). This opens the client to new, more flexible ways of responding to difficult thoughts and feelings.

After creative hopelessness, we usually move to dropping the struggle (also in chapter 8), and from there, we can segue into any unhooking skill, such as defusion, acceptance, self-compassion, or dropping anchor. All these mindfulness skills teach clients new ways of responding to their painful thoughts and feelings, with an attitude of openness and willingness rather than avoidance.

Overcoming Our Own Self-Doubt and Fear of Failure

Do you have self-doubt about introducing experiential exercises to clients? Are you worried that the techniques will be ineffective or the client will see them as lame or feel invalidated? The inconvenient truth is, such unwanted outcomes are always possible. (And this is nothing special about ACT; it's true for any intervention in any model of therapy.) So if fear of failure or self-doubt is holding us back, we want to apply ACT to ourselves. We might say to the client:

> I really want to help you to XYZ. *(XYZ are the client's behavioral goals for therapy.)* And I have an idea of something that could help. The problem is, my mind is trying to talk me out of it. My mind is saying, *You'll find this lame or silly or invalidating.* And I'm feeling anxious about introducing it to you; I notice my heart is racing, and my stomach is churning. And my mind is saying, *Shut up! Don't say anything else. Change the topic.* But I'm also listening to my values as a therapist; my aim is to help people. And if I don't introduce this to you because I'm not willing to make room for my own anxiety about it, then I'm not being true to my values, and I don't think I'm doing you the service you came for. So even though I feel anxious, and my mind's saying you won't like this, I'd like to introduce you to something that I think can really help you to XYZ.

Again, notice how the fundamentals must be in place: we need to have established behavioral goals for therapy, and have informed consent for ACT, in order to make this work.

We also want to introduce the idea of experiments: "Can we treat this as an experiment? I never know what will happen in advance. I think it will be helpful for you; otherwise I wouldn't suggest it. It usually is for most people, but I can never know for sure. Can we do this as an experiment and see what happens? And afterward, you tell me if it's helpful or not."

Overcoming Resistance to Exercises

If your client seems unwilling to do experiential exercises or learn new skills in session, check:

Have you gotten informed consent?

Have you established behavioral goals?

Are you giving a clear rationale for each and every exercise—making it clear as to how it will help the client with her behavioral goals?

Are you setting up each exercise up as an experiment?

Are you responding effectively when interventions backfire?

For more on these topics, read chapter 4: Beastly Barriers.

If the client is hesitant to do exercises due to her anxiety, then first validate and normalize the anxiety. Then ask if you can focus the session on learning new skills to handle anxiety; be clear that the reason for doing this is to help your client achieve her therapy goals. Explicitly tease out that the way she is responding to her anxiety in session is preventing her from achieving those very goals. Once she agrees, your next step will usually need to be creative hopelessness (chapter 8).

Doing ACT vs. Talking About ACT

Check with yourself: are you actively practicing core skills in session with your client? Or are you just talking about ACT? Don't fall into the trap of thinking metaphors are enough. If you introduce a metaphor such as hands as thoughts and feelings (appendix 5) or pushing away paper (appendix 6), you must then go on to actively practice defusion skills or acceptance skills. (If your client doesn't want to practice skills, then see the previous point.)

Get crystal clear: what does the client want from therapy? If she doesn't want ACT, then you have to make a choice: use a different model or refer her to someone else.

Dropping Anchor

If your client is experiencing extreme fusion, emotional dysregulation, dissociative states, flashbacks, or other intense emotional and cognitive reactions that interfere with therapy, then make your sessions about dropping anchor (chapter 7: Dodgy Dropping Anchor). Build anchoring skills first, before going on to other aspects of the model.

Defusion from Hopelessness

If your client is feeling hopeless about himself, life, the future, or therapy itself, this is obviously going to interfere with progress. So our first step is usually going to involve defusion from the hopelessness itself. See chapter 12: Measly Motivation. See also chapter 9: Dastardly Defusion, especially the Q&A on "What techniques work best with extreme fusion?"

Building Motivation

If your client is lacking motivation to do the challenging work of therapy, first get buy-in through informed consent (appendix 2) and establishing behavioral goals (chapter 3). Then work on defusion from hopelessness and other barriers to therapy as described in the previous point. And then, as soon as possible, bring in values to build motivation. For more on this topic, see chapter 12: Measly Motivation.

Reinforcing Change Between Sessions

If your client is failing to make changes between sessions, then your first step is to find out why. Start your next session by exploring what the barriers are, and then target them. For failure to do "homework," use the strategies in chapter 12: Measly Motivation.

Keeping Sessions Focused and Productive

If your client keeps going off topic, switching problems, jumping from worry to worry, changing the subject, or filling up the session with worrying and ruminating, there are a few steps to take. Assuming you have informed consent and have established behavioral goals for therapy, the next two steps are to (a) get permission to "press pause" and start using it to interrupt such fused behavior as it arises, and (b) set an agenda for the session.

Once all this is in place, use press pause to interrupt fused behavior, and then target the fusion itself. Often, for such extreme fusion, it's good to start with simple but powerful exercises such as those in chapter 9: Dastardly Defusion, especially the ones described in the Q&A on "What techniques work best with extreme fusion?"

Functional Analysis

Last but definitely not least, don't forget about good old-fashioned functional analysis (chapter 5: Freaky Functional Analysis). If you're finding it difficult to constructively influence any type of problematic behavior—whether it's happening in session or between sessions—take the time and effort to analyze it in terms of ABCs (antecedents, behavior, and consequences). This will usually give you a wealth of ideas for effectively interrupting the problematic behavior and reinforcing a more workable behavior as an alternative.

References

Albom, M. (1997). *Tuesdays with Morrie.* New York, NY: Random House.

American Psychiatric Association. (2013). *Diagnostic and statistical manual of mental disorders* (5th ed.). Washington, DC: Author.

Ciarrochi, J., Bailey, A., & Harris, R. (2013). *The weight escape: How to stop dieting and start living.* Boulder, CO: Shambhala Publications.

Craske, M. G., Kircanski, K., Zelikowsky, M., Mystkowski, J., Chowdhury, N., & Baker, A. (2008). Optimizing inhibitory learning during exposure therapy. *Behaviour Research and Therapy*, 46(1), 5–27.

Dahl, J., & Lundgren, T. (2006). *Living beyond your pain: Using acceptance and commitment therapy to ease chronic pain.* Oakland, CA: New Harbinger.

Harris, R. (2009a). *ACT made simple: An easy-to-read primer on acceptance and commitment therapy.* Oakland, CA: New Harbinger.

Harris, R. (2009b). *ACT with love: Stop struggling, reconcile differences, and strengthen your relationship with acceptance and commitment therapy.* Oakland, CA: New Harbinger.

Harris, R. (2012). *The reality slap: Finding peace and fulfillment when life hurts.* Oakland, CA: New Harbinger.

Harris, R. (2013). *Getting unstuck in ACT.* Oakland, CA: New Harbinger.

Hayes, S. C., Strosahl, K. D., & Wilson, K. G. (1999). *Acceptance and commitment therapy: An experiential approach to behavior change.* New York, NY: Guilford Press.

Kübler-Ross, E. (1975). *Death: The final stage of growth.* New York, NY: Touchstone.

Neff, K. D., & Vonk, R. (2009). Self-compassion versus global self-esteem: Two different ways of relating to oneself. *Journal of Personality*, *77*(1), 23–50.

Polk, K., & Schoendorff, B. (2014). *The ACT matrix: A new approach to building psychological flexibility across settings and populations.* Oakland, CA: New Harbinger.

Ramnerö, J., & Törneke, N. (2008). *The ABCs of human behavior: Behavioral principles for the practicing clinician.* Oakland, CA: New Harbinger.

Rauch, S., van der Kolk, B. A., Fisler, R., Alpert, N. M., Orr, S. P., Savage, C. R.,…Pitman, R. K. (1996). A symptom provocation study of posttraumatic stress disorder using position emission tomography and script-driven imagery. *Archives of General Psychiatry*, *53*(5), 380–387.

Strosahl, K. D., Robinson, P., & Gustavsson, T. (2012). *Brief interventions for radical change: Principles and practice of focused acceptance and commitment therapy.* Oakland, CA: New Harbinger.

Turrell, S., & Bell, M. (2016). *ACT for Adolescents.* Oakland, CA: New Harbinger.

World Health Organization. (1992). *International statistical classification of diseases and related health problems, 10th Revision.* Geneva, Switzerland: Author.

Free Resources and Online Training

Below is information about free resources you can access as well as my online training courses.

Free Resources

I have created many free resources for you to use with and share with your clients. You can download the complete set of worksheets, handouts, and appendices from this book, plus many other resources, from the free resources page on http://www.ImLearningACT.com.

Online Training

I've also created a range of beginners- and advanced-level online training courses in ACT. These 6- to 8-week interactive courses, which run several times each year, include:

- ACT for Beginners
- ACT for Adolescents
- ACT and Mindfulness for Trauma
- ACT for Depression and Anxiety Disorders

You can find information about these courses on http://www.ImLearningACT.com.

Russ Harris is a medical practitioner, psychotherapist, and world-renowned acceptance and commitment therapy (ACT) trainer. He has trained over 27,000 practitioners in ACT, and authored nine books, including *ACT Made Simple*, *ACT with Love*, *The Reality Slap*, and the international bestseller, *The Happiness Trap* (now translated into thirty languages). He lives and practices in Melbourne, Australia.

Index

C

D

E

F

G

H

I

J

K

L

M

N

O

P

Q

R

S

W

Y